AF605847

THE HISTORY OF AL-ṬABARĪ

AN ANNOTATED TRANSLATION

VOLUME XIII

The Conquest of Iraq,
Southwestern Persia, and Egypt

THE MIDDLE YEARS OF ʿUMAR'S CALIPHATE

A.D. 636–642/A.H. 15–21

The History of al-Ṭabarī

SUNY

SERIES IN NEAR EASTERN STUDIES

Said Amir Arjomand, Editor

The preparation of this volume was made possible in part by a grant from the National Endowment for the Humanities, an independent federal agency.

Bibliotheca Persica
Edited by Ehsan Yar-Shater

The History of al-Ṭabarī
(Ta'rīkh al-rusul wa'l-mulūk)

VOLUME XIII

The Conquest of Iraq, Southwestern Persia, and Egypt

translated and annotated
by

Gautier H. A. Juynboll

State University of New York Press

Published by
State University of New York Press, Albany

Printed in the United States of America

For information, address State University of New York Press, State University Plaza, Albany, N.Y. 12246

Library of Congress Cataloging-in-Publication Data
Ṭabarī, 838?-923.
[Ta'rīkh al-rusul wa-al-mulūk. English. Selections]
The conquest of Iraq, Southwestern Persia, and Egypt/translated and annotated by Gautier H. A. Juynboll.
p. cm. — (SUNY series in Near Eastern studies) (Bibliotheca Persica) (The history of al-Ṭabarī = Ta'rīkh al-rusul wa'l-mulūk ; v. 13)
Translation of extracts from: Ta'rīkh al-rusul wa-al-mulūk.
Bibliography: p.
Includes index.
ISBN 0-88706-876-6. ISBN 0-88706-877-4 (pbk.)
1. Islamic Empire—History—622-661. I. Juynboll, G. H. A. II. Title. III. Series. IV. Series: Bibliotheca Persica (Albany, N.Y.) V. Series: Ṭabarī, 838?-923. Ta'rīkh al-rusul wa-al-mulūk. English ; v. 13.
DS38.2.T313 1985 vol. 13
[DS38.1]
909'.1 s—dc19
[909'.09767101] 88-2262
CIP

Preface

THE HISTORY OF PROPHETS AND KINGS (*Ta'rīkh al-rusul wa'l-mulūk*) by Abū Ja'far Muḥammad b. Jarīr al-Ṭabarī (839–923), here rendered as the *History of al-Ṭabarī*, is by common consent the most important universal history produced in the world of Islam. It has been translated here in its entirety for the first time for the benefit of non-Arabists, with historical and philological notes for those interested in the particulars of the text.

Ṭabarī's monumental work explores the history of the ancient nations, with special emphasis on biblical peoples and prophets, the legendary and factual history of ancient Iran, and, in great detail, the rise of Islam, the life of the Prophet Muḥammad, and the history of the Islamic world down to the year 915. The first volume of this translation will contain a biography of al-Ṭabarī and a discussion of the method, scope, and value of his work. It will also provide information on some of the technical considerations that have guided the work of the translators.

The *History* has been divided here into 38 volumes, each of which covers about two hundred pages of the original Arabic text in the Leiden edition. An attempt has been made to draw the dividing lines between the individual volumes in such a way that each is to some degree independent and can be read as such. The page numbers of the original in the Leiden edition appear on the margins of the translated volumes.

Al-Ṭabarī very often quotes his sources verbatim and traces the chain of transmission (*isnād*) to an original source. The chains of transmitters are, for the sake of brevity, rendered by only a dash

(—) between the individual links in the chain. Thus, According to Ibn Ḥumayd—Salamah—Ibn Isḥāq means that al-Ṭabarī received the report from Ibn Ḥumayd who said that he was told by Salamah, who said that he was told by Ibn Isḥāq, and so on. The numerous subtle and important differences in the original Arabic wording have been disregarded.

The table of contents at the beginning of each volume gives a brief survey of the topics dealt with in that particular volume. It also includes the headings and subheadings as they appear in al-Ṭabarī's text, as well as those occasionally introduced by the translator.

Well-known place names, such as, for instance, Mecca, Baghdad, Jerusalem, Damascus, and the Yemen, are given in their English spellings. Less common place names, which are the vast majority, are transliterated. Biblical figures appear in the accepted English spelling. Iranian names are usually transcribed according to their Arabic forms, and the presumed Iranian forms are often discussed in the footnotes.

Technical terms have been translated wherever possible, but some, such as dirham and imām, have been retained in Arabic forms. Others that cannot be translated with sufficient precision have been retained and italicized as well as footnoted.

The annotation aims chiefly at clarifying difficult passages, identifying individuals and place names, and discussing textual difficulties. Much leeway has been left to the translators to include in the footnotes whatever they consider necessary and helpful.

The bibliographies list all the sources mentioned in the annotation.

The index in each volume contains all the names of persons and places referred to in the text, as well as those mentioned in the notes as far as they refer to the medieval period. It does not include the names of modern scholars. A general index, it is hoped, will appear after all the volumes have been published.

For further details concerning the series and acknowledgments, see Preface to Volume I.

Ehsan Yar-Shater

Contents

Abbreviations

BOS: Bonner Orientalistische Studien.
EI[2]*: Encyclopaedia of Islam,* 2nd ed., Leiden, 1960—.
GAS: F. Sezgin, *Geschichte des arabischen Schrifttums,* Vol 1, Leiden, 1967.
IJMES: International Journal of Middle East Studies.
JESHO: Journal of the Economic and Social History of the Orient.
JSAI: Jerusalem Studies in Arabic and Islam.
WKAS: Wörterbuch der klassischen arabischen Sprache, ed. M. Ullmann *et al.,* Wiesbaden, 1970.
ZDMG: Zeitschrift der Deutschen Morgenländischen Gesellschaft.

Translator's Foreword

This volume is almost exclusively associated with Sayf b. ʿUmar (d. between 170/786 and 193/809), that controversial collector of material mainly dealing with the early conquests. With Oriental scholars in the Middle Ages as well as with western scholars during the last one hundred years or so, Sayf's material has always been a matter of debate as to whether or not it has any historical basis. However, this volume does not offer historical analysis; that I gladly leave to others better qualified. There is only one thing that I should like to dwell on briefly; that is the question of Sayf's seemingly inflated numbers.

If one reads through a volume such as this, one cannot help but wonder from where Sayf got his numbers. Presumably from his authorities. But who is responsible for inflating them? Now, whether it is Sayf himself, or an authority between him and Ṭabarī, or Ṭabarī himself (which seems the least likely), or an authority from Sayf down to the eyewitness of the event, who is responsible for multiplying the original numbers by a certain figure in order to inflate them is a matter of guesswork. In fact anybody qualifies; the question defies answering. But I cannot help feeling that if, just for the sake of argument, we assume that the anonymous multiplier consistently used *one and the same* multiplication coefficient for all the numbers, for sums of money as well as for numbers of soldiers participating in a certain battle, the modern reader would be able to reconstruct Sayf's numbers by dividing them by this same coefficient. The main problem we are left with, then, is to decide on a hypothetical coefficient which, once applied, reduces Sayf's figures in such a way that the historical account becomes somewhat more plausible.

I have found that the constituting elements of the historical reports presented here become a great deal more believable when a certain division coefficient is applied. Then most of the reports begin to make historical sense, or at least, they cease to be utterly grotesque.

While I was doing the translation, it occurred to me that the figure one hundred could be deemed a suitable coefficient. Every number in a Sayf report divided by one hundred produces a result, the proportions of which are at least believable. Since nearly all Sayf's numbers are above one thousand, this could be done on a wide scale. Suddenly the accounts of "skirmishes" involving 5,000, say, become skirmishes (without quotes) in which only fifty take part, figures of one million dirhams become 10,000 dirhams, etc. Even if there is not a shred of evidence for this surmise, reading an historical account which is in so many other aspects delightful and in which the numbers assume believable proportions is, I think, a much more rewarding pastime than being constantly reminded of the compulsive inflation of the figures due to the interference of a collector/transmitter, who was under the impression that inflated numbers made his story more heroic and thus more popular.

But then, what do we do with figures that produce numbers too low to fit the context when divided by the coefficient one hundred? I have found that figures lower than one thousand, which divided by one hundred no longer make sense, do produce a plausible number when divided by, say, ten.

The figures ten and one hundred are not entirely random. There is one passage in which a certain vacillation with the transmitter in the multiplying of his figures seems to be discernible. See what happens: At a dangerous river crossing, the advance party sent ahead is first described as numbering six hundred, then from them a selection of sixty is made, but in the end the advance party actually identified by name as having established the beachhead comprises six people (plus one anonymous youngster). Six hundred–sixty–six. This last figure begins to make sense. So my choice of the coefficients ten and one hundred seems to work in this particular context. Is it not tempting to consider this passage, which is presented by Ṭabarī at [p. 2433] below, also as one that allows us a peep into the workshop of our unknown multiplier with a seemingly obvious predilection for the decimal system?

There is another incident, not contained in this volume, but in Volume XII of this series, that conceivably might be taken as an indication that the coefficients one hundred, or with lower figures ten, have something to commend them (see Volume XII, [p. 2305]).

At a certain point in the battle of al-Qādisiyyah, reinforcements of 6,000 troops arrive from Syria to lend support. One of Sayf's heroes, al-Qaʿqāʿ b. ʿAmr, leads 1,000 of them to a particular spot, divides his riders into units of ten, and sends them into the fray. These tens, according to the account, make all the difference, and the Muslims, thus "reinforced," carry the day.

One may wonder, then, why the entire force of one thousand was not ordered to attack all at once? The overall outcome of the battle of al-Qādisiyyah could have been decided then and there. But no, it had to be achieved at the hands of units of ten. At the same time, we are asked to believe that units of ten, sent to reinforce an army of tens of thousands, make all that much difference, and if we assume that as large a number as one hundred or more units of ten were mobilized consecutively and sent into battle one after the other, we must realize that that is what the story sets out to convey, although it does not say so in so many words.

If we take this information at face value, we are asked to lend credence to the description of a battle, involving tens of thousands of troops on either side, in which *not* reinforcements totalling 6,000, but small units of ten, determine the outcome. Well, after all the numbers of Persians and Muslims on either side have been divided by one hundred, we are shown a battlefield and a military activity in which fresh injections of ten warriors each may conceivably have swayed the balance in favour of one of the warring parties toward victory, rather than stalemate or defeat. After this division coefficient has been applied, the story is no longer marred by "embellishments" in the shape of inflated numbers, which tend to put the reader off rather than entertain him. Other suitable division coefficients can be expected to give satisfactory results, as in the case of collectors other than Sayf. Ten and one hundred have worked very well for me in this volume.

For a historiographical evaluation of Sayf's collection, see the recently published translation of A. A. Duri's classic, *The Rise of Historical Writing Among the Arabs,* index s.v. The *isnāds*, which Sayf frequently uses, are analyzed in Martin Hinds's paper "Sayf b. ʿUmar's Sources on Arabia" in *Studies in the History of Arabia,* I/2, 3–16. In his *The Early Islamic Conquests,* 446, F. M. Donner announces the forthcoming publication of a general study on early Arabic historical sources, which may be expected to contain new insights into the Sayf saga. Donner also grapples with the convoluted chronology of Sayf which is very much in evidence in this volume. The final word about this controversial issue has not been said, however.

In this translation, my principal objective has been to make Sayf's (or some other anonymous redactor's) difficult and at times ultra concise Arabic available in *readable* English. On numerous occasions that entailed having to add in parentheses words or phrases meant to facilitate comprehension (although, much to my regret, very many of these parentheses were subsequently removed by an editor). Readers interested in the ancient and often quaint Arabic prose of the original need simply skip these insertions. But by reading it in this way, one will quickly realize that, without the insertions, understanding what the early historian or eyewitness was driving at is no mean task. What makes the Arabic in this volume especially difficult is the often seemingly insoluble mishmash of unidentified pronominal suffixes and subject markers. Suffixes like *–hum, –hu,* and *–hā,* as well as their corresponding pronouns, occur by the dozen in relatively brief passages that abound in verbs whose subjects are left unspecified, thereby causing the translator many problems which at first defy solution. I was helped by realizing that many of these difficult passages may have begun as stories told by early Islamic storytellers (*quṣṣāṣ*), who facilitate their audiences' comprehension with the help of gestures. By pointing, for example, in one direction he indicates "the Muslims," in the other direction "the enemy," and so on, whereas in print we may only find the suffix *–hum* used in both cases.

In order to avoid stiltedness as much as possible, I have made use of the following devices: I have cut up extended parataxis by resorting to hypotaxis conveying the same meaning. That has also entailed translating main clauses as if they were *ḥāl*s or relative clauses. Conversely, I have tried to enhance readability by translating many secondary clauses, *ḥāl*s and *ṣilah*s as main clauses. Thus I have often rendered secondary clauses introduced by *ḥattā* followed by a perfect with "Finally. . . ." Furthermore, in many instances, it seemed a good idea to translate *ḥāl*s as relative clauses and vice versa. But on the whole I have kept close to the original Arabic.

However, with the numerous poetic fragments scattered over this volume, I have taken the liberty of rendering them somewhat more freely. The reason for this, as well as the methods followed, are outlined in Appendix I. Here we also find a running commentary on the verses, as well as less free renderings, where that has been deemed necessary.

Appendix II contains an early twentieth-century plan of the situation around the city of Tustar, once allegedly besieged by Muslim forces, a siege described in this volume. This description tallies so remarkably well with the details given in Sayf's account that I have decided to include it.

Apart from Sayf, whose reports constitute the bulk of this volume, we occasionally encounter Ibn Isḥāq, al-Wāqidī, al-Madā'inī and a few others. But on the whole, this is a Sayfian volume, as the style in which most of the reports are composed makes abundantly clear to those familiar with Ṭabarī's *Annales.* Sayf's material has rarely been drawn upon by other historians. Ibn al-Athīr copied, or better excerpted, Ṭabarī's Sayf material for his own work, but the fact that he left out virtually every passage whose interpretation posed the slightest problem in my view justifies the surmise that Ibn al-Athīr did not himself grasp the meaning, or if he did, perhaps he thought that his readers would not. At any rate, parallel passages in other historical works are few and offer barely any textual overlap that might have helped in the interpretation of Sayf's original. The only other historical work containing extensive Sayf passages is still in manuscript; I mean the *Kitāb al-Maghāzī* by ʿAbd al-Raḥmān b. Muḥammad b. ʿAbdallāh Ibn Ḥubaysh (d. 584 [1147]). This work is preserved in two manuscripts, one in Berlin and one in Leiden.

Apart from two Istanbul manuscripts containing sections of Ṭabarī's *Annales* called C and Co, which can be considered as fairly defective, Eugen Prym, the editor of the Ṭabarī volume of which this book is a partial translation, had no more manuscript material at his disposal than the manuscripts of Ibn Ḥubaysh's work.

While translating this volume, I have made frequent use of the Leiden Ibn Ḥubaysh (Or. 342). In spite of repeated efforts, I have not been able to obtain microfilms of the Istanbul manuscripts. In the end, I had to make do with Prym's text as it stands. Although I have the greatest admiration for that scholar's obviously phenomenal knowledge of, and feeling for, this ancient Arabic, his edition still contains many passages with which there are some things wrong and which seem to defy any attempt at emendation. Even so, on a few occasions I have proposed corrections duly discussed in the notes.

Of all the friends and colleagues who have given a hand in the solving of the numerous problems encountered in a translation of this kind I shall name here just a few. Thus I should like to thank Peri Bearman (Leiden) and Robert Hillenbrand (Edinburgh) for the care they exercised in going over parts of this translation to rid it of infelicities of style.

But, more than anybody else, Martin Hinds (Cambridge) helped me with constant advice. He read the entire volume and gave me freely of his incomparable expertise. His numerous judicious suggestions and ingenious emendations are scattered throughout the footnotes. He also drew my attention to a number of secondary sources and studies unknown to me, which proved to be valuable in the interpretation of many obscure passages. His untimely death in December of 1988 was a great shock to me, as to all his friends. In deep gratitude and affection I dedicate this volume to his memory.

G. H. A. Juynboll

The Events of the Year 15 (cont'd)

(February 14, 636–February 1, 637)

Now we will enumerate the reports about those battles, that is the battles that took place until the end of the year. As I mentioned, scholars differed about what took place.[1] [2419]

According to al-Sarī[2]—Shuʿayb—Sayf—Muḥammad, al-Muhallab, ʿAmr and Saʿīd: ʿUmar enjoined Saʿd, when he ordered him to march on al-Madāʾin, to leave the women and children in al-ʿAtīq[3] and to station an army contingent with them. This Saʿd did. ʿUmar also charged him to let these soldiers share in whatever booty there was, as long as they followed the Muslims with the latters' families. They said: After the conquest Saʿd stayed two months in al-Qādisiyyah, corresponding with ʿUmar concerning the measures he had to take. He dispatched Zuhrah to al-Lisān, that is to Lisān al-Barr, which is like a tongue of land laid

1. From here up to and including the battle at Jalūlāʾ (p. 2470), the account has been summarized in Wellhausen, *Skizzen*, VI, 72 ff, and Morony, *Iraq*, 191–4.

2. For an appraisal of the *isnād*s in this volume, see the translator's foreword.

3. According to Wellhausen, *Skizzen*, VI, 71, this is a canal of the Euphrates near the place where al-Kūfah was later built.

down in the countryside.[4] Al-Kūfah is situated there nowadays; previously the main city there was al-Ḥīrah. Al-Nakhīrajān was encamped there. However, he left when he heard that Zuhrah was on his way, and he then joined his companions.

They continued: Among the songs that the children chanted in the camp and the women sang out to them while on the riverbank of al-ʿAtīq,[5] was something the women also sang in Zarūd,[6] Dhū Qār[7] and other watery places.[8] That was when they were ordered to march again to al-Qādisiyyah[9] in the month Jumādā II. This cryptic song, which the women sang, was like a nonsense verse, because there is no time between the months Jumādā and Rajab (in *rajaz*):

O wonder of all wonders!
    Between Jumādā and Rajab
[2420] There's something that needs doing.
    Have seen it those who've perished.
Buried in dust and clamor.[10]

The Battle of Burs

The transmitter said: After concluding the operations at al-Qādisiyyah and sending Zuhrah b. al-Ḥawiyyah forward at the head of the vanguard to al-Lisān, Saʿd set off. Then he dispatched ʿAbdallāh b. al-Muʿtamm after Zuhrah, next Shuraḥbīl b. al-Simṭ after ʿAbdallāh, and finally Hāshim b. ʿUtbah after all these. Saʿd had appointed the last-named as his deputy in the area in which Khālid b. ʿUrfuṭah was commander. Khālid was given command of the rearguard. Then, in late Shawwāl (November 636), Saʿd set out himself, together with all the Muslims, mounted and well-equipped, God having made available to them all the weapons,

4. This "tongue of land" was formed by two arms of the Euphrates, one leading along al-Ḥīrah, the other was more to the east, see Le Strange, *Lands* map II, and also Yāqūt, *Muʿjam*, IV, 355; see also *WKAS*, II/1, 625, right column, penult.

5. There used to be a village, ʿAtīq al-Sājah, which disappeared in the Tigris, see Yāqūt, *Muʿjam*, III, 613.

6. See *ibid.*, II, 928.

7. See *ibid.*, IV, 10.

8. This specification seems to indicate that all these villages were (partly) surrounded by water.

9. Wellhausen, *Skizzen*, VI, 74, n. 1, probably correctly, suggests reading al-Madā'in here, as above in line 6 of the Arabic text. See also *Glossarium*, p. DCXIX.

10. See Wellhausen, *Skizzen*, VI, 74, n. 1. For some introductory remarks on how I have translated the poetry in this volume, see Appendix I.

mules and riches found in the Persian camp. Zuhrah marched until he stopped at al-Kūfah. A *kūfah* is a place wholly covered with pebbles mixed with red sand. Then ʿAbdallāh and Shuraḥbīl arrived, and Zuhrah set out for al-Madāʾin. When he reached Burs, Buṣbuhrā confronted him at the head of a troop of soldiers. They engaged him in a skirmish and Zuhrah routed them. Buṣbuhrā and those men with him fled to Bābil, where those who had escaped from al-Qādisiyyah had gathered together with the rest of their commanders, al-Nakhīrajān, Mihrān al-Rāzī, al-Hurmuzān and their peers. They stayed there, choosing al-Fayruzān to command them. Buṣbuhrā arrived there also, but, having escaped with a spear wound, he died thereof.

According to al-Sarī—Shuʿayb—Sayf—al-Naḍr b. al-Sarī—Ibn al-Rufayl—his father: Zuhrah speared Buṣbuhrā at the battle of Burs. He fell into the river and then died of his wound after [2421]
reaching Bābil. When Buṣbuhrā was routed, Bisṭām, the dihqān of Burs, approached Zuhrah and entered into an agreement with him. He made pontoon bridges for Zuhrah and brought him news of those who had assembled at Bābil.

The Battle of Bābil

They said: When Bisṭām brought Zuhrah the news about those who had escaped from al-Qādisiyyah and were now gathered at Bābil, Zuhrah took the time to write[11] this news to Saʿd. When Saʿd stopped with those who were staying with Hāshim b. ʿUtbah at al-Kūfah and the news from Zuhrah reached him that the Persians were gathered under the command of al-Fayruzān at Bābil, he sent ʿAbdallāh (b. al-Muʿtamm) ahead, followed by Shuraḥbīl and Hāshim. Then he departed with the remaining troops. When he arrived at Burs, he sent Zuhrah ahead, followed by ʿAbdallāh (b. al-Muʿtamm), Shuraḥbīl and Hāshim. Then Saʿd followed them. They descended upon al-Fayruzān at Bābil, having said, "We will fight them in strength,[12] before we disperse." Thus they fought at

11. The Arabic has *aqāma wa-kataba*, which may mean "camped and wrote." If we substitute *qāma* for *aqāma*, we might translate "he wrote forthwith."

12. That is the meaning of *dast*, suggested by *Glossarium*. On the basis of the connotations given in Lane, it is feasible to translate also "with cunning." Dozy, *Supplément*, s.v., suggests among other meanings "a round of wrestling," which seems to fit too. But not one of these possibilities can be substantiated.

Bābil and routed the Persians in a shorter time than (required for) taking off one's cloak. The Persians fled in all directions, nothing else mattered to them. Al-Hurmuzān set off toward al-Ahwāz, seized the province and taxed[13] it as well as Mihrijān Qadhaq.[14] Al-Fayruzān moved out with him and then turned up at Nihāwand, where the treasures of the Persian king were stored. Thus al-Fayruzān took Nihāwand and taxed the two regional centres Māhān.[15] Al-Nakhīrajān and Mihrān al-Rāzī retreated toward al-Madā'in until, after they had passed Bahurasīr,[16] they crossed to the other bank of the Tigris; then they cut the pontoon bridge. For several days Sa'd remained in Bābil, where the news reached him that al-Nakhīrajān had deputed Shahriyār, one of the dihqāns of the Gate,[17] over Kūthā with a troop of men. So Sa'd sent
[2422] Zuhrah ahead followed by the main army. Zuhrah marched on until he came upon Shahriyār in Kūthā, having first killed Fayūmān and al-Farrukhān in the region between Sūrā and al-Dayr.

According to al-Sarī—Shu'ayb—Sayf—al-Naḍr b. al-Sarī—Ibn al-Rufayl—his father: Sa'd had sent Zuhrah ahead from al-Qādisiyyah. Zuhrah marched with his soldiers and warriors[18] divided in different formations. Every band of men he met, who had been pursuing the fleeing enemy, was sent ahead. Zuhrah ordered his own men to follow; they were not to pass by any (Persian) whom they caught up with without killing him. Sometimes Zuhrah would stay put until, this time, when he was sent ahead from Bābil, he sent Bukayr b. 'Abdallāh al-Laythī ahead and also Kathīr b. Shihāb al-Sa'dī, the brother of al-Ghallāq. This was

13. This rendering was suggested by *Glossarium*. It seems to me that the translation "he consumed (everything in) it" may not be ruled out.

14. See Yāqūt, *Mu'jam*, IV, 698.

15. That is Nihāwand and al-Dīnawar; see *Ibid.*, IV, 405.

16. Bahurasīr is the name of one of the seven "cities" (in Arabic *al-madā'in*) situated on the west bank of the Tigris which, together with six other "cities" (such as Sābāṭ) situated on the east bank, make up the city of al-Madā'in, see *ibid.*, I, 768; Le Strange, *Lands*, 34; see also p. 12 below.

17. It is tempting to assume that these are the Persian forerunners of the later Muslim functionaries (guards, chamberlains) the *ḥujjāb* (sing. *ḥājib*), see Morony, *Iraq*, 79–83.

18. This is a meaningless distinction, of course. The Arabic has two terms *jund* and *ḥarb*. One senses that the two groups may constitute specific military units such as "occupation forces" and "assault and defense units." This hunch is based on the contexts in which these words mostly figure, but these connotations are not borne out by evidence from the standard dictionaries.

when Zuhrah crossed the Ṣarāt, so that they would catch up with the rest of the enemy, among whom were Fayūmān and al-Farrukhān; the former was from Maysān, the latter from al-Ahwāz. Bukayr killed al-Farrukhān and Kathīr killed Fayūmān at Sūrā. Then Zuhrah marched on until he passed through Sūrā. He then made camp. Hāshim drew near until he alighted there too. Saʿd also came that way and made camp there. Then Zuhrah was sent ahead and caught up with some men who had been waiting for him between al-Dayr and Kūthā. Al-Nakhīrajān and Mihrān had deputed Shahriyār, the dihqān of the Gate, over their armies and they themselves went to al-Madā'in. Shahriyār remained a while among his troops.

When the Arabs encountered the army of Shahriyār and the vanguard of his cavalry in the neighborhood of Kūthā, Shahriyār came forward and shouted, "Let any man or rider from among you big and strong enough come forward to me in order that I may [2423]
teach him a lesson." Zuhrah retorted, "A moment ago I had in mind to meet you in combat, but now that I have heard what you said, I won't send anyone but a mere slave out to you; if you wait for him, he will kill you—God willing—, because of your effrontery. If you flee from him, you flee from a slave!" Thus he baited Shahriyār. Then he ordered Abū Nubātah Nā'il b. Juʿshum al-Aʿrajī, a courageous Tamīmī, to go out and face his adversary. Each had his spear. Both were of sturdy build, except that Shahriyār was (tall) as a camel. When he saw Nā'il, he flung his spear down in order to grab him by the neck. Nā'il did likewise. They drew their swords and hacked at each other. Then they took each other by the throat and crashed down from their mounts. Shahriyār fell on top of Nā'il like a ton of bricks and held him down under one thigh. He drew his dagger and started to undo the fastenings of Nā'il's coat of mail. Shahriyār's thumb happened to land in Nā'il's mouth and Nā'il crushed the bone in it (with his teeth). He noticed a (momentary) slackening (in his opponent's assault) and, attacking him furiously, whipped him off onto the ground, sat on his chest, drew his own dagger and tore Shahriyār's coat of mail from his belly. Then he stabbed him in his abdomen and side until he died. Nā'il took his horse, his bracelets[19] and his

19. Bracelets were part of the Persian nobility's distinctive accessories, see Morony, *Iraq*, 186.

spoils. The dead man's companions withdrew and fled in all di-
[2424] rections and Zuhrah stayed on in Kūthā until Saʿd arrived there.

Nā'il was brought before Saʿd, who said, "I have taken the following decision with regard to you, Nā'il b. Juʿshum: After you have put on this Persian's bracelets, cloak and coat of mail, I want you to mount his horse." Thus Saʿd assigned to him all that as his booty. Nā'il went aside, put on the captured armor and then came forward to Saʿd, carrying Shahriyār's weapons while riding his mount. Saʿd said to him, "Do not don bracelets except when you are actively engaged in a war; wear them only then." Thus Nā'il was the first Muslim in Iraq to wear bracelets.

According to al-Sarī—Shuʿayb—Sayf—Muḥammad, Ṭalḥah, al-Muhallab, ʿAmr and Saʿīd: Saʿd stayed in Kūthā for some days. He went to the spot where Abraham used to sit in Kūthā and alighted at the place of the people who used to preach (the religion of) Abraham.[20] Saʿd came to the house in which Abraham had been kept prisoner, he inspected it, invoked God's blessing upon His Messenger, upon Abraham and God's Prophets, and recited, "Those days which we send down alternatively upon the people."[21]

The Story of Bahurasīr in the Month Dhū al-Ḥijjah of the Year 15 (January 637) as Related by Sayf

According to al-Sarī—Shuʿayb—Sayf—Muḥammad, Ṭalḥah, al-Muhallab, ʿAmr, Saʿīd and al-Naḍr—Ibn al-Rufayl: Then Saʿd sent Zuhrah ahead toward Bahurasīr. Zuhrah left Kūthā at the head of the vanguard until he arrived at Bahurasīr, having had a meeting at Sābāṭ with Shīrazādh, who offered him a truce and the payment of the *jizā'*.[22] Zuhrah sent Shīrazādh to Saʿd and went with him,

20. This is what it says in the text. Although emending the text should be resorted to only when no other solution seems to present itself, it is indeed tempting to reconstruct this particular passage in such a way that it reads ". . . people to whom Abraham used to preach." Instead of . . . *alladhīna kānū yubashshirūna Ibrāhīma,* the Arabic should then read . . . *alladhīna kāna Ibrāhīmu yubashshiruhum.*

21. The Qur'ānic verse III, 140, pertains allegedly to the successes and adversities of, respectively, the Muslims and the Meccans at the battles of Badr (2/624) and Uḥud (3/625). The verse may be thought of as conveying how Abraham's initial bad luck (see Ṭabarī, II, 263) took a turn for the better later in life.

22. *Jizā'* is a plural of *jizyah,* the tax paid by non-Muslims in exchange for "protection" (in Arabic *dhimmah*). Sayf seems to distinguish between the singular and the plural.

followed by the wings of the army.[23] Hāshim went forth, followed by Saʿd. In the meantime, the contingent formed by Queen [2425]
Būrān[24] had fled from Zuhrah in the vicinity of al-Muẓlim. Hāshim arrived finally at Muẓlim near Sābāṭ and waited for Saʿd to join him. That coincided with the return of al-Muqarraṭ, a tamed lion belonging to the king. Al-Muqarraṭ was chosen from the lions of al-Muẓlim. In al-Muẓlim there were several detachments of (a former) Kisrā, a woman called Būrān. Everyday they used to swear by God, "The kingdom of Fārs shall never perish as long as we live." When Saʿd arrived, Al-Muqarraṭ rushed toward the Muslim forces. Hāshim jumped down from his mount and killed it. Therefore his sword was named the Strong One.[25] Saʿd kissed Hāshim on the head; Hāshim kissed Saʿd's foot. Then Saʿd sent him ahead to Bahurasīr. Hāshim camped at al-Muẓlim and recited, "Had you not sworn previously that you would never perish?"[26] When a part of the night had passed, Saʿd departed and marched against the enemy at Bahurasīr. Every time the cavalry advanced on the way to Bahurasīr, the Muslims staying behind would stop what they were doing and shout, "God is great." They continued in that manner until the last warrior accompanying Saʿd had passed by. In all, he stayed with the army, attacking Bahurasīr for two months, and they crossed the river in the third.

ʿUmar b. al-Khaṭṭāb led the people on the pilgrimage that year. His governor over Mecca was ʿAttāb b. Asīd. Al-Ṭā'if was governed by Yaʿlā b. Munyah, al-Yamāmah and al-Baḥrayn by [2426]
ʿUthmān b. Abī al-ʿĀṣ. ʿUmān was governed by Ḥudhayfah b. Miḥṣan, and the districts of Syria by Abū ʿUbaydah b. al-Jarrāḥ. Al-Kūfah and its environs were given to Saʿd b. Abī Waqqāṣ, with Abū Farwah[27] in charge of the judiciary there, while al-Mughīrah b. Shuʿbah had charge over al-Baṣrah and its environs.

---

23. Or, conceivably, "horses," see Lane, II, 408.

24. See immediately below and also Morony, *Iraq*, 193.

25. In Arabic, al-Matn; a variant reading has the sword called al-Matīn, which means the same.

26. Q. XIV, 44.

27. *Glossarium*, p. DCXIX, suggests reading Abū Qurrah; this is confirmed by Wakīʿ, *Akhbār al-quḍāt*, II, 397.

The Events of the Year 16

(February 2, 637–January 22, 638)

Al-Ṭabarī said: In this year the Muslims entered the city of Bahurasīr and conquered al-Madā'in from which (king) Yazdajird b. Shahriyār fled.

The Remainder of the Account of the Muslims' Entering the City of Bahurasīr

According to al-Sarī—Shu'ayb—Sayf—Muḥammad, Ṭalḥah and al-Muhallab: When Sa'd descended upon Bahurasīr, he deployed his cavalry, which raided the people, who lived between the Tigris and those of the people along the Euphrates, who had concluded a treaty. These horsemen came upon 100,000 peasants who were duly counted. Each horseman gained control over one peasant, the situation being that everyone living near Bahurasīr was of Persian origin. The peasants dug protective trenches for them. Shīrazādh, the dihqān of Sābāṭ, said to Sa'd, "Do not maltreat them, they are only underlings of the Persians, and would never undertake anything against you. Leave them to me, until you find a (better) solution. So Shīrazādh wrote down their names for Saʿd, whereupon Saʿd handed them over. Then Shīrazādh told them, "Go back to your villages."

Saʿd wrote to ʿUmar, "We have (finally) arrived in Bahurasīr after what has happened to us on the way from al-Qādisiyyah to here. No one has engaged us in combat. I have deployed the cavalry (in all directions) and I have brought together the peasants from the villages and marshes.[28] Give me your opinion." ʿUmar replied, "Whoever of those peasants comes over to you, if they stay put (and) do not assist (your enemies) against you, then that constitutes their guarantee of safety. But whoever flees and you catch him, do with him as you think fit." When this letter reached Saʿd, he let the peasants go. The dihqāns sent messengers to him, whereupon he invited them to embrace Islam and then to return (to wherever they came from) or to pay the *jizā*ʾ, as a consequence of which they would enjoy full protection. One after the other they opted for the latter proposition. But no one entered into the same covenant who belonged to the entourage of the Persian king or his family. There did not remain (in the countryside stretching) from the west (bank) of the Tigris to the country of the Arab tribes one single person who did not live in guaranteed safety or who was not satisfied with the sovereignty of Islam. The Arabs received the *kharāj*. They laid siege to Bahurasīr, bombarding its people with catapults, closing in on them with armoured siege devices and fighting them with all available gear. [2427]

According to al-Sarī—Shuʿayb—Sayf—al-Miqdām b. Shurayḥ al-Ḥārithī—his father: The Muslims descended upon Bahurasīr. The city was protected by trenches, guards and all sorts of military gear. The Muslims bombarded them with catapults and smaller mangonels.[29] Then Saʿd asked Shīrazādh to build catapults, so he set up twenty such devices against the people of Bahurasīr; in this way they kept them busy. [2428]

According to al-Sarī—Shuʿayb—Sayf—al-Naḍr b. al-Sarī—Ibn al-Rufayl—his father: When Saʿd arrived at Bahurasīr, the Arabs lay in a circle around it with the Persians secure inside. Occasion-

28. That is how I interpret *ājām*, (lit. "thickets," "brushwoods") in this context; it could conceivably also be interpreted as the plural of *ujum* ("fortress"), but that does not seem to fit here, see Morony, *Iraq*, 189.

29. In this translation, I summarize the explanation of this word given in the margin of the Berlin manuscript of Ibn Ḥubaysh used for the edition.

ally, the Persians would venture outside, walking across the dams overlooking the Tigris in armed platoons, ready to wage battle with the Muslims, but they did not stand up to their besiegers. Finally they (all) came out, infantry and archers, fully resolved to wage battle, and having promised one another not to yield. So the Muslims fought with them and the Persians were not able to stand their ground. They failed in their attempt, turned around and fled. Zuhrah b. al-Ḥawiyyah was wearing a coat of mail with a gash in it. Some people said to him, "If you give the order, you could have this hole stitched up." Zuhrah said, "Why should I?" They answered, "On account of this gash we fear for your safety." Zuhrah replied, "I am a noble man in the eyes of God. Do you think that one Persian arrow from their entire army could be shot in such a way that it actually hits me through this crack and lodges in me?[30] He, Zuhrah b. al-Ḥawiyyah, was the first of the Muslims to be killed that day by an arrow, which lodged in him through that very gash. Some people said, "Pull the arrow out of him." But he said, "Leave me be; I may stay alive as long as it remains there. Perhaps I can make a victim on the other side with a spear thrust, a blow with my sword, or with an arrow."[31] So he rushed forward toward the enemy and, with his sword, he struck Shahrbarāz,[32] a man from Iṣṭakhr, killing him. Then he was surrounded and killed himself.[33] Thereupon his killers withdrew.[34]

According to al-Sarī—Shuʿayb—Sayf—ʿAbdallāh b. Saʿīd b.
[2429] Thābit—ʿAmrah, the daughter of ʿAbd al-Raḥmān b. Asʿad—ʿĀ'ishah, the mother of the believers: When God had granted victory and Rustum and his men were killed in al-Qādisiyyah and their multitudes dispersed, the Muslims pursued them until they dismounted at al-Madā'in. In the meantime, groups of Persians had scattered and reached their mountain regions. Their soldiers and cavalry spread in all directions except for the king, who stayed in their city with those Persians who had remained under his orders.

---

30. This is a tentative rendering of a seemingly corrupt text.

31. I have adopted Wellhausen's reading *ḥazwah*, "arrow," see *Glossarium*, p. DCXX, and Nöldeke, in *ZDMG*, XXV (1871):257.

32. Ibn al-Athīr, II, 397: Shahriyār.

33. Below on p. 20, Zuhrah will emerge again, alive and well.

34. In Ibn al-Athīr, II, 397, this final phrase is negated ". . . and they did not withdraw." Another interpretation might be ". . . were defeated."

According to al-Sarī—Shuʿayb—Sayf—Simāk al-Hujaymī—his unknown father and Muḥammad b. ʿAbdallāh—Anas b. al-Ḥulays: While we were besieging Bahurasīr after their sally and subsequent retreat, a messenger appeared (on the battlement) above us who said, "Thus speaks our king to you. Will you agree to a peace agreement that entitles us to (our side of) the Tigris and our mountain and you to your side as far as your mountain; will you not be satisfied with this? (If not), may God never satisfy your appetites!" Then Abū Mufazzir al-Aswad b. Quṭbah, to the surprise of the people, (answered back), God making him utter words of which he did not know the meaning, nor we, for that matter. So the man withdrew (from the battlements) and we saw the Persians crossing the river back to al-Madā'in. "What did you say to him, Abū Mufazzir?," we asked. He replied, "By Him who sent us Muḥammad with the true message. I do not know what it was except that a divine tranquility[35] had come over me; I hope that I, [2430] one day, will be made to speak even better words." So the people continued firing questions at him, until Sa'd heard about this. He came to us and said, "Abū Mufazzir, what did you say? By God, the Persians have all fled!" Abū Mufazzir gave Saʿd the same explanation he had given us.

Then Saʿd rallied the people and marched with them (toward the enemy) while our catapults rained projectiles upon them. Nobody appeared on the city ('s walls) and no one came out toward us except the one man who called out to us that his life be spared. This we granted. He said, "There is no one left, what is holding you back?" Then our men scaled the walls. Thus we conquered the city. We did not find anything or anyone in it except some prisoners whom we brought outside the city in fetters. We interrogated them, as well as that man, as to why the Persians had all fled. They answered, "The king sent a messenger to you, offering you a peace agreement, but you replied to him that there never would be peace between you and us until we would eat honey of Ifrīdhīn[36] mixed with citrons of Kūthā. Then the king said, "Woe unto us, only angels, speaking with their

35. The Arabic word *sakīnah* used here has an equivalent in the Hebrew *shekhinah*.

36. This is perhaps identical to Ifrandīn, see Yāqūt, *Muʿjam*, I, 324, a region between al-Rayy and Naysābūr.

[2431] tongues, descending upon us, would answer us (in this way) on behalf of the Arabs! If this is not as I say (, I'll be damned[37]). This cannot be anything other than words put into the mouth of this man, (i.e., by someone or something else) so that we give up the struggle." Then they fell back upon the other not yet conquered section of the city (of al-Madā'in on the other bank of the river).

Al-Sarī—Shuʿayb—Sayf—Saʿīd b. al-Marzubān—Muslim gave more or less the same account as that of Simāk; and according to al-Sarī—Shuʿayb—Sayf—Muḥammad, Ṭalḥah, al-Muhallab, ʿAmr and Saʿīd: When Saʿd and the Muslims entered Bahurasīr, he made the people settle there and the base camp of the army was moved to it. When they attempted to cross the river, they found that the Persians had concentrated all the ships (on the other bank and tied them up all the way) between al-Baṭā'iḥ and Takrīt.[38]

When the Muslims entered Bahurasīr, in the middle of the night, they saw something white. Ḍirār b. al-Khaṭṭāb exclaimed, "God is great, this white thing there must be the palace[39] of the king, as God and His messenger have promised us." The people never stopped shouting "God is great!" until dawn. Muḥammad and Ṭalḥah added: That was in the night when they descended upon Bahurasīr.

According to al-Sarī—Shuʿayb—Sayf—al-Aʿmash—Ḥabīb b. Ṣuhbān Abū Mālik: We pressed forward toward al-Madā'in, that is Bahurasīr, that part of the city nearest (to us on the west bank of the Tigris) and we besieged their king and his followers until they ate dogs and cats. The report goes on: The Muslim army did not enter (the city), however, until a Persian called out, "By God, there is no one here." Then they moved in and, indeed, there was no one inside.

The Report Concerning al-Madā'in al-Quṣwā, That Is, That Part (on the East Bank of the Tigris) in Which the King Had His Residence

Sayf added: That was in Ṣafar of the year 16 (March 4–April 1,
[2432] 637). The transmitters said: When Saʿd arrived in Bahurasīr, that

37. This elided apodosis was suggested by Prym (. . . *nihil intelligo*).

38. This elaborate interpretation seems to be suggested by the Arabic terms *ḍammū al-sufun.*

39. My hunch that the White Palace may be meant here is prompted by the mention of *al-qaṣr al-abyaḍ* on p. 16 below; see also p. 20.

is, that part of the city (of al-Madā'in on the) near (west bank of the Tigris), he looked for boats to cross with his men to the city (on the eastern or far side of the Tigris). But he did not find any. He found that the Persians had concentrated all the boats (on the eastern bank).[40] So the Arabs stayed in Bahurasīr for several days of that month of Ṣafar, urging Sa'd to make the crossing. Concern for the lives of the Muslims prevented him from making the crossing, until some local people came to him.[41] It was they who showed him a place where one could wade through onto *terra firma.* Sa'd was disinclined at first, and hesitated to do that, when suddenly a rise of the water surprised them. Now, Sa'd had had a dream describing how the horses of the Muslims rushed into a river to cross it, advancing against the rising water (as if spurred) by a gigantic force. Also, in order to have this dream explained, he had set his mind on crossing the river, and that in a year of uninterrupted summer rain! So Sa'd assembled the people, praised God and extolled Him, and said, "Your enemy has taken refuge from you across this river, so you cannot get at them,[42] whilst they can get at you if they want, and engage in skirmishes with you from their boats. Behind you there is nothing, however, that you have to fear an attack from. The veterans of our past battles[43] have protected you against them, wrecked their frontier garrisons and annihilated those who protected them. I think it would be the proper course to embark upon a holy war against the enemy aided by your strong intentions, before unforeseen circumstances prevent you from doing so.[44] Therefore I have decided to cross this river towards them!" Thereupon they all said, "May God decide

40. The crossing of the Tigris depicted here induced Wellhausen to compare it with a miraculous crossing of a large stretch of seawater during the *riddah* campaign in al-Baḥrayn, see *Skizzen*, VI, 23, 72. I do not think that that is called for; the admittedly risky crossing described in the following pages seems in my opinion perfectly plausible and need not be seen as *Auflockerung der Berichterstattung*, as Noth calls such a device.

41. In Arabic, *a'lāj*, plural of *'ilj*, "non-Arab."

42. I cannot find a suitable rendering for *ma'ahu* in this sentence; if we decide to read *minhu* instead of *ma'ahu*, which does not seem to be substantiated by the available manuscripts, we can render it "across it," that is "across the river."

43. In Arabic, *ahl al-ayyām;* this points to warriors who had been present at battles preceding that of al-Qādisiyyah.

44. Literally, "before the world encircles/besieges you." Some variants listed in the apparatus "to break," "to harvest" and "to arrive at" do not make much sense either. It must be obvious that any rendering is tentative.

to give right guidance to us as well as you. Do as you say you will!"

Saʿd ordered the men to cross, saying, "Who will go first to (take possession of and) keep occupied the city's loading quays for us
[2433] (on the bank of the river[45]), until the (other) warriors can join him, lest the enemy prevent them from reaching the other bank[46])?" So ʿĀṣim b. ʿAmr, the valiant, volunteered and, after him, six hundred men of tested steadfastness.[47] Saʿd made ʿĀṣim their commander, who marched in their midst until he came to a halt on the bank of the Tigris. Then ʿĀṣim said, "Who will volunteer to go with me so that we may keep the city's loading quays free from the enemy and give you protection until you have all crossed?" Sixty people showed their willingness, among them Aṣamm from the Banū Wallād and Shuraḥbīl, as well as several equally valiant others. ʿĀṣim divided them into two squadrons of cavalry, one consisting of only mares and one of only stallions so that they might be more tractable when urged to swim. Then they plunged into the Tigris with the rest of the six hundred on their heels.

The first to advance on their own, ahead of those sixty, were Aṣamm al-Taym, al-Kalaj, Abū Mufazzir, Shuraḥbīl, Jaḥl al-ʿIjlī, Mālik b. Kaʿb al-Hamdānī and a young lad from the Banū al-Ḥārith b. Kaʿb. When the Persians saw them and realized what they were doing, they made for the same horses as those used against Saʿd. Having mounted them, they also plunged into the Tigris, urging them to swim toward the Muslims. They came face to face with ʿĀṣim among his vanguard, who had almost come abreast with the loading quays of the city. ʿĀṣim shouted, "Use your spears, use your spears! Point them at those horses, aim at their eyes!" Then they became engaged in man–to–man combat, going for one another with their spears, the Muslims aiming at their enemies' eyes. The latter retreated toward the shore with
[2434] the Muslims on their heels, urging their mounts at them, and the

45. In modern military terms this might be called "establishing a beachhead."

46. I have opted for Ibn al-Athīr's reading *ʿubūr* instead of *khurūj* (II, 398).

47. In Arabic, *ahl al-najadāt*; according to the *Tāj*, *najdah* is not the sort of courage that urges a warrior to surge recklessly forward into battle, but rather shows his composure in times of *shiddah*, "hardship." Donner (344) interprets "champions"; this does not seem entirely satisfactory.

Persian horsemen unable to withstand the attack. So the Muslims caught up with them on the shore and killed most of them, while some of them got away having lost an eye in the process. Their horses staggered away with them until the loading quays were vacated.

None the worse for wear, the six hundred caught up with those sixty vanguard. When Saʿd saw ʿĀṣim in control of the loading quays, he gave permission to his men to take the plunge themselves, calling to them, "Say aloud: We ask God for support, we rely on Him; He suffices us, an excellent guardian is He; there is no power nor strength except in God, the exalted, the great!" Thus the main force of the army followed closely, riding the waves, the otherwise dark colored water of the Tigris throwing up spume. Indeed, the men kept on talking to one another while they swam across, in close-knit groups, without a care, conversing as if they were on the march on dry ground. Thus they surprised the Persians in a way the latter had not thought possible. They were quickly driven (out of the city), leaving behind the bulk of their possessions. The Muslims entered the city in Ṣafar of the year 16 (March 637) and confiscated all that had remained in the royal quarters: three billion (dirhams' worth) and what Shīrōē and those who had come after him had amassed.

Abū Bujayd Nāfiʿ b. al-Aswad composed the following poem on this event (in *khafīf*):

We urged (our) horses to Madā'in,
    Its waters like its dry land fruitful.
We cleansed the coffers of this Kisrā,
    They fled that day, like he, despairing.

According to al-Sarī—Shuʿayb—Sayf—al-Walīd b. ʿAbdallāh b. [2435]
Abī Ṭaybah—his father: When Saʿd camped at the Tigris, a local man came to him and asked, "Why do you stay here? Before three days have passed, Yazdajird may have fled with all his possessions from al-Madā'in." That is what incited Saʿd to sound the call to make the crossing.

According to al-Sarī—Shuʿayb—Sayf—a certain man—Abū ʿUthmān al-Nahdī (who reported on) how Saʿd stood up among his men calling upon them to make the crossing in more or less similar terms. Then he said: We covered the Tigris with men, horses and (other) animals to such an extent that, standing on the bank, you could no longer see the water. Our horses carried us to the enemy, shaking their manes, whinnying. When the Persians saw this, they ran away, no longer concerned with anything. We finally arrived at the White Palace, in which some people had fortified themselves. One of them looked out and addressed us. We called out to them and made them various propositions. We said, "There are three possibilities, from which you may choose whatever you want." They asked, "What are they?" We answered, "Islam first of all; if you embrace our religion, you will have the same privileges and obligations as we. If you reject this, then you may pay the *jizyah.* And finally, if you reject that too, you will have to do battle with us until God decides between us and you." A spokesman for them replied, "We have no use for the first or the last proposition, but we will accept the middle one." Al-Sarī—Shuʿayb—Sayf—ʿAṭiyyah reported a similar account, adding that their ambassador who negotiated with the Persians was Salmān (al-Fārisī).[48]

According to al-Sarī—Shuʿayb—Sayf—al-Naḍr b. al-Sarī—Ibn al-Rufayl: When they had routed the Persians in the water and chased them onto the loading quays, from which they subse-
[2436] quently expelled them too, they took away all their treasures except those which the Persians had been able to send ahead. Three billion (dirhams worth) had been in the king's treasure chambers (in all), and this three times over;[49] half of this had been sent away with Rustum, the other half they left in the treasure chambers.

According to al-Sarī—Shuʿayb—Sayf—Badr b. ʿUthmān—Abū Bakr b. Ḥafṣ b. ʿUmar: On that day, before asking the bulk of his army to take the plunge, looking at the advance party[50] battling on the loading quays, Saʿd stood up and spoke, "By God, had those

---

48. Of Persian origin, he is alleged to have gone from his native country to seek out the Prophet. Captured and sold as a slave, he embraced Islam and was manumitted, see Ibn Ḥajar, *Iṣābah*, III, 141.

49. Whether or not these last few words belong to the text seems dubious, see *Glossarium*, p. DCXX.

50. Literally, "the protectors," to wit, of a safe landing site for their fellow warriors.

fighters over there been the Kharsā' brigade,[51] the detachment in which were enlisted al-Qaʿqāʿ b. ʿAmr, Ḥammāl b. Mālik and al-Ribbīl b. ʿAmr, and had the Kharsā' fought those Persian horsemen in exactly the same manner as those out there, then that would (also) have been amply sufficient.[52] Now, ʿĀṣim's detachment was known as that of al-Ahwāl;[53] Saʿd simply compared the Ahwāl brigade with that of the Kharsā'[54] because of the struggle he witnessed in the water as well as on the beachhead."

The report goes on: Then, after they had taken a series of simple measures against the enemy and at the same time improved their own position, the "beachhead" party shouted across the water,[55] so the Kharsāʿ brigade[56] moved out and joined up with them. When they and the whole Ahwāl detachment had safely reached the loading quays, Saʿd ordered the rest of the men to plunge into the water. The one who crossed the water alongside Saʿd was Salmān al-Fārisī. While the horses swam the men across, Saʿd said, "God suffices us; an excellent guardian is He; by God, may He grant victory to His agent and may He render His religion victorious and defeat His enemy; if there are no offenders or sinners in His army, their merits alone will defeat the enemy." Then Salmān said, "Islam generates good fortune. By God, crossing [2437]
rivers has become as easy for them as crossing the desert. By Him in whose hand Salmān's soul lies, may they emerge from the water in the same numbers in which they entered it!" They crowded the surface so closely that, from the bank, one could no longer see the water. And all the way they chatted, even more so then had they been on land. They got out of the water as Salmān had prayed, having lost nothing and no one having drowned.

According to al-Sarī—Shuʿayb—Sayf—Abū ʿUmar Dithār—

51. Literally "the silent" or "dumb," see Lane, 722, middle column, for several different connotations.

52. I take this to mean: Then they would not have done the job more efficiently.

53. Literally "the horrors."

54. Presumably because they were famous for battling without too much clamor.

55. Translation tentative.

56. Although the Kharsā' brigade is not explicitly mentioned as the subject of the verb "moved out," from a report listed below I deduce that it was they who were the first to follow, see p. 20.

Abū ʿUthmān al-Nahdī: To the last man, they safely made the crossing except for one man from the tribe of Bāriq called Gharqadah, who slid off the back of his chestnut-colored mare which—I still see it clearly before my own eyes—shook its mane free.[57] While the man floated in the water, al-Qaʿqāʿ b. ʿAmr urged his horse toward him, grabbed his hand and dragged him along, until they safely reached the bank. The man from Bāriq, himself a very sturdy fellow, said, "Even my own sisters would not be able to give birth to someone like you, Qaʿqāʿ!" It so happened that al-Qaʿqāʿ did have maternal uncles among Bāriq!

According to al-Sarī—Shuʿayb—Sayf—Muḥammad, Ṭalḥah, al-Muhallab, ʿAmr and Saʿīd: On that day, nobody lost anything, save a cup, tied (to someone's luggage) with a frayed piece of string that broke, and was swept away in the water. Then the man who was making the crossing alongside the cup's owner said, upbraiding him, "God's decree[58] struck it, so it was lost." The cup's owner answered, "By God, I am just one individual; God would never take away only my cup from among all the people in
[2438] the army." When they had arrived at the other side, they came upon a man who had been one of those who initially had established the "beachhead." This man had gone down to the water's edge, until he met the first of the people emerging from the water. The wind and the waves had tossed the cup to and fro, until it landed on the bank. This man retrieved it with his lance and brought it to the troops. The owner recognized it as his and took it from him, saying to his former companion, "Did I not tell you. . . ?" The cup's owner was a confederate of the Quraysh from ʿAnz called Mālik b. ʿĀmir, and the one who had said, "Your cup is lost" was called ʿĀmir b. Mālik.

According to al-Sarī—Shuʿayb—Sayf—al-Qāsim b. al-Walīd—ʿUmayr al-Ṣāʾidī: When Saʿd urged his men to plunge into the Tigris, they all teamed up in pairs. Salmān was Saʿd's companion, making the crossing at his side. Saʿd said, "That is the decree of the Almighty, the Omniscient."[59] They floated thus in the water, all horses erect, in perfect balance. When a horse would become

57. Presumably from the man clinging to it.
58. In Arabic *qadar*; the alliteration with *qadaḥ* ("cup") is perhaps deliberate.
59. Q. VI, 96; XXXVI, 38; XLI, 12.

tired, it would (suddenly find itself) treading on to an elevation (i.e., in the river bottom) on which it could regain its breath as if it were on firm ground. That was the most astonishing thing that happened in the taking of al-Madā'in. That was the Day of the Water, also called the Day of the (Underwater) Humps.

According to al-Sarī—Shuʿayb—Sayf—Muḥammad, al-Muhallab, Ṭalḥah, ʿAmr and Saʿīd: The day they rode the Tigris was called the Day of the (Underwater) Humps, as soon as anyone became tired he would suddenly find himself walking onto an elevation (i.e., in the river bottom) on which he could regain his [2439]
breath.

According to al-Sarī—Shuʿayb—Sayf—Ismāʿīl b. Abī Khālid—Qays b. Abī Ḥāzim: We plunged into the Tigris, which was (at that time of the year) full. When we got to the deepest passages, the water did not reach higher than a horseman's belt, as long as he remained standing (in his stirrups).

According to al-Sarī—Shuʿayb—Sayf—al-Aʿmash—Ḥabīb b. Ṣuhbān Abū Mālik: When Saʿd entered the city on this side of the river (Bahurasīr), and as a consequence its people had destroyed the bridge and concentrated the boats (of which the bridge was made on the other, eastern, bank) the Muslims said, "What are you waiting for at this puddle?"[60] So one man rushed into the water and the others plunged in after him. No one drowned or lost any of his belongings, except one Muslim who lost a cup, the string (tying it to the luggage) had broken. I saw the cup floating in the water.

According to al-Sarī—Shuʿayb—Sayf—Muḥammad, al-Muhallab and Ṭalḥah: The defending Persians did not stop fighting on the loading quays until someone came to them who said, "Why are you killing yourselves? By God, al-Madā'in is deserted!"

According to al-Sarī—Shuʿayb—Sayf—Muḥammad, Ṭalḥah, al-Muhallab, ʿAmr and Saʿīd: When the unbelievers[61] saw the Muslims and what they had in mind, they sent troops who had to defend (the loading quays) against the Muslims' crossing. The others loaded their animals and fled away from the city. Before

60. The Arabic word is *nuṭfah*, "sperm"; in the present context clearly an insignificant quantity of liquid is meant.

61. The Arabic has *mushrikūn*, which literally means "polytheists." I have opted for "unbelievers" because I think it fits the English translation better.

that, after Bahurasīr had been conquered, Yazdajird had sent the members of his household away to Ḥulwān. Then he himself left later, journeyed until he arrived at Ḥulwān and joined his house-
[2440] hold, Mihrān al-Rāzī and al-Nakhīrajān the former keeper of the treasury at al-Nahrawān having been left in control. But they also departed, with the last troops, carrying as much as they could of the most precious and portable commodities, together with as much as they could possibly carry with them from the treasury. In addition, they took the women and children. However, in the treasure chambers they left behind clothes, other commodities, vessels, trinkets,[62] presents[63] and oils, all of inestimable value. They also left the cattle, sheep, food and drink, which they had held in readiness in case of a siege. The first to enter al-Madā'in were the Ahwāl brigade, followed by the Kharsā' brigade. They spread out over its streets, but they did not encounter or hear anyone but those left in the White Palace. So the Muslim brigades surrounded the Persians and called upon them to surrender. They responded to Sa'd's proposition accepting "protection" in exchange for *jizā'*. One after the other, the inhabitants of al-Madā'in eventually returned to the city on the same conditions, but in this agreement there were no terms pertaining to the royal family or its entourage.

Sa'd took up quarters in the White Palace. He sent Zuhrah at the head of the vanguard in pursuit of those who had fled to al-Nahrawān. So Zuhrah set forth until he arrived at al-Nahrawān. Sa'd[64] dispatched similar numbers in all directions in pursuit of those who had fled.

According to al-Sarī—Shu'ayb—Sayf—al-A'mash—Ḥabīb b. Ṣuhbān Abū Mālik: On the day of al-Madā'in when the Muslims
[2441] crossed the Tigris, the Persians, staring at them in the water, burst out shouting in Persian, "The devils have come!" (*dīwān āmad*).[65] Then they said to one another, "By God, you and I are

62. The Arabic word is *fuḍūl*, the plural of a word denoting "remainder," "rest." I arrived at my interpretation by inferring that what is left behind as superfluous or dispensable may well have consisted of trinkets. Ibn al-Athīr (II, 400) has *fuṣūṣ* "precious stones."

63. In Arabic, *alṭāf*, plural of *laṭaf*, see *Tāj*, s.v. *l-ṭ-f*.

64. Zuhrah can conceivably also be taken as the subject of this sentence.

65. In the Leiden manuscript of Ibn Ḥubaysh there is a marginal gloss of Abū Bakr b. Sayf (would he be the son of our Sayf?), which reads in translation, "Satan

not about to wage battle with ordinary people, instead, you and I will have to fight nothing but jinn." So they fled.

According to al-Sarī—Shuʿayb—Sayf—ʿAṭiyyah b. al-Ḥārith and ʿAṭāʾ b. al-Sāʾib—Abū al-Bakhtarī: The Muslims' scout[66] was Salmān al-Fārisī. They had nominated him to the function of middleman[67] with the people of Persia.

ʿAṭiyyah said: They had given him the order to invite the people of Bahurasīr to an agreement. The same order was given on the day of the White Palace's siege. So Salmān invited them to an agreement three times in all.

ʿAṭiyyah and ʿAṭāʾ both went on: The words Salmān called out to them ran as follows: "I have the same origin as you, I shall be compassionate toward you; you have three options to which I invite you, which may bring about a peace treaty for you: Either you embrace Islam, then you will be our brethren, you will have the same privileges and obligations as we. Or you pay the *jizyah.* And if these two propositions are not acceptable, then we will declare war on you . . . . likewise[68]; God does not care for the treacherous."

ʿAṭiyyah went on: When it was the third day, the people in Bahurasīr refused to accept any proposition, so the Muslims fought them. On the third day in al-Madāʾin, however, the occupants of the White Palace gave in and came outside. Saʿd took up his quarters in the White Palace and designated the Great Hall as prayer site.[69] In this hall there were several statues of plaster, but they were left in their place.

According to al-Sarī—Shuʿayb—Sayf—Muḥammad, Ṭalḥah and al-Muhallab, complemented by Simāk al-Hujaymī: The Persian king had sent his household to Ḥulwān, when Bahurasīr was [2442]

---

has arrived." Notice the singular and compare it with the plural used in the original Persian.

66. In Arabic, *rāʾid;* this term denotes originally "someone sent ahead to seek herbage." In a military context it also means "guide" or "reconnoiterer."

67. Literally, "propagandist."

68. A quotation from Q. VIII, 58. This "likewise," here seemingly out of context, makes good sense when the text immediately preceding it in the Qurʾān is considered: "If you fear that people (with whom you have a pact) may betray you, you should throw (that pact) back at them, likewise."

69. For a reconstruction of what this Great Hall (in arabicized Persian, *īwān*) may have looked like and what function it may have had in Sasanian times, see *EI*[2], s.v. *Īwān* (Grabar).

conquered. When the Muslims crossed the water, the king (and his entourage) left in flight, while his cavalry, at the water's edge, tried to prevent the Muslims and their horsemen from landing. So they and the Muslims fought fiercely, until someone called out to them, "Why get yourselves killed? By God, there is no one left in al-Madā'in!" So they were put to flight, pursued by the Muslim cavalry who rushed into the city. Sa'd made the crossing amidst the remainder of the army.

According to al-Sarī—Shu'ayb—Sayf—Muḥammad, Ṭalḥah and al-Muhallab: The vanguard of the Muslims caught up with the rearguard of the Persians. A certain Muslim called Thaqīf, one of the 'Adī b. Sharīf, caught up with a Persian warrior. He came face to face with him on one of the roads, while the latter was covering his companions' retreat. The Persian spurred his horse into attacking the Muslim, but it refused and would not budge. Then he spurred his horse to flee, but it was recalcitrant. Finally, the Muslim caught up with him, chopped off his head and took his armour as spoils.

According to al-Sarī—Shu'ayb—Sayf—'Aṭiyyah, 'Amr and Dithār Abū 'Amr: That day a certain Persian horseman from al-Madā'in happened to be in the vicinity of (a village called) Jāzir.[70] He was told that the Arabs had invaded the territory and that the Persians had fled. But, being a self-confident man, he did not pay heed to this news and went on until he entered the house of some of his serfs. They were busily packing their clothes. He said, "What is the matter with you?" They answered, "Hornets have driven us out of our houses and taken possession of them." So this man asked for (a crossbow and) clay bullets to be brought and he started
[2443] shooting at the hornets until he had killed many of them, glued to the walls. Then fear finally struck him. He got up and ordered a serf to saddle a mount for him. The saddlegirth broke, but he quickly refastened it and mounted. Then he left the village and stopped when another man passed him by. This man drove his spear into the Persian saying, "Take this, I am Ibn al-Mukhāriq,[71]" and he killed him. Then he went on his way, not paying heed to his victim.

According to al-Sarī—Shu'ayb—Sayf—Sa'īd b. al-Marzubān: In

70. Near al-Nahrawān, see Yāqūt, *Mu'jam*, II, 7.

71. If the name means anything in this context, unfortunately, this could not be established. Form III of *kharaqa* is listed nowhere.

a similar report: the man turned out to be Ibn al-Mukhāriq b. Shihāb.

They said: A certain Muslim warrior met a Persian, together with a band of people who were reproaching one another, saying, "For what are we fleeing?" One of them said to another, "Give me a ball."[72] Then he threw it (at a certain target), not missing it. When he saw this, he and the others headed in another direction, with himself in front. So they went until they came face-to-face with the aforementioned Muslim. The Persian shot the ball at him from a shorter distance than the first time, this time missing him. Then the Muslim went for the Persian and split his skull, saying, "I am Ibn Musharriṭ al-Ḥijārah.[73]" One after the other his companions fled away from the Persian (who lay there slain).

They said: When Saʿd entered al-Madā'in, he saw that it was vacated. Finally, he came to the Great Hall of the king's palace and started to recite, "How many gardens and springs (flowing therein) have they abandoned, how many sown fields and noble habitats, how many comforts in which they took delight! The situation was thus. We bequeathed them (and their properties) to another people[74])." Then he performed a prayer ritual commemorating the conquest; this was no congregational prayer meeting. He performed eight *rakʿa*s without pauses between them. He adopted the Great Hall as site for the prayer ritual. There were plaster statues there, of men and horses, but that did not prevent Saʿd, nor the other Muslims, (from praying there) and they were left as they were.

They said: Saʿd performed the prayer ritual on the day he entered the city; that was because he intended to stay there for the time being. [2444] The first Friday prayer ritual held in Iraq was the one held in congregation in al-Madā'in in Ṣafar of the year 16 (March 637).

---

72. In Arabic, *kurah*, obviously some sort of projectile is meant. A polo ball?

73. If, following the edition, we read Musharriṭ, we may interpret this with Lane "scarifier, someone who makes incisions (sc. here in stones, *ḥijārah*)." There is some confusion, though, as to whether we should read a second or a fourth form; the *Tāj*, s.v. *b-z-gh* (that is the synonym suggested by Lane) reads a first. The connotation "twisting," also found in connection with *sharaṭa* IV (see also *sharīṭah* in Lane), does not seem to fit in with *ḥijārah*.

74. Q. XLIV, 25–8. The words in brackets were gleaned from Qur'ān commentaries.

Mention of the Booty Amassed from the People of al-Madā'in

According to al-Sarī—Shu'ayb—Sayf—Muḥammad, al-Muhallab, 'Uqbah, 'Amr, Abū 'Umar and Sa'īd: Sa'd settled in the Great Hall of the King and dispatched Zuhrah with the order to go straightaway to al-Nahrawān. In addition, he sent similar detachments in every direction to expel the unbelievers and collect the spoils. After three days he moved to the palace. He entrusted 'Amr b. 'Amr b. Muqarrin with control over what was confiscated and ordered him to collect what was in the palace, the Great Hall and the private compounds. He also had to count what the search parties had produced. The inhabitants of al-Madā'in, at the time of the defeat, had quickly snatched up what they could before fleeing in every direction. Not one of them, however, escaped with anything that did not eventually turn up in the camp of Mihrān at al-Nahrawān; not even a piece of string. The search parties chased after them to the extent that they retrieved everything that those fleeing had taken with them; the Muslims brought back what the latter had snatched up in order to add all that to what already had been amassed. The first objects to be collected on that day were from the White Palace, the living quarters of the king and the other compounds of al-Madā'in.

According to al-Sarī—Shu'ayb—Sayf—al-A'mash—Ḥabīb b. Ṣuhbān: We marched into al-Madā'in and came upon Turkish
[2445] tents filled with baskets sealed with leaden seals. At first, we did not think they would contain anything but food, but later they were found to contain vessels of gold and silver. These were later distributed among the men. At the time, Ḥabīb (b. Ṣuhbān) went on, I saw a man running around shouting, "Who has silver or[75] gold in his possession?" We also came upon large quantities of camphor which we mistook for salt.[76] So we began to knead it (in our dough) until we discovered that it made our bread taste bitter.

According to al-Sarī—Shu'ayb—Sayf—al-Naḍr b. al-Sarī—Ibn al-Rufayl—his father al-Rufayl b. Maysūr: Zuhrah left with his

---

75. In the Arabic text we read *bi-ṣafrā'* "with gold." Is this a use of *bi-* referred to in Wright, II, 164, l. 1, sc. *li'l-muṣāḥabah*?

76. Indeed, an easy mistake to make, since both camphor and salt are commonly found as white crystals in nature.

vanguard, ordering them to follow him. Finally, they came to the bridge at al-Nahrawān. The Persians were actually on it, packed together. Suddenly a mule fell into the water. With great effort, the Persians hastened to retrieve it. Zuhrah exclaimed, "I swear by God, there must be something important about that mule. They would not have put in so much effort to retrieve it, nor would they have endured our swords in this dangerous situation, unless there was something special they did not want to give up." And sure enough, on this mule were packed the king's finery, his clothes, gems, swordbelt and coat of mail encrusted with jewelry. The king used to don all these when sitting in state. Then Zuhrah dismounted to fight. Thereupon, after he had routed them, he ordered his men to retrieve the mule. They lifted it (out of the water) and brought its baggage. Zuhrah returned this to the spoils, he and his men still unaware of its contents. On that day Zuhrah recited the following verses in *rajaz:*

My uncles be ransom today for my fighters,
 Recoiling from leaving me there at the river.
They cleft for (the prize of) the mule in the struggle
 With every sword blow the cranial sutures.
The Persians were slain covering their own hillocks, [2446]
 As if they were (nothing but mere) heads of cattle.[77]

According to al-Sarī—Shuʿayb—Sayf—Hubayrah b. al-Ashʿath—his grandfather al-Kalaj: I was among those who went out to look for the Persians who had fled. Suddenly I came upon two mule drivers who had repelled the cavalry with arrows. They had nothing but two arrows left. When I persevered in pursuing them, they deliberated, the one saying to the other, "When you shoot him, I'll cover you, or shall I shoot him while you cover me?" So each of them chose to cover the other. The result was that they shot off both arrows. Then I attacked them and killed them. Not realizing what they were carrying, I led the two mules back to our army, where I presented them to the overseer of the spoils. This man was writing down what the warriors brought him and what the treasure chambers and dwellings contained. He said, "Wait a moment,

77. This seemingly simple poem contains a metrical peculiarity and one or two double entendres, which receive detailed treatment in Appendix I.

we will see what you have brought." I began to unload them. On one of the mules there were two baskets containing the crown of the king, which could only be held aloft by two jewel-incrusted props.[78] On the other mule there were (also) two baskets containing the king's garments, in which he used to dress up, brocaded with interwoven gold thread and adorned with gems, as well as other garments made of different fabrics similarly interwoven and adorned.

According to al-Sarī—Shuʿayb—Sayf—Muḥammad, Ṭalḥah and al-Muhallab: Al-Qaʿqāʿ b. ʿAmr also went out that day in search of those who had fled. He caught up with a Persian covering the retreat of the others. They engaged in combat and al-Qaʿqāʿ slew
[2447] him. At the side of the dead man was a pack animal that carried two leather bags and two bundles, the latter containing five and six swords respectively, the former containing coats of mail. Among these coats of mail, there turned up the one of the king, his helmet, greaves and armplates, as well as the coats of mail of Heraklius,[79] Khāqān,[80] Dāhir,[81] Bahrām Shūbīn,[82] Siyāwakhsh,[83] and al-Nuʿmān.[84] What the Persians had not inherited, they had acquired as spoils, in the days of their raids on Khāqān, Heraklius and Dāhir. As for those of al-Nuʿmān and Bahrām, those were acquired when they dissented from the king and fled. One of the aforementioned

78. The crown was hanging above the king's head by a chain from the ceiling, or perhaps, as seems to be suggested here, from the two props. For more information on royal crowns at the Sasanian court, see Kurt Erdmann, "Die Entwicklung der Sāsānidischen Krone," in *Ars Islamica, XV–XVI* (1951):87–123; Christensen, *L'Iran*, 392–3; R. Ettinghausen, *From Byzantium to Sasanian Iran and the Islamic world* (Leiden 1972), 23, 28–9 (with pictures).

79. Presumably, this was a trophy captured in the course of the Byzantine campaign into Sasanian territory in the late 620's.

80. This is the title of a foreign monarch; in Ibn al-Athīr, II, 402, he is identified as the king of the Turks.

81. In Ibn al-Athīr, *loc. cit.*, Dāhir is identified as the king of India; on p. 2593 below he is mentioned as the king of Mukrān, or Makrān, the coastal area in southeast Iran, see Le Strange, *Lands*, 329–33. For more on Dāhir, see Yohanan Friedmann, "The Origins and Significance of the Chach Nāma," in *Islam in Asia*, I, Jerusalem, 1984, 23–37.

82. A usurper of the Persian throne, see Morony, *Iraq*, index (Bahrām Chūbīn).

83. Identified by De Goeje as Bahrām Shūbīn's grandson, see Ṭabarī's general index.

84. He is al-Nuʿmān b. al-Mundhir, the last of the Lakhmid kings (d. 602), see Morony, *Iraq*, 220.

bundles contained the swords of the king, Hurmuz,[85] Qubādh[86] and Fayrūz,[87] and the other swords turned out to be those of Heraklius, Khāqān, Dāhir, Bahrām, Siyāwakhsh and al-Nuʿmān.

Al-Qaʿqāʿ brought all these spoils to Saʿd who said, "Pick one of these swords." So al-Qaʿqāʿ selected the one of Heraklius. Saʿd also gave him Bahrām's coat of mail. The rest of this weaponry he distributed freely among the Kharsā' brigade, except for the swords of the king and al-Nuʿmān, which were sent to ʿUmar. This was so that the tribesmen, who had previous knowledge of the existence of these swords, would hear of this feat. Thus Saʿd and his men retained as part of the distributable booty[88] those two swords, the king's finery, his crown, and his garments. Then they sent these objects to ʿUmar for the Muslims to see and for the nomadic tribesmen to hear about. In this way, Khālid b. Saʿīd acquired the (famous) sword al-Ṣamṣāmah[89] belonging to ʿAmr b. Maʿdī Karib in the "apostasy" war [*al-Riddah*], Amr's fellow tribesmen asking that their lives be spared as a consequence.[90] [2448]

According to al-Sarī—Shuʿayb—Sayf—ʿUbaydah b. Muʿattib—someone from the Banū al-Ḥārith b. Ṭarīf—ʿIṣmah b. al-Ḥārith al-Ḍabbī: I marched among those who left in search of the Persian fugitives. I took a well-traveled path and found myself suddenly face-to-face with a man driving a donkey. When he saw me, he urged it forward, caught up with another man driving a donkey ahead of him and together they surged forward, spurring their donkeys to greater speed. Finally, they came to a stream. Its bridge was broken. They remained standing there until I reached them, then they parted ways. One shot at me, but I pursued and killed him. The other escaped. I returned to the donkeys and

85. Hurmuz is identified by De Goeje as the son of the king.

86. Identified by De Goeje as the son of Fayrūz.

87. Identified by De Goeje as the son of Yazdajird b. Bahrām Gūr.

88. In Arabic, *akhmās*, to be distinguished from *anfāl*, which is the booty handed out *freely* as some sort of special reward to the most deserving warriors, not necessarily in equal portions. Distribution in equal portions of the *khums* (=one-fifth sent to Medina) and the *akhmās* (=four-fifths divided among the participating soldiers) is called in Arabic *qasm* or *iqtisām*, to be distinguished from the handing out of *anfāl*, which is *nafl* or *tanfīl*. See also n. 94 below.

89. This is a sword which does not bend, see Lane, 1724, left column.

90. Conceivably, this last sentence admits of an alternative interpretation: "as a result of which ʿAmr's fellow tribesmen were put to shame."

brought them to the overseer of the booty. He inspected what the one was carrying. It turned out to be two baskets. In one of these there was a golden figure of a horse, saddled with a silver saddle; on its crupper and breast girth there were rubies and emeralds encased in silver. Its bridle was likewise embellished. There also was a figure of a horseman made of silver encrusted with gems. The other basket contained a figurine representing a silver she-camel; on it were a saddlecloth and a strap of gold. It also had a halter or bridle made of gold, all this studded with rubies. On the camel a man, made of gem-encrusted gold, was seated. The king used to attach these two figures to the props used for holding his crown aloft.

According to al-Sarī—Shuʿayb—Sayf—Hubayrah b. al-Ashʿath
[2449] —Abū ʿUbdah al-ʿAnbarī: When the Muslims descended upon al-Madāʾin and collected the booty, a man came forward carrying a box. He handed this to the overseer of the spoils who with the others said, "We have never seen anything like it; it is not like anything we have, not even remotely." They asked that man whether he had taken away for himself anything from the contents, whereupon he exclaimed, "Of course not, had it not been for God, I would not have brought this box to you." So they began to realize that this was a man of importance. "Who are you?," they asked, to which the man replied, "I won't tell you in anticipation of your praise, nor anyone else in order to solicit his eulogy. I praise God and am satisfied with His reward." (Still curious,) they had him followed by someone. When he finally reached his people, the man (who had shadowed him) made inquiries as to his identity. He turned out to be ʿĀmir b. ʿAbd Qays.[91]

According to al-Sarī—Shuʿayb—Sayf—Muḥammad, Ṭalḥah, al-Muhallab, ʿAmr and Saʿīd: Saʿd said, "By God, the army is truly honest! If it had not been for the prestige of the fighters at Badr[92] earned in the past—and I swear by God, I uphold their merit!—time and again I came across trifles (from the booty amassed at Badr) too many to enumerate, which several of them had kept for

91. He seems a relatively nondescript figure. He plays a minor role in vol. XV of this series.

92. Name of a well where the famous first battle of the year 2 (624) took place between Muḥammad helped by his Medinan following and a far superior Meccan force accompanying a richly laden caravan.

themselves, whereas I never heard that the warriors (involved in this battle) did anything of the sort!"

According to al-Sarī—Shuʿayb—Sayf—Mubashshir b. al-Fuḍayl— Jābir b. ʿAbdallāh: "By God beside Whom there is no other god, it has not come to our notice that anyone of the fighters present at al-Qādisiyyah wanted this world's riches beside the [2450]
Hereafter." Although we did suspect three men, Ṭulayḥah b. Khuwaylid, ʿAmr b. Maʿdī Karib and Qays b. al-Makshūḥ,[93] we ourselves, nor the enemy whom we attacked, had ever seen anything like their honesty and moderation.

According to al-Sarī—Shuʿayb—Sayf—Muḥammad b. Qays al-ʿIjlī—his father: When the king's sword, belt and finery were brought to ʿUmar, he exlaimed, "People who hand in such precious booty are indeed honest!" Then ʿAlī said, "It is your own virtuous conduct that is imitated by the people."

According to al-Sarī—Shuʿayb—Sayf—ʿAmr and al-Mujālid—al-Shaʿbī: When ʿUmar saw the king's weaponry, he said, "People who hand in such costly spoils are indeed honest!"

How the Booty Acquired at al-Madā'in Was Distributed among the People Present at Its Conquest, Who Numbered, as Sayf Claims, in All Sixty Thousand

According to al-Sarī—Shuʿayb—Sayf—Muḥammad, Ṭalḥah, ʿAmr, Saʿīd and al-Muhallab: When Saʿd, after his arrival in al-Madā'in, had dispatched people in pursuit of the Persians who had fled, the search party reached al-Nahrawān. Then they gradually retreated and the unbelievers marched on to Ḥulwān. After he had set aside the fifth, Saʿd distributed the booty among the people. Every horseman [2451]
received a share to the value of twelve thousand (dirhams). In fact, all of them were mounted, no infantry having participated in the conquest. The number of pack animals in al-Madā'in was large.

Al-Sarī—Shuʿayb—Sayf—al-Mujālid—al-Shaʿbī gave a similar account. All the transmitters agree in that he distributed freely

93. All three of these were notorious for having "apostatized," i.e. refused to pay the taxes imposed by Medina, upon the death of the Prophet. They were subdued again during the reign of Abū Bakr in the course of the *Riddah* wars, the so-called "apostasy wars."

from the (remaining four-fifths of the) spoils, without letting only the men who had displayed particular valor have more than their exact share.[94]

They said: Sa'd distributed the houses of al-Madā'in among the people and made them move into them. The man who exercised control over the collecting of the spoils was 'Amr b. 'Amr al-Muzanī. The man in charge of the booty's distribution was Salmān b. Rabī'ah. Al-Madā'in was conquered in Ṣafar of the year 16 (March 637).

They said: When Sa'd invaded al-Madā'in, he firmly established regulations concerning the performance of the prayer ritual, and he also fasted. He issued orders that the people were to come to the Great Hall of the Royal palace. This hall was made into a place of worship for the religious festivals. He had a pulpit erected in it. Sa'd used to perform the prayer ritual in this hall while there were still (Persian) statues standing there. He also used to convene the congregational Friday prayer in it. When a fast was broken, it was commonly said, "Show yourselves, for the established norm concerning the two festivals is that you come into the

---

94. This is a difficult passage and perhaps needs some explanation. The "people of particular valor" is my rendering of the Arabic *ahl al-balā'*. On p. 2412 of vol. XII of this series we find in the details of 'Umar's *dīwān* ("stipend register") a reference to them, which permits us to see them as fighters who received more than their normal share from the spoils, because they had especially distinguished themselves in the battle of al-Qādisiyyah and the main battles in Syria (e.g. al-Yarmūk), but who had *not yet* been mobilized into the Muslim armies fighting the battles immediately *preceding* that of al-Qādisiyyah and its Syrian counterpart. Those battles were called *al-ayyām* (lit. "the days"). In other words, they fell just short of the prestige accorded to the *ahl al-ayyām*.

"Distributing freely" is my rendering of the verb *naffala*. Contrary to the verb *qasama*, which means "dividing into exactly equal shares among. . . ," *naffala* means "giving each according to his individual merits," or "handing out in unequal shares." This interpretation is based on *Tāj*, s.v. *n-f-l*, where we read among other things: *naffalahu tanfīlan faḍḍalahu 'alā ghayrihi* and *naffilū akbarakum ay zīdūhu 'alā ḥiṣṣatihi*, see also Noth, index s.v. *nafal*. On p. 2412 of Vol. XII, where the *ahl al-balā'* were previously mentioned, we read how to the *bāri'* ("excellent") from among them a larger share is allotted. For the fifth form of this root in the *Tāj* we come across the connotation *tabarra'a bi'l- 'aṭā' tafaḍḍala bi-mā lā yajibu 'alayhi*. Finally, in this at first sight obscure, passage, we are lumbered with the terms *wal-lam yajhadhā*, which constitutes Prym's otherwise nearly always judicious vocalization. Contrary to what has been my policy adopted throughout, I had to reject this vocalization, because it does not seem to make sense. I propose to read a fourth form: *wa-lam yujhidhā*; Lane gives for IV also "to give away here and there," see *Tāj*, s.v. *j-h-d*.

open."[95] Sa'd said, "Perform your prayer rituals in the Great Hall." It is reported that he himself did so. He also said, "(Come to the Great Hall for the congregational prayer) no matter whether you happen to be in the very centre of your village."[96]

According to al-Sarī—Shu'ayb—Sayf—'Amr—al-Sha'bī: When Sa'd had settled in al-Madā'in and had divided the living quarters, he sent for the families[97] and settled them in the houses. These had privies and the like.[98] They stayed on in al-Madā'in until the Muslims had finally finished at Jalūlā', Takrīt and al-Mawṣil. After that they moved to al-Kūfah.

According to al-Sarī—Shu'ayb—Sayf—Muḥammad, Ṭalḥah, Ziyād and al-Muhallab, 'Amr and Sa'īd shared with them the same account: Sa'd brought together the fifth part of the booty. Therein was included everything with which he wanted to surprise 'Umar: to wit the king's garments, finery, his sword and the like, [2452]
and what might delight Arab tribesmen as well, if it fell into their hands.[99] Then he freely distributed[100] from the remaining four-fifths (among the people of valor). After also the more strict division among the rest of the people was carried out and after he had set apart the fifth (destined for Medina), he was left with the *qiṭf*,[101] but dividing that up could not be achieved in any fair way. So Sa'd addressed the Muslims saying, "What do you think, if we were to manage without dividing among us four-fifths of this *qiṭf*, so that we could dispatch it to 'Umar for him to dispose of as he deems fit? For we are of the opinion that it cannot be divided successfully among us, because we (would only end up each of us

---

95. With this there seems to be an implication that Sa'd wanted to give the congregational aspect of the performance of the prayer ritual more emphasis; history confirms that every nascent religion has benefitted from accentuating this aspect.

96. In other words, far away from the Great Hall.

97. Sc. those families left behind at the 'Atīq, see pp. 1-2 above.

98. That is how I interpret *marāfiq* here, a word which, according to Lane, stands for any appurtenances of a house, such as the kitchen or washing facilities. My choice of the interpretation "privy" may be justified with the occurrence of *kanīf*, plural *kunuf*, in Ibn Hishām, *Sīrah*, III, 312, indicating a "privy" in use with non-Arabs.

99. The intention seems to be that 'Umar might be thus enabled to persuade nomadic tribesmen to convert to Islam more readily.

100. Again we have the term *naffala*, rather than *qasama*, the latter implying a division in strictly equal shares; see n. 94 above.

101. What this *qiṭf* is will be explained below.

owning) a small piece, whereas it would suit the people of Medina admirably."[102] "But of course, we agree," the people answered. So Sa'd sent it to 'Umar as he had found it.

This *qiṭf,* measuring sixty by sixty cubits, was one (gigantic) carpet, one *jarīb*[103] in size. On it were pictures of roads and inlays like rivers; among them were pictures of houses. The edges looked like cultivated lands planted with spring vegetables, made of silk on stalks of gold. Their blossoms were of gold and silver, etc.

When the fifth finally reached 'Umar, he freely distributed from it among certain people and said, "From the main four-fifths of the booty those of the people of valor, who were or were not present at the battle, received their free shares, in all totaling two-fifths.[104] But I am of the opinion that (here in Medina none of) the Medina fifth should be divided up in *free* shares."[105] Then he distributed it in exactly equal shares among those who were entitled to it.[106] Thereupon 'Umar asked, "Advise me as to what to
[2453] do with this carpet." Medina's elders all agreed on one solution and said, "The fighters out there have made that matter over to you,[107] so you do as you think fit." They all agreed on this except 'Alī, who had another suggestion to offer. "Commander of the Faithful," 'Alī said, "the matter stands indeed as they have said,

---

102. If my translation is correct, with this there seems an implication that granting this *qiṭf* a permanent place in Medina, for everybody to enjoy, appeared to Sa'd a better solution than cutting it up in so many pieces in al-Madā'in.

103. A *jarīb* is a land measure of 958 m^2, see Hinz, 60; if we assume it was square, that means that it was a carpet of more than 30 meters long and broad. A cubit is a little over 50 cm in this context. The wording of the following few lines seems defective.

104. This figure of two-fifths may imply *either* that the other two-fifths minus the *qiṭf* were distributed according to the *qasm* method, *or* that two-fifths constituted all the booty distributed among the warriors, the remaining two-fifths representing the value of the *qiṭf.*

105. The text reads *jahadū 'l-khumsa bi'l-nafli;* again I propose to read a fourth form rather than a first (see above, n. 94), or we may deduce that I and IV may have the same meaning: treating booty as to be divided up, not according to the *qasm* method, but rather to the *nafl* method, not in strictly equal shares and commensurate with the achievements or prestige of the recipients.

106. Q. VIII, 41, stipulates that the fifth ("God's share") is to be distributed among the Prophet's relatives, as well as orphans, poor people and travelers, while one-fifth of the fifth, originally destined for the Prophet himself, was now to be deposited in the treasury.

107. The verb used is *ja'ala,* which also implies "giving a soldier his wages."

so there remains no other solution than to ponder this matter somewhat more. If you accept it today as it is, (there does not seem to be anybody who objects, but) tomorrow you will certainly come across people who are entitled to something of the booty that is not in their possession." "You are quite right," ʿUmar said, "that is sound advice." So he cut up the carpet and distributed the pieces among them.

According to al-Sarī—Shuʿayb—Sayf—ʿAbd al-Malik b. ʿUmayr: On the day of the conquest of al-Madāʾin the Muslims acquired "the king's spring,"[108] which they found too cumbersome[109] to take along. They had been keeping it ready for use in winter for the time when their provisions were all but exhausted. When they wanted a drinking party, they would sit and drink on this carpet. Then they would feel as if they were sitting in a garden. It was a carpet measuring sixty by sixty (cubits); its background[110] was gold-colored, its brocade was inlaid, the fruits depicted on it were precious stones, its foliage silk and its waters golden. The Arabs used to call it the *qiṭf*. When Saʿd had divided the booty among them, he was left with this carpet; he could not bring himself to cut it up. So Saʿd gathered the Muslims and said to them, "God has filled your hands, but dividing this carpet is not so easy; nobody could possibly purchase it.[111] Therefore, I consider it a good idea that you should relinquish it freely to the Commander of the Faithful; let him dispose of it as he wants." Thus they decided. When the carpet had reached ʿUmar in Medina, he had a dream. He convened the people, praised God and extolled Him, and, having told them what this was all about, he asked them their opinion. Some people suggested that ʿUmar keep it for himself, others that he be the arbiter thereof,[112] and still others created disagreement.[113] When ʿAlī saw that ʿUmar was about to reject each of these suggestions, he stood up, went to him and said, "Why do you pretend not to know or to have doubts? Nothing of this material [2454]

108. *Bahār-i Kisrā* is the Persian name of the carpet the Arabs called *qiṭf*.

109. The word used here, *thaqula*, has two connotations "to be heavy" and "to be difficult." The double entendre is perhaps intentional.

110. According to Lane, the Arabic word *arḍ* can mean "carpet."

111. Or "sell it," the Arabic *shirāʾ* being a *ḍidd* admitting of either interpretation.

112. Translation tentative.

113. Translation tentative.

world really belongs to you except what you have been given and then you spend it all, or the clothes with which you dress yourself which you then wear thin, or the food you eat which you then digest." "You are perfectly right," 'Umar replied. So he cut the carpet up into equal pieces and distributed these among the people. 'Alī also acquired a fragment which he sold for twenty thousand (dirhams). And that was not even the best piece!

According to al-Sarī—Shu'ayb—Sayf—Muḥammad, Ṭalḥah, al-Muhallab, 'Amr and Sa'īd: The one who took charge of the four-fifths, namely those of al-Madā'in, was Bashīr b. al-Khaṣṣāṣiyyah. The one who relayed news of the conquest of the city was Ḥulays, of unknown parentage, from Asad, and the one overseeing the amassing of the plunder was 'Amr (b. 'Amr al-Muzanī). Its distribution was in the hands of Salmān (b. Rabī'ah). They continued: When the carpet had been cut up and distributed among the people, they profusely praised the warriors of al-Qādisiyyah. 'Umar said, "Of all the Arabs, they are the prominent ones, the champions. For them, religion goes hand in hand with many dangers. They are truly the warriors of the early battles and of al-Qādisiyyah and its aftermath."[114] They continued: When the king's finery, as well as his attire when he sat in state and his garments destined for other occasions (he had a number of different ceremonial dresses, one set for every occasion), reached Medina, 'Umar ordered that Muḥallim be brought forward. At that time this man was the most corpulent Bedouin in the region of Medina. Muḥallim was crowned with the royal crown, held aloft on its two wooden props, dressed up in his sashes, necklaces and garments, and seated in front of the people. 'Umar looked at him; so did the people. They saw something magnificent belonging to this material world and its allure. Then Muḥallim stepped out of those and he was dressed up in the next set of regalia. The people looked at all that without interest[115] until all the royal garments

114. The Arabic reads *ahl al-ayyām wa-ahl al-qawādis*; for the first category of people, see p. 13, n. 43 above. Al-Qawādis, which means literally "the Qādisiyyas," I interpreted as comprising the battles of al-Qādisiyyah as well as immediately subsequent battles and skirmishes. See also Yāqūt, *Mu'jam*, IV, 196.

115. This rendering is a tentative one; the Arabic *fī ghayri nū'in* or *naw'in* is listed nowhere in the dictionaries consulted. The *Lisān* suggests "hunger" or "thirst" for *nū'*, which I have used here.

had been tried on. Then Muḥallim was asked to arm himself with the king's weapons and to gird himself with his sword. The people kept staring. Then ʿUmar ordered him to take everything off [2455] and said, "By God, people who surrender (such precious objects instead of keeping them for themselves) are truly honest." Then he handed the king's sword to Muḥallim as his share of the spoils and said, "How stupid is the Muslim who is beguiled by material possessions! Surely, does anyone thus beguiled attain anything except less than this his present share or even just as much? What good is there for any Muslim in that which previously harmed the king and was of no use to him? The king did not go beyond devoting himself to what he was told about his afterlife. Thus he gathered riches for the (future) husband of his wife (after his death) or for his daughter's husband or his son's wife. For himself he did not set anything aside. Here a man has provided for himself and has secured that which he does not immediately need in storage, so that that might provide for him later and if not, then in any case for the three (comparable descendants) coming after him. How stupid is he who gathers riches for the sole benefit of his descendants or (simply) for an enemy to scoop up!"[116]

According to al-Sarī—Shuʿayb—Sayf—Muḥammad b. Kurayb—Nāfiʿ b. Jubayr: At the time when the spoils[117] were brought, while looking at the king's weaponry, garments and finery—together with the sword of al-Nuʿmān b. al-Mundhir—ʿUmar said to Jubayr (b. Muṭʿim), "Verily, people who submit (precious booty such as) this are truly honest. What clan did al-Nuʿmān belong to?" Jubayr answered, "The Arabs used to trace his lineage to a few remaining members of Qanaṣ; he was one of

116. This entire speech of ʿUmar is quite unclear and my rendering is a tentative one. One wonders whether ʿUmar's audience understood one iota of it, that is, if it is historical.

117. The text has *akhmās* "the fifths"; I take this not as an erroneous reading for *khums* "one-fifth," the normal fraction to be sent back to Medina, but I interpret this as implying that, because al-Madīnah received on top of the usual fifth that costly carpet described above, it received spoils to the value of a few That we do not have a simple mistake (*akhmās* instead of *khums*) is borne out by the occurrence of the term *akhmās* describing the al-Madā'in booty sent to Medina also on a later occasion, see p. 36 below. It is, of course, also conceivable that we have to interpret the plural *akhmās* as an indication of the different *khums* parts acquired as a result of different conquests or battles.

the Banū ʿAjam b. Qanaṣ." ʿUmar said, "Take his sword," granting it as booty to Jubayr. Not aware of the name ʿAjam, the people always said Lakhm. They went on: ʿUmar entrusted Saʿd b. (Abī Waqqāṣ) Mālik with organizing the *ṣalāt* in the territory conquered and leading the military actions in it. Saʿd did so. Furthermore, ʿUmar charged al-Nuʿmān and Suwayd with the levying of
[2456] the land tax. They were sons of ʿAmr b. Muqarrin. Suwayd took charge of the land irrigated by the Euphrates and al-Nuʿmān of that irrigated by the Tigris. They also constructed bridges. Then ʿUmar sent as overseers—whereupon they resigned—Ḥudhayfah b. Asīd and Jābir b. ʿAmr al-Muzanī. Thereupon he sent as overseers of the latter two Ḥudhayfah b. al-Yamān and ʿUthmān b. Ḥunayf.

Ṭabarī said: In this year, I mean the year 16 (637), the battle of Jalūlāʾ took place. This was reported to me by Ibn Ḥumayd, who said that he had been informed by Salamah on the authority of Ibn Isḥāq. Also al-Sarī wrote to me about this, mentioning that Shuʿayb had informed him about this on the authority of Sayf.

The Report about the Battle of Jalūlāʾ al-Waqīʿah[118]

According to al-Sarī—Shuʿayb—Sayf—Ismāʿīl b. Abī Khālid—Qays b. Abī Ḥāzim: After we had descended upon al-Madāʾin and distributed the spoils that were there, having sent more than[119] one-fifth to ʿUmar, and having populated it again with our own people, we stayed there for a while. Then there came to us the news that Mihrān had made his camp in Jalūlāʾ after he had a trench dug around it, and also that the people of al-Mawṣil had made their camp in Takrīt.

Al-Sarī—Shuʿayb—Sayf—al-Walīd b. ʿAbdallah b. Abī Ṭaybah al-Bajalī—his father, gave the same report with the addition: Saʿd wrote to this effect to ʿUmar, who wrote back, "Send Hāshim b. ʿUtbah to Jalūlāʾ with twelve thousand men; give the command over the vanguard to al-Qaʿqāʿ b. ʿAmr, that over the right wing to
[2457] Siʿr b. Mālik and that over the left wing to ʿAmr b. Mālik b.

118. See Yaqūt, *Muʿjam*, II, 107: *al-waqīʿah* is a word for "onslaught," the battle of Jalūlāʾ allegedly resulting in large numbers of casualties.

119. The Arabic reads *akhmās* rather than what we would expect, *khums;* see n. 117 above.

ʿUtbah; place the infantry of the army under the command of ʿAmr b. Murrah al-Juhanī."

According to al-Sarī—Shuʿayb—Sayf—Muḥammad, Ṭalḥah, al-Muhallab and Ziyād: ʿUmar wrote to Saʿd, "If God defeats the two armies, the army of Mihrān and that of al-Anṭāq, order al-Qaʿqāʿ to march on until he gets to (the region) between the Sawād and al-Jabal[120] at the farthest (position reached by) your armed forces."

ʿAmr and Saʿīd concurred with the account of the abovementioned transmitters: It was said about the men involved at Jalūlāʾ that, when the Persians, after their flight from al-Madāʾin, finally reached Jalūlāʾ and the people of Ādharbayjān and al-Bāb were about to go their separate ways from the people of al-Jibāl and those of Fārs, they started to incite one another to fight saying, "If you disperse now, you will never get together again; this is a spot that sends us in different directions. So, come on, let us unite to face the Arabs here and let us fight them. If we win, that is what we want, and if we lose, then we will have performed our duty, thus creating an excuse for ourselves."[121] So they dug a moat and assembled within its perimeter under the command of Mihrān al-Rāzī. Yazdajird had passed through to Ḥulwān, where he alighted. He provided them with men and also left some of his wealth behind (in Jalūlāʾ). They stayed within their trench, which, except for its exits, was completely surrounded by hedges consisting of wooden pointed stakes.

According to ʿAmr—ʿĀmir al-Shaʿbī: Abū Bakr never used to ask anyone from the "people of the apostasy" [*ahl al-Riddah*] to help him in his warfare until he died. ʿUmar did request their assistance, but he never entrusted a command to any of them except over a small contingent or even smaller units. He never gave up his custom of entrusting commands to Companions when he found someone worthy enough to wage his war for him. [2458]
And if he did not find anyone (from among the Companions) cut out for this task, then he would readily scout around for a suitable Successor. But, until Islam had become firmly established, no one

120. Al-Jabal (lit. "the mountain"), also called al-Jibāl (the plural of *jabal*) is the name of the mountainous region northeast of the Tigris between Iṣfahān and Hamadhān, see Yaqūt, *Muʿjam*, II, 15 f., 22f.; see also Le Strange, *Lands*, ch. XIII. Sawād means "cultivated area (sc. of Iraq)."

121. Or "having showed our valor," see Lane, 256, left column.

who had participated in the "war of the apostasy" was encouraged with a command, their commanders in those wars having been riff-raff in any case.

'Amr, Muḥammad, al-Muhallab, Ṭalḥah and Sa'īd concurred: Hāshim b. 'Utbah departed from al-Madā'in in Ṣafar of the year 16 (March 637) at the head of twelve thousand men, among whom were leading Emigrants and Helpers as well as eminent tribesmen, people who had not joined the "wars of the apostasy," but also those who had. Thus Hāshim marched from al-Madā'in to Jalūlā' in four days, until he arrived at the Persians' camp. He surrounded the camp and besieged them, the Persians at first holding out, not venturing out on sorties, unless they saw an advantage therein. The Muslims charged the Persian fortress in Jalūlā' in eighty raids, God granting them victory on every occasion. They showed themselves to be stronger than the unbelievers in spite of their wooden stakes; so the Persians surrounded themselves with ones made of iron.

According to al-Sarī—Shu'ayb—Sayf—'Uqbah b. Mukram—Biṭān b. Bishr: When Hāshim swooped down upon Mihrān in Jalūlā', he laid siege to them lying behind their trench. The Persians mounted raids against the Muslims in large numbers and with much clamor. Hāshim made it his custom to tell his men, "The emergency (in which we find ourselves) will be decisive for the future."[122] Sa'd began to reinforce Hāshim's troops with horsemen who, when the last of these had arrived, finally presented themselves to the Muslims and, with them, marched against the enemy. Hāshim stood up among his men and said,
[2459] "Show God your valor, that He may fulfill therewith your recompense and booty. Strive for God." So they went to face the enemy and fought. God sent a whirlwind over them which darkened the enemy('s free observation of the) terrain. The only thing open to them was to try and prevent the Muslims from engaging them in combat. Their cavalry tumbled down into their own trench and did not see any other way out than to make breaches (in the barricades) at the very spot where they were,[123] enabling their

122. In Noth, 118, this expression is identified and analyzed as a *topos*.

123. Sc. presumably not wandering about in the trench until they arrived at one of its thoroughfares.

horses to climb (onto the bank), thus ruining their defense system. A rumor that that was going on reached the Muslims. They looked at the scene and said, "Let us attack them a second time; perhaps we can invade their stronghold or else we are prepared to die in the effort." So, when the Muslims moved in on them a second time, the enemy came out and set up around the trench, facing the Muslims, a barricade of iron-pointed stakes, so as to prevent the Muslim cavalry from attacking them. They left one spot in this barricade open for easy access by which they went out to face the Muslims. These last fought ferociously, more so than they had ever fought before except for the "night of clamor,"[124] only this time with even more determination and speed. Al-Qaʿqāʿ b. ʿAmr finally took a direction along which he fought his way forward toward the thoroughfare of the Persians' trench. He took up a position there and ordered someone to proclaim the following message: "Listen, Muslim warriors, this is your commander speaking; he has entered the enemy's trench and established a stronghold there. So now you move in on it, and let no one whom you find on your way prevent you from going down into it." He gave this order just to boost the morale of the Muslims. These last attacked, not doubting for a moment that Hāshim had indeed established a position in the trench.[125] Nothing withstood their attack until they ended up at the passage through the trench. Who else but al-Qaʿqāʿ b. ʿAmr did they find there! He had established himself firmly. The unbelievers started fleeing right and left, away from the clearance facing their trench. They perished in (the iron stakes) which they had set up against the Muslims. Their [2460]
horses were injured and they had to return on foot, pursued[126] by the Muslims. Only an insignificant number got away. That day God killed one hundred thousand of them. The whole clearing was covered with corpses, in all directions. Hence Jalūlāʾ was called Jalūlāʾ al-Waqīʿah[127] on account of the dead bodies covering it.[128]

According to al-Sarī—Shuʿayb—Sayf—ʿUbaydallāh b. Muḥaf-

---

124. Sc. at al-Qādisiyyah.

125. Again I have adopted the reading of Ibn al-Athīr, II, 405, which in my opinion gives a better text.

126. I read *ittabaʿahum* instead of *atbaʿahum*.

127. *Waqīʿah*, as we saw, has the connotation "massacre" or "onslaught."

fiz—his father: I was among the first of the Muslim hordes at the time they entered Sābāṭ and al-Muẓlim nearby.[129] I was also among the first to cross the Tigris and enter al-Madā'in. It was there that I acquired a statue which, had it been divided as booty among all the members of the Bakr b. Wā'il, it certainly would have satisfied them, what with all its precious stones. But I handed it over (to be added to the other spoils). We only stayed a short while in al-Madā'in until the news reached us that the Persians had gathered an immense force against us at Jalūlā'. They had sent their families ahead to al-Jibāl,[130] but had kept their riches with
[2461] them. Sa'd sent 'Amr b. Mālik b. 'Utbah b. Uhayb b. 'Abd Manāf b. Zuhra to them.[131] The army of the Muslims that fought at Jalūlā' was twelve thousand strong. The commander of its vanguard was al-Qa'qā' b. 'Amr. Also, eminent people and horse-owning knights[132] marched in this army. When they passed Bābil Mahrūdh,[133] its dihqān concluded a peace treaty on the condition that he cover a *jarīb*[134] of land with dirhams (for the Muslim army). This he did, in this way obtaining a safeguard for his people.[135] Then the Muslim army moved on until it confronted the Persians at Jalūlā', where it appeared that these had dug a protecting trench around themselves, and especially their treasury.[136] By the fires

128. Perhaps the double entendre implied in the verb "to cover" (*jallala*), used in connection with the battle of Jalūlā', a name which is derived from the same root, is quite intentional.

129. Two localities near al-Madā'in; see Yāqūt, *Mu'jam*, IV, 569.

130. See n. 120 above.

131. He seems to be confused with 'Amr b. 'Utbah b. Nawfal b. Uhayb, who in this context is the general mentioned in Balādhurī; see the note in the text edition.

132. Horses were so valuable, and at the same time so expensive to keep in desert areas, that not all warriors could afford them. Compare the pitifully small number of warriors on horseback participating in the first *maghāzī* listed, for instance, in the *Sīrah* of Ibn Isḥāq.

133. The combination of these two geographical names cannot be explained with the help of Yāqūt, where the one and the other are not mentioned in tandem. Above, on p. 2421, a place Bābil was mentioned. Is the story of this peace treaty to be identified with the peace treaty concluded on p. 3?

134. See n. 103 above.

135. See also Yāqūt, *Mu'jam*, IV, 700.

136. See above p. 2457, where it is related that the king had left some of his treasures behind in Jalūlā'.

they had lit they swore one another solidarity and loyalty that no one was to take to his heels.[137]

The Muslims made their camp near the enemy. Every day troops (dispatched by the king) from Ḥulwān began to arrive at the fortress of the unbelievers. He thus reinforced them with as many people from al-Jibāl as he could find. The Muslims appealed to Saʿd for reinforcements too, which he duly dispatched, three times a contingent of two hundred cavalry. When the Persians became aware of the Muslims' being reinforced, they hastened to wage battle. That day the commander of the Muslim cavalry was Ṭulayḥah, the son of an unnamed father, one of the Banū ʿAbd al-Dār. The Persian cavalry commander was Khurrazādh b. Khurrahurmuz. Both armies fought a tremendous battle, the Muslims never having been engaged in anything like it before. They first [2462]
used up all the darts and arrows.[138] Then all the spears broke, whereupon they resorted to wielding their swords and battleaxes. Thus they fought all morning until noon. When it was time for the noon prayer ritual, the fighters performed this by just nodding their heads.

(They went on fighting) until, about halfway between noon and the mid-afternoon prayer ritual,[139] one Muslim detachment retreated and another came and took its place. Then, addressing himself to these men, al-Qaʿqāʿ b. ʿAmr said, "Has this battle scared you out of your wits?"[140] "Yes," they replied, "we wear ourselves out while they rest; when someone is exhausted, he is always afraid that his strength will fail him, unless his place is regularly taken by others."[141] So al-Qaʿqāʿ said, "We will attack them, we will press hard on them, we will not retreat or draw back until God decides between us. So let us charge them as one

137. This is probably a description of a Zoroastrian ritual accompanying the swearing of oaths.

138. The Arabic has *nabl* and *nushshāb*; the first mentioned are short and shot with a crossbow or a bow equipped with an arrow guide, the second are longer and shot with a standard handbow, see J. D. Latham and W. F. Paterson, *Saracen archery*, London, 1970, index s.v. and esp. 188.

139. Approximately 2 p.m.

140. Which means, perhaps, ". . . to the point that you want to sneak away?"

141. I base this translation of *yuʿqabu* on Lane, 2098, left column, three lines from the top.

man would,[142] until you are actually in the enemy's midst and let no one of you fail to live up to expectations!"[143] He advanced, the enemy's ranks were opened, not a single Muslim warrior budged from the passage through the trench, until the night drew its curtain over them. They ventured right and left. Then Ṭulayḥah, Qays b. al-Makshūḥ, ʿAmr b. Maʿdī Karib and Ḥujr b. ʿAdī approached among the reinforcements and arrived on the scene as night fell when the Muslims had just stopped fighting. Then al-Qaʿqāʿ b. ʿAmr had someone make a loud announcement, "Why do you desist from fighting, whilst your commander is actually down in the trench?" Then the unbelievers began to flee and the Muslims attacked again. I[144] go down into the trench,[145] (I enter their camp) and come to a tent in which there are pillows and clothes. Suddenly (I sense the presence of) a human form hidden under some blankets. I tear them away and what do I find? A
[2463] woman, like a gazelle, radiant as the sun! I took her and her clothes and surrendered the latter as booty, but put in a request for the maid, that she may be allotted to me. Thus I acquired her as a concubine; she later bore me a child.

According to al-Sarī—Shuʿayb—Sayf—Ḥammād al-Burjumī—his otherwise unknown father: That day, Khārijah b. al-Ṣalt chanced upon a figurine of a she-camel of gold or silver, adorned with pearls and rubies, about as big as a young goat when placed on the ground. There was a figure of a rider on it, made of gold and similarly adorned. Khārijah brought both objects (to the spot where the loot was accumulated) and surrendered them.

According to al-Sarī—Shuʿayb—Sayf—Muḥammad, Ṭalḥah, al-Muhallab, ʿAmr, Saʿīd, al-Walīd b. ʿAbdallāh, al-Mujālid and ʿUqbah b. Mukram: Hāshim ordered al-Qaʿqāʿ b. ʿAmr to go after those Persians who had run away, so he searched for them all the way until he got to Khāniqīn.[146] When news of the defeat reached Yazdajird, he traveled from Ḥulwān to al-Jibāl. In the meantime,

---

142. That is, in a mass charge.

143. I adopt the interpretation of *takdhīb* listed in *WKAS*, I, 93, right column, below.

144. This is Muḥaffiz, the eyewitness of this account, see pp. 39–40 above.

145. Since the Arabic has here and in what follows, the verbs in the imperfect, I have chosen to translate them as a historical present.

146. See Yāqūt, *Muʿjam*, II, 393: a locality between al-Madā'in and Hamadhān.

al-Qaʿqāʿ arrived at Ḥulwān, and this because of something that ʿUmar had written to Saʿd, "In case God defeats both armies, that of Mihrān and the one of al-Anṭāq, send al-Qaʿqāʿ ahead until he gets to a region between the Sawād and al-Jabal at the furthest (position taken by) your armed forces. So al-Qaʿqāʿ stopped at Ḥulwān with an army of men from different clans and from the Ḥamrā'[147] and he remained there until there was a general move from al-Madā'in to al-Kūfah. When Saʿd left al-Madā'in for al-Kūfah, al-Qaʿqāʿ joined him. He had entrusted the administration of the border region to Qubādh, one of the Ḥamrā' who originally hailed from Khurāsān, and he had freely handed out booty from the area to those who had been present at its subjugation as well as to some of those who had stayed out at al-Madā'in.

They continued with similar accounts: Then they[148] wrote to ʿUmar giving the news of the conquest of Jalūlā' and of al-Qaʿqāʿ's arrival in Ḥulwān, and they asked ʿUmar's permission to follow [2464] him to this place. But ʿUmar refused, saying, "I wish there was a barrier between the Sawād and al-Jabal stopping the Persians from reaching us, and us from going out to them. The Sawād constitutes quite sufficient cultivable land for us; I prefer peace for the Muslims to plunder." They continued: When al-Qaʿqāʿ was dispatched by Hāshim in pursuit of the Persians who had run away, he overtook Mihrān in Khāniqīn, where he killed him. Then he caught up with al-Fayruzān, but this man jumped (off his horse), letting it go, and clambered out of sight away into the mountains. Al-Qaʿqāʿ made prisoners of war and sent some of them to Hāshim; so the latter and his men allocated these among themselves as part of the booty. The women among them were taken as concubines and bore their Muslim masters children. Since those prisoners of war are associated with Jalūlā', they are called "the captives of Jalūlā'." One of these women taken pris-

147. The Ḥamrā' (literally, "the Red") were Persian defectors who settled with the Muslims in, among other places, al-Kūfah, where they were assigned special living quarters. They occupied a position among the Muslim forces comparable with that of the Asāwirah, Persian cavalry men, who settled among the Muslims in al-Baṣrah. See Balādhurī, *Futūḥ*, 280; Pellat, *Le milieu*, 22, 35; Morony, *Iraq*, 197 f.; Juda, 76.

148. Presumably, this word "they" refers to other victorious Muslim warriors who had stayed on in Jalūlā'.

oner was al-Sha'bī's mother, who was first allotted to a man from the Banū 'Abs. She gave birth to a child, but the father died. Then Sharāḥīl took her unto him and she also bore him a child, 'Āmir,[149] who grew up among the Banū 'Abs.

According to al-Sarī—Shu'ayb—Sayf—Muḥammad, Ṭalḥah and al-Muhallab: The chattels[150] of Jalūlā' were distributed among them, each horseman receiving nine thousand (dirhams' worth) and nine animals. Then Hāshim returned to Sa'd with the war booty.

According to al-Sarī—Shu'ayb—Sayf—'Amr—al-Sha'bī: God singled out as *fay'* booty[151] for the Muslims what they found in the Persians' camp at Jalūlā', what the Persians carried on their persons, as well as all the animals they had stationed there with the exception of a small number. In fact, those who did get away had not been able to take anything of their riches with them. The distribution of all that among the Muslims was in the hands of
[2465] Salmān b. Rabī'ah, who in those days supervised the entire intake of the booty.[152] Therefore the Arab tribesmen used to call him "Salmān of the cavalry," especially since it was to that contingent of the fighting forces that he distributed in strictly equal portions, whereas in the allotment to other warriors he did not take such great pains. Thus he distinguished three different types among the thoroughbreds. The share of each cavalryman at Jalūlā' approached that acquired at al-Madā'in.

According to al-Sarī—Shu'ayb—Sayf—al-Mujālid and 'Amr—

---

149. In other words, this 'Āmir is 'Āmir b. Sharāḥīl al-Sha'bī (d. 103–10/721–8), the man who became later one of al-Kūfah's most famous legal experts. Moreover, Ṭabarī has preserved a large number of al-Sha'bī's historical reports.

150. The Arabic word used here is *fay'*, a problematic term. Strictly speaking, it should not have been used here, *fay'* denoting mostly immovable property obtained from the enemy after the concluding of a peace treaty: land, estates, etc., not the movable booty acquired after a fight. See Yaḥyā b. Ādam, *Kitāb al-kharāj*, ed. Th. W. Juynboll, Leiden, 1896, 3: . . . *al-ghanīmah mā ghalaba 'alayhi al-muslimūna bi'l-qitāl ḥattā ya'khudhūhu 'anwatan wa'l-fay' mā ṣūliḥū 'alayhi . . . mina'l-jizyah wa'l-kharāj.* But its use here by al-Sha'bī in the following report may indicate a very early interpretation of the Qur'an *locus.* We might say that we find *fay'* here in its preclassical usage.

151. See previous note; this time not the noun *fay'* but the Qur'ānic verb *afā'a* is used.

152. The Arabic reads here *al-aqbāḍ wa'l-aqsām*; this seems to suggest that the terms convey different notions. We could conceivably read in *aqbāḍ* "all the takings including the fifth to be sent off later to Medina," and in *aqsām* "that part of the booty to be divided up into equal parts among the warriors."

al-Shaʿbī: The booty[153] to be distributed among the men at Jalūlā' amounted to thirty million (dirhams minus) the fifth which amounted to six million.

According to al-Sarī—Shuʿayb—Sayf—Muḥammad, Ṭalḥah, al-Muhallab and Saʿīd: Saʿd handed out free gifts[154] from the booty of Jalūlā' to those who had fought most bravely from among those warriors who had actually been present at that battle and also those valiant ones who were out at al-Madā'in. The fifth parts[155] of the booty consisting of gold and silver coins, vessels and garments he sent away with Quḍāʿī b. ʿAmr al-Du'alī and he sent the prisoners of war with Abū Mufazzir al-Aswad. So on their way they went.

According to al-Sarī—Shuʿayb—Sayf—Zuhrah and Muḥammad b. ʿAmr: (Saʿd) sent the fifth parts of the booty away with Quḍāʿī and Abū Mufazzir and the written record with Ziyād b. Abī Sufyān. The latter was the one who acted as the people's scribe and entered their names in the *dīwān*. When they had made their way to ʿUmar, Ziyād spoke to him about what had happened and he gave him descriptions (of the situation in Iraq). Then ʿUmar said, "Are you willing to address the people and tell them the same story as you have told me?" "To my mind," Ziyād [2466]
answered, "there is no one on earth more respected than you; but, apart from you, why should I not be capable of giving this account?" So he stood up among the people and related to them what had happened (to the troops in Iraq), what these had achieved, and also that they were seeking ʿUmar's approval to penetrate even more deeply into enemy territory. ʿUmar said, "This is truly an eloquent speaker,"[156] and recited the verse (in *khafīf*):

Our forces have loosened
    our tongues with their exploits.

---

153. Again the word *ghanīmah*, rather than the word *fay'* used here, would have suited the context better, see n. 150 above.

154. This means, not as part of the distribution into strictly equal portions to be carried out later.

155. In Arabic, *akhmās;* this indicates here probably the fifth parts of the booty acquired at various battles. We might also interpret the plural as referring to the five parts into which the Medina *khums* is divided.

156. Whatever the merit of the hypothesis may be that historians under the ʿAbbāsids "purged" early historical accounts of all the *faḍā'il* elements eulogizing

According to al-Sarī—Shuʿayb—Sayf—Zuhrah and Muḥammad—Abū Salamah: When the booty from Jalūlā'[157] was brought to ʿUmar, he said, "This should not be hidden in any house until I have divided it." So ʿAbd al-Raḥmān b. ʿAwf and ʿAbdallāh b. Arqam spent the night standing guard over it in the courtyard of the mosque. When morning had come, ʿUmar came with a large crowd and took away the covers (which had kept the booty out of sight), they having used mats. When he saw the rubies, chrysalites peridots and (other) gems, he burst into tears. Then ʿAbd al-Raḥmān (b. ʿAwf) said to him, "Why do you weep, Commander of the Faithful, is this not rather an occasion to be grateful?" Said ʿUmar, "No, for heaven's sake, that is not the reason why I cry. By God, He never gave (such as) this to any people without that giving rise to mutual envy and hatred. I pray God that they won't quarrel over it; otherwise fighting will be their lot." ʿUmar had agonized over the distribution of all the plunder acquired at al-Qādisiyyah, until the Qur'ānic verse "The spoils God has assigned. . ." (LIX, 7) occurred to him, i.e., in respect of the fifth.[158] So ʿUmar assigned that fifth part of the booty to those people who were entitled to it, and he dealt with the fifth from Jalūlā' in exactly the same manner as he
[2467] had done with that of al-Qādisiyyah, namely, convening the elders, asking their advice and obtaining a consensus from the Muslims. But first, among some Medinans he handed out free gifts[159] from that fifth.

According to al-Sarī—Shuʿayb—Sayf—Muḥammad, Ṭalḥah, al-Muhallab, Saʿīd and ʿAmr: Saʿd gathered the people living around al-Madā'in and gave orders to count them. They were found to number more than 130,000, comprising more than 30,000 families. He calculated that that amounted to assigning to every Arab warrior (the supervision over) three Persian peasants with their families. Saʿd wrote to that effect to ʿUmar. ʿUmar wrote back

---

the Umayyads and their henchmen, this undeniable glorification of Muʿāwiyah's "adopted brother" escaped deletion.

157. In Arabic, *akhmās;* strictly speaking, this should have read *khums,* see n. 155 above.

158. Sc., the fifth part of the spoils which were to go to the Prophet for him to distribute among himself, his relatives, the orphans, the poor, and eligible travelers.

159. In other words, before distributing the rest in strictly equal portions among those entitled.

saying, "Keep the (local) peasants in their present state except those who are hostile or the ones who ran away from you to your enemy and whom you subsequently captured. Treat the peasants (outside al-Madā'in) in the same way you treated the other peasants before them. When I write to you about (dealing with subjugated) people, always treat them in the same manner."[160] Then Sa'd wrote 'Umar asking him what to do with people who did not farm the land. 'Umar replied, "As for all those who are not peasants, you are to make your own decision concerning them,[161] as long as you have not already acquired their belongings as booty, that is to say, divided that up as such. As for the Persian who is hostile, abandons his land and vacates it, his land shall be yours (to do with as you like). When you summon them (to convert to Islam or else pay the *jizā'*) and you receive the *jizā'* from them and you send them back (to their homesteads even) before the allotment (of the moneys thereby collected), then that constitutes "protection." In addition, if you do not summon them to convert to Islam, then everything they own constitutes lawful booty for you, destined for him whom God has indicated." The people who had been present at the battle of Jalūlā' received the largest share in the territorial booty (*fay'*), appropriating all the *fay'* land beyond al-Nahrawān and sharing with all the other fighters in the *fay'* divided before the Jalūlā' (battle).[162] They confirmed the peasants (on their land) and summoned the stubborn (to conclude a treaty with the Muslims). They imposed a land tax on the peasants and [2468]
on those who, (after having run away first) returned to their land and accepted "protection." They singled out as special booty[163] what had belonged to the king, his family and those of his retinue who had remained stubborn, as destined for those indicated by God. It was not permitted to sell any piece of land situated be-

160. This last imperative is in the plural, an abrupt change from the imperatives in the singular preceding it. If we do not adopt the singular imperative listed in the apparatus as occurring in one manuscript (*fa-ajri*), the plural (*fa-ajrū*), for which Prym opted, may be taken as an indication that 'Umar did not only mean Sa'd to carry out his directives but also other Arabs in leading positions, perhaps including those who were yet to be posted in newly created administrative positions. For more details on tax matters, see Dennett, *Conversion*, 14–42.

161. Or conceivably, everything they own is yours.

162. Or conceivably, this way of an-Nahrawān.

163. The term used is *istiṣfā'*, see *EI*², s.v. *Ghanīma* (Løkkegaard).

tween al-Jabal (in northern Iraq) and the mountains in the land of the Arabs except to those to whom God had granted this as *fay'* land. Similarly, they did not permit any piece of that land among the other people, at least not among those to whom God had not granted it as *fay'* land, namely those who were merely in the employ of the official tenants,[164] to whom (in other words) God had not assigned a share in the *fay'* land. The Muslims preserved *fay'* land in this manner and did not divide it up, because the benefit of a division would not be theirs. The same procedure was applied to marsh lands,[165] fire temple domains, postal stations, to what the king used to own and to the possessions of those who used to associate with him, also to the properties of those who were killed, as well as to stretches of rugged ground. Later on, some evil men asked the Sawād's administrative officers (*wulāt*) to divide that land, but the majority of Arab warriors, having rejected that, prevented them from so doing; then the *wulāt* espoused the majority's view and did not accede to the request saying, "Had it not been for the fact that you would come to blows, then we would have complied." If this request for the division of that land had come about as the result of a joint decision,[166] then it would have been divided among them.

[2469] According to al-Sarī—Shu'ayb—Sayf—Ṭalḥah b. al-A'lam—Māhān: No one of the people of the Sawād, except the inhabitants of some villages that were conquered by force, stuck to the agreement concluded with the Arab veterans, all *sawādī*s violating the agreements except those villages. When these others had been prompted to return (to obedience), they were once more placed under "protection." They had to pay the *jizā'* but enjoyed the Arabs' safeguard in exchange, except those regions formerly belonging to the royal family and those of their entourage, for those

164. This admittedly wordy rendering of the Arabic *mimman yu'āmiluhum* is based on the indication in *Tāj*, VIII, 36, l. 9, that, in Iraq, *mu'āmalah* is the equivalent of the term *musāqāt* used in the Ḥijāz. The latter term denotes some sort of land lease, Schacht, *Introduction*, index; Løkkegaard, *Taxation*, 94.

165. That is how I interpret the expression *ājām* "thicket" (in this case, of reeds) used in tandem with *maghīḍ al-miyāh* "places sometimes inundated, sometimes dry."

166. The Arabic expression used, *'an mala'in. Mala'* is "assembly of elders." My translation is based on Lane, 2730, left column.

became *ṣāfiyah*[167] properties, namely, those situated between Ḥulwān and Iraq.[168] From the beginning, ʿUmar had been content with the cultivable lands of the Sawād.[169]

According to al-Sarī—Shuʿayb—Sayf—Ṭalḥah—Māhān: They[170] wrote to ʿUmar asking him what to do with the *ṣawāfī*, so he wrote back, "Repair to the *ṣawāfī* that God has singled out for you and distribute their revenues among those whom God has indicated; four-fifths are to go to the army and one-fifth to me for me to distribute among those entitled to it. If the Arab fighters prefer to settle in the *ṣawāfī*, then that is their prerogative." When ʿUmar had thus left the decision to them, they thought it best not to scatter over Persian territory.[171] Rather they kept the *ṣawāfī* as a *ḥabīs*[172] belonging to them, which they had someone, whom they all agreed on, administer. They would divide their revenues once every year and they would not have it supervised except by someone they unanimously agreed on. It turned out that they only used to agree on governors holding office in al-Madāʾin and later those of al-Kūfah, after they had all moved thither.

According to al-Sarī—Shuʿayb—Sayf—al-Walīd b. Abdallāh b. Abī Ṭaybah—ʿAbdallāh b. Abī Ṭaybah: ʿUmar wrote (to the people in Iraq) a letter, saying, "Take possession of your *fay*ʾ lands, for if you don't, (the normal course of) affairs will grind to a halt because (too) much time has elapsed. By God, I have taken the necessary decision; I ask you[173] to be my witness before them, so [2470]
testify!"

167. Its plural is *ṣawāfī*; this is a technical term denoting conquered lands and properties placed under special tutelage of the *imām* who, at his discretion, favored with the administration thereof those people who deserved to be rewarded particularly for special services rendered. These lands formerly belonged to either the ruling family of the enemy which, having been defeated, could no longer exert their rights over it, or other enemy families who had either perished or had abandoned their properties definitively. See Hinds, "Alignments," 350; Ṭabaṭabāʾī, *Kharāj*, 8f.

168. Presumably, the area between Ḥulwān and the north bank of the Tigris.

169. See p. 43 above.

170. Presumably, "the Arab leaders in Iraq."

171. In the apparatus and in *Glossarium*, p. CDII, it is suggested to read *an lā yaftariqū fayʾa bilādi ʾl-ʿajam*, that is ". . . not to divide the Persian *fay*ʾ land among themselves."

172. A technical term for an inalienable allotment or bequest, in this case consisting of enemy territory.

173. Presumably Saʿd is meant.

According to al-Sarī—Shuʿayb—Sayf—al-Walīd b. ʿAbdallāh—ʿAbdallāh (b. Abī Ṭaybah): The peasants were to take care of the roads, bridges, markets, tilling of the soil and guide services. Besides, in exchange for protection,[174] they had to pay the *jizā'* commensurate with their economic ability. Also the dihqāns had to afford *jizyah* in exchange for Arab protection and they also had to watch all building activities. Furthermore, it was everyone's duty to show traveling Emigrants the way and receive them hospitably. Being shown hospitality was something God had bestowed upon them as an inherited privilege.

Al-Sarī—Shuʿayb—Sayf—ʿAbd al-ʿAzīz b. Siyāh—Ḥabīb b. Abī Thābit gave a similar account: They said: The conquest of Jalūlā' occurred in Dhū al-Qaʿdah of the year 16 on its first day,[175] nine months having elapsed between this event and the conquest of al-Madā'in. They all said: ʿUmar's treaty concluded with the people enjoying "protection" stipulated that the state of "protection" would be considered as having ceased should they betray the Muslims to their enemies. Furthermore, if they should revile a Muslim, the terms of the treaty demanded that they would receive a crushing punishment. If they should fight with a Muslim, they would be killed. ʿUmar in his turn took it upon himself to guard their safety, although he was not to be held responsible for any ignominious deed committed by passing troops against anyone named in the treaty.

Al-Sarī—Shuʿayb—Sayf—Muḥammad b. ʿAbdallāh and al-Mustanīr—Ibrāhīm gave a similar report.

According to al-Sarī—Shuʿayb—Sayf—Ṭalḥah—Māhān: Of all the Persians at Jalūlā', the people of al-Rayy had the most difficult
[2471] time. They had been the defenders of the local people, but as a result of the battle of Jalūlā' they were wiped out.

They all went on to say: When the fighters at Jalūlā' had returned to al-Madā'in, they settled in their land concessions.[176] All

174. My rendering of the expression *ʿan aydīhim* is suggested by Bravmann, *Background*, 199–212. See also Paul G. Forand in *JESHO*, XIV (1971):32ff.; Dennett, 21.

175. November 24, 637.

176. The Arabic technical term is *qaṭīʿah*, plural *qaṭāʾiʿ*, see *EI*[2], s.v. *Ḳaṭīʿa* (Cahen). One of the manuscripts has the term *iqṭāʿāt* instead of *qaṭāʾiʿ*, this is probably a retrojection of what later also became an administrative term for concessions granted to meritorious servants of the state, who enjoyed, at first, the

of the Sawād had become "protection" territory for them, except those properties formerly belonging to the Persian royal household and their staunch supporters, which God had set aside as *ṣawāfī*.[177] They all went on to say: When the news had reached the Persians of what ʿUmar had said and deemed fit in respect of the Sawād and the land beyond, they said, "We'll be content with the same conditions that the Arabs are content with," whereas the Kurds[178] of every township were dissatisfied with the damage done to their arable lands.

According to al-Sarī—Shuʿayb—Sayf—al-Mustanīr b. Yazīd and Ḥakīm b. ʿUmayr—Ibrāhīm b. Yazīd: The selling[179] of *ṣawāfī* lands between Ḥulwān and al-Qādisiyyah is not permitted, because they belong to whom God has given them.

Al-Sarī—Shuʿayb—Sayf—ʿAmr b. Muḥammad—al-Shaʿbī gave a similar report.

According to al-Sarī—Shuʿayb—Sayf—Muḥammad b. Qays—al-Mughīrah b. Shibl: Jarīr (b. ʿAbdallāh al-Bajalī) once purchased a piece of *ṣawāfī* land situated in the Sawād on the bank of the Euphrates. Thereupon he went to ʿUmar and told him. ʿUmar, disapproving of the sale, rescinded it and thereupon forbade the selling of any property that had not been divided among those with a right to it.

According to al-Sarī—Shuʿayb—Sayf—Muḥammad b. Qays: I asked al-Shaʿbī, "Was the Sawād conquered by force?" "Yes," he said, "all the land, except for some fortresses and strongholds, for some of these concluded peace treaties and some others were simply overpowered." I asked, "Did the people of the Sawād enjoy [2472]
a form of 'protection' laid down in a treaty before some of them ran away?" "No," said al-Shaʿbī, "but when they were summoned to embrace Islam or else pay tax, and consented to the latter

revenues out of *kharāj* (land tax levied from the legal owners) minus the tithe imposed by the *zakāt* regulations, and later the usufruct of these concessions, see *EI*², s.v. *Iḳṭāʿ* (Cahen).

177. See n. 167 above.

178. Wellhausen exclaimed (*Skizzen*, VI, 155), "Was sollen hier die Kurden?" Yes, indeed what! Does this passage suggest that the Sawād had pockets of Kurdish inhabitants? Hinds suggests that we should read *akarah*, the plural of *akkār* "land cultivator."

179. Or "buying"; like *sharā* and *bāʿa* (see n. 103 and pp. 47–48 above) *ishtirāʾ*, which is used here, is a *ḍidd*.

which was duly collected, they then enjoyed official 'protection.' "

According to al-Sarī—Shuʿayb—Sayf—ʿAbd al-ʿAzīz—Ḥabīb b. Abī Thābit: None of the Sawād's inhabitants had an official peace treaty drawn up for them except the Banū Ṣalūbā, and the people of al-Ḥīrah, Kalwādhā, and some villages on the Euphrates. Then they broke faith, whereupon they were summoned to accept official "protection" but this was only after they had broken their agreement. Hāshim b. ʿUtbah recited the following lines of poetry on the occasion of the battle of Jalūlā'[180] (in *rajaz*):

The fight at Jalū́lā', the battle of Rustum,[181]
  And, prior to that, the march on al-Kūfah,
The day of that wide, formidable[182] river[183]
  Among other fierce fights of days now gone by,
Have colored my temples with hoar, they look aged,
  Like white *thaghām*[184] flowers in honored Arabia.

Likewise, Abū Bujayd (Nāfiʿ b. al-Aswad) composed about this the following verses (in *ṭawīl*):

On th' day of the kill at Jalū́lā' our squadrons
  Rushed forward, attacking like glowering lions[185]
They crushed all the Persians, while I killed them off;
  So perish, you impure cadavers of Magians!
Al-Fayruzān did get away by the skin
  Of his teeth; but Mihrān they slew on th' day skulls were cleft.
They stayed in a spot where they were to meet death,
  Interred under whirlwinds of dust.

---

180. As everywhere, an attempt has been made to render the following poems in rhythmic English; the admittedly ungrammatical stress mark on the second syllable of Jalū́lā' has been placed there just for the sake of the rhythm.

181. He is Rustum b. al-Farrukhzādh, the general of Yazdajird III; the battle referred to is that of al-Qādisiyyah.

182. Literally, it says "holy" or "sacrosanct," but an Arab poet would probably not conceive of a river outside the peninsula as such.

183. This is probably a reference to that successful crossing of the Tigris prior to the conquest of al-Madā'in described above; see pp. 12 ff.

184. A certain white flower with which greying hair is often compared; according to Lane it grows in the mountains of Tihāmah and Najd.

185. See n. 180 above.

According to al-Sarī—Shuʿayb—Sayf—Muḥammad, Ṭalḥah, al- [2473]
Muhallab, ʿAmr and Saʿīd: ʿUmar had written Saʿd a letter in
which he said, "If God conquers Jalūlāʾ for you, send al-Qaʿqāʿ b.
ʿAmr in pursuit of those who may get away, until he arrives at
Ḥulwān, so that he may be able to help those Muslims arriving
there later. May God preserve for you your Sawād land!" So when
God had defeated the enemy at Jalūlāʾ, Hāshim b. ʿUtbah posi-
tioned himself there. Al-Qaʿqāʿ b. ʿAmr went forth in pursuit of
the Persian soldiers as far as Khāniqīn with an army of men from
different clans as well as from the Ḥamrāʾ. He made several pris-
oners and killed off those fighting men he caught up with. Mihrān
was slain, but al-Fayruzān escaped. When news of the defeat of
the people of Jalūlāʾ and the death of Mihrān reached Yazdajird, he
moved out of Ḥulwān, departing in the direction of al-Rayy. In
Ḥulwān he left behind a cavalry squadron under the command of
Khusrawshunūm. Al-Qaʿqāʿ drew nearer. When he reached Qaṣr-i
Shīrīn,[185a] still a full parasang away from Ḥulwān, Khusrawshu-
nūm marched out toward him, having sent al-Zaynabī, the dih-
qān of Ḥulwān, ahead. Al-Qaʿqāʿ encountered the latter and they
engaged in battle. Al-Zaynabī was killed, with both ʿAmīrah b.
Ṭāriq and a certain ʿAbdallāh[186] contending for the credit of hav-
ing killed him. So al-Qaʿqāʿ gave that credit as well as the man's
spoils to both, for them to divide between themselves. ʿAmīrah
viewed this with disdain. Khusrawshunūm fled and the Muslims
took possession of Ḥulwān. Al-Qaʿqāʿ settled the Ḥamrāʾ there
and installed Qubādh as their head. Al-Qaʿqāʿ remained there in [2474]
control of the border garrison as well as the *jizāʾ*, that is, after he
had summoned them to convert to Islam or pay tax. Gradually
they returned to their homesteads and conceded to pay the *jizāʾ*,
until Saʿd moved from al-Madāʾin to al-Kūfah. Al-Qaʿqāʿ joined
him there after having left Qubādh in control of the garrison.
Qubādh was of Khurāsānī origin.

In this year, I mean the year 16 (637), according to Sayf's account, the conquest of Takrīt (also) took place. That was in the month Jumādā (May–June).

185a. For a description of this palace, see Le Strange, *Lands*, 63.

186. He cannot be identified with certainty. Prym suggests that the name should be deleted. Is he perhaps the son of al-Muʿtamm?

The Account of the Conquest of Takrīt

According to al-Sarī—Shuʿayb—Sayf—Muḥammad, Ṭalḥah, al-Muhallab and Saʿīd, al-Walīd b. ʿAbdallāh b. Abī Ṭaybah concurred with them: Saʿd wrote a letter (to ʿUmar) concerning the inhabitants of al-Mawṣil, who had rallied under al-Anṭāq and advanced as far as Takrīt. They had dug a trench around themselves in order to defend its lands against Saʿd. He also wrote regarding the people rallying under Mihrān at Jalūlā'. So ʿUmar replied concerning the matter of Jalūlā' as we have described already, and he also wrote about Takrīt and the rallying of the people of al-Mawṣil under the command of al-Anṭāq, saying, "Send ʿAbdallāh b. al-Muʿtamm forth to al-Anṭāq, set Ribʿī b. al-Afkal al-ʿAnazī over his vanguard, al-Ḥārith b. Ḥassān al-Dhuhlī over his right wing and Furāt b. Ḥayyān al-ʿIjlī over his left wing. Furthermore, give the command over the infantry to Hāni' b. Qays and that over the cavalry to ʿArfajah b. Harthamah." Thus
[2475] ʿAbdallāh b. al-Muʿtamm set out from al-Madā'in at the head of five thousand men. He marched to Takrīt until he descended upon al-Anṭāq in four days. This commander had with him, apart from (his) Byzantine contingent, some tribesmen from the Iyād, Taghlib and al-Namir tribes,[187] as well as some local dignitaries. They were all dug in behind trench fortifications. ʿAbdallāh b. al-Muʿtamm besieged them for forty days, during which the Muslims stormed them in twenty-four successive attacks. These forces were possessed of less military prowess than the opposition at Jalūlā' and were dealt with more easily. (Realizing this), ʿAbdallāh b. al-Muʿtamm dispatched a messenger to the Arab tribesmen (siding with al-Anṭāq), to summon them to embrace his cause and to give him assistance in the fight against the Byzantines, to which they wholeheartedly agreed. When the Byzantines saw that every sortie they made was a failure and that they were routed every time they marched against their enemy, they deserted their leaders and carried their belongings to their boats. Spies from Taghlib, Iyād and al-Namir brought ʿAbdallāh b. al-

187. For the Iyād and their involvement with these Byzantine forces, see *EI*², s.v. Iyād (Fück); for Taghlib and al-Namir, see Caskel, II, 541 f. and 444 (an-Namir b. Qāsiṭ). See also W. E. Kaegi, "Heraklius and the Arabs," in *The Greek Orthodox Theological Review*, XXVII (1982):109–33.

Muʿtamm news of this and asked him to agree to peace with their fellow tribesmen. They informed him of their (and their fellow tribesmen's) willingness to embrace his cause. Ibn al-Muʿtamm sent word back telling them, "If you seriously desire peace, then testify that there is no god except God and that Muḥammad is His messenger; confirm what he has brought you from God. Then let us know what you think." The spies submitted these conditions to their respective tribes, who sent them back to Ibn al-Muʿtamm asserting they would accept Islam. Ibn al-Muʿtamm then told the delegation to go back to their people with the following order, "As soon as you hear us cry out, God is great!, know that we will have rushed to the gates nearest to us in order to attack the enemy by forcing our way in through them. You yourselves must then take up a position at the gates facing the Tigris, shout at the top of your voices, God is great!, and kill as many defenders as you can. Go now and see to it that your men carry this out." Then [2476] Ibn al-Muʿtamm, with the Muslims, rushed toward those gates facing them and started to shout, God is great! Thereupon the Taghlib, Iyād and al-Namir followed suit, having taken position at the gates assigned to them. But the defenders thought that the Muslims had launched an attack on them from behind, having forced their way in via the gates facing the Tigris. They hastened in the direction of the gates at which the Muslims had taken position, where swordsmen, that is Muslim swordsmen, stopped them in their tracks. But also the swordsmen of Rabīʿah, who had embraced Islam the previous night, (descended upon them) from behind. Of all those who had defended the trench, no one escaped except those of the tribes of Taghlib, Iyād and al-Namir who had converted to Islam.

Before that, ʿUmar had enjoined Saʿd, in case the enemy was defeated, to have ʿAbdallāh b. al-Muʿtamm send Ibn al-Afkal al-ʿAnazī to al-Ḥiṣnān.[188] ʿAbdallāh b. al-Muʿtamm therefore dispatched Ibn al-Afkal al-ʿAnazī to al-Ḥiṣnān. When the latter was

188. According to Yāqūt, *Muʿjam*, II, 275, al-Ḥiṣnān, which means literally "the two fortresses," was the name of a certain locality without indicating where that was. Ibn al-Athīr, II, 408, who for once gives more information than Ṭabarī, says that with these are meant Nīnawā (= Niniveh) and al-Mawṣil, twin cities on the Tigris. Checking this information in Yāqūt, we only find under Nīnawā a single reference to the "two fortresses" (*Muʿjam*, IV, 870, ult.).

about to set out, Ibn al-Muʿtamm said to him, "Try to outrun the news (of the conquest of Takrīt). Travel without taking a rest in the afternoon, or at night for that matter." Along with him, Ibn al-Muʿtamm dispatched the Taghlib, Iyād and al-Namir tribesmen. Ibn al-Afkal positioned them up front under the command of ʿUtbah b. al-Waʿl, one of the Banū Saʿd b. Jusham, Dhū al-Qurṭ, Abū Wadāʿah b. Abī Karib, Ibn Dhī al-Sunayna, who was later to
[2477] die of rabies, Ibn al-Ḥujayr al-Iyādī and Bishr b. Abī Ḥawṭ, each one of these commanding his own contingent. They did arrive at al-Ḥiṣnān ahead of the news (that Takrīt had been taken), and when they were at a short distance (from the twin cities), they sent ʿUtbah b. al-Waʿl forward who immediately demanded that victory be conceded to him, in addition to booty and a free opportunity to return.[189] After that, Dhū al-Qurṭ was sent forward, then Ibn Dhī al-Sunayna, Ibn al-Ḥujayr and Bishr. They halted at the gates, after having taken up a position there. The swiftest horsemen approached, with Ribʿī b. al-Afkal hurtling down upon the enemy in al-Ḥiṣnān. No sooner had they drawn up abreast with the cities, than the besieged shouted out their willingness to conclude a peace treaty. Those who were willing to accept a treaty stayed on, while those who refused fled. Finally, ʿAbdallāh b. al-Muʿtamm approached. When he had arrived at the cities, he summoned those who had been obstinate until that moment, as well as those who had departed to accept Islam, and he pledged that he would fulfil his promises to those who had stayed on. Gradually, those who had run away returned, those who had stayed behind rejoiced, and all of them were granted "protection" and safety.

They divided the spoils of Takrīt up into lots, each of one thousand dirhams, every mounted soldier receiving three thousand and every infantry man one thousand. Then they sent the fifths away in the care of Furāt b. Ḥayyān and news of the victory (to ʿUmar) with al-Ḥārith b. Ḥassān. Ribʿī b. al-Afkal was entrusted with further military operations at al-Mawṣil, and tax gathering was in the hands of ʿArfajah b. Harthamah.

---

189. *Qafala* "to return" also conveys the sense that the enemies give the assurance that they will not pursue the retreating Muslim fighters, see *Lisān*, s.v. *q-f-l*.

In this same year, I mean the year 16 (637), the conquest of Māsabadhān also took place.

The Account of the Conquest of Māsabadhān

According to al-Sarī—Shuʿayb—Sayf—Ṭalḥah, Muḥammad, Muhallab, ʿAmr and Saʿīd: When Hāshim b. ʿUtbah returned from Jalūlā' to al-Madā'in, the news reached Saʿd that Ādhīn b. al-Hurmuzān had brought together a military force with which he had marched to the plain. Saʿd wrote about this development to ʿUmar who wrote back, "Send Ḍirār b. al-Khaṭṭāb with an army to stop them; set over its vanguard Ibn al-Hudhayl al-Asadī and over its two wings ʿAbdallāh b. Wahb ar-Rāsibī, a confederate of the Bajīlah tribe, and al-Muḍārib al-ʿIjlī, son of so-and-so." So Ḍirār b. al-Khaṭṭāb, who was one of the Banū Muḥārib b. Fihr, marched out with a military force with Ibn al-Hudhayl over the vanguard, until he reached the plain of Māsabadhān. The armies came face-to-face at a spot called Bahandaf where they engaged in combat. The Muslims pounced on the unbelievers. Ḍirār took Ādhīn captive and held him. The latter's army was routed, so Ḍirār placed Ādhīn in front[190] and had him beheaded. Then he marched forward in pursuit (of those who had run away) until he came to al-Sīrawān. Thus he took Māsabadhān by force. Its inhabitants scattered in al-Jibāl. Ḍirār summoned them to embrace his cause, to which they consented. He stayed on the spot until Saʿd moved out of al-Madā'in. After receiving the latter's message, he came to al-Kūfah and deputed Ibn al-Hudhayl over Māsabadhān, which was one of the access routes to al-Kūfah. [2478]

In this year, the battle of Qarqīsiyā' also occurred, in the month Rajab (August).

The Account of the Battle That Took Place at Qarqīsiyā' [2479]

According to al-Sarī—Shuʿayb—Sayf—Ṭalḥah, Muḥammad, al-Muhallab, ʿAmr and Saʿīd: Hāshim b. ʿUtbah returned from Jalūlā' to al-Madā'in. In the meantime, concentrations of people of al-

190. Does that mean "for everybody to see?"

Jazīrah had gathered and assisted Heraklius against the garrison of Ḥimṣ, and they sent a military force to the people at Hīt. Saʿd wrote to this effect to ʿUmar, who wrote back, "Send ʿUmar b. Mālik b. ʿUtbah b. Nawfal b. ʿAbd Manāf with an army to fight them. Appoint over its vanguard al-Ḥārith b. Yazīd al-ʿĀmirī, and Ribʿī b. ʿĀmir and Mālik b. Ḥabīb as commanders of its two wings. So ʿUmar b. Mālik marched off with his army in the direction of Hīt, having placed al-Ḥārith b. Yazīd over the vanguard, until he descended upon those who had positioned themselves at Hīt, where they had dug themselves in behind a trench. When ʿUmar b. Mālik saw their resistance in this trench and how they had found shelter there, he became impatient. He left his tents as they were pitched, with al-Ḥārith b. Yazīd in command of the remaining troops of the besieging forces, and marched out with the other half of his army, taking a direct route until he descended out of the blue on Qarqīsiyā', which he conquered by force. The inhabitants agreed to pay the *jizā'*. Then he wrote to al-Ḥārith b. Yazīd saying, "If those (to whom you are laying siege) agree to a settlement, leave them and let them out. If not, dig a trench around their trench with your gates facing theirs, until I make up my mind (what to do next)." The besieged agreed, however, to consent to a peace treaty, so the besieging warriors joined ʿUmar (b. Mālik's) army again, while the locals were united once more with the people of their places of origin.

Al-Wāqidī said: In this same year, ʿUmar banished Abū Miḥjan
[2480] al-Thaqafī[191] to Bāḍiʿ.[192] He went on: Also in this year, ʿUmar's son[193] married Ṣafiyyah bint Abī ʿUbayd.[194] He continued: In this year, Māriyah, the *umm walad*[195] of the Messenger of God and the mother of (his son) Ibrahim passed away. ʿUmar performed the funeral prayer for her and had her buried in the month Muḥarram

191. For some amusing anecdotes about this man, see Ibn Ḥajar, *Iṣābah*, VII, 260–5.

192. According to Yāqūt, *Muʿjam* I, 471, this is the name of an island off the Yemen coast.

193. This is ʿAbdallāh b. ʿUmar, who died in 73 (693).

194. She is the sister of the notorious rebel al-Mukhtār.

195. An *umm walad* is a female slave who has borne a child to her master and who automatically becomes a free person upon his death. On Māriyah, see Kaj Öhrnberg, "*Māriya al-qibṭiyya* unveiled," in *Studia Orientalia Societatis Fennicae, LV* (1983):14.

(February) in the Baqīʿ.[196] He went on: Also in this year, the (Islamic) dating system was inaugurated as from Rabīʿ I/April–May.

He continued: According to Ibn Abī Sabrah—ʿUthmān b. ʿUbaydallāh b. Abī Rāfiʿ—(Saʿīd) b. al-Musayyab: The first to fix the (Islamic) dating system was ʿUmar after two and a half years of his caliphate had elapsed. This was written as of the year sixteen after the Hijrah, in consultation with ʿAlī b. Abī Ṭālib.[197]

According to ʿAbd al-Raḥmān b. ʿAbdallāh b. ʿAbd al-Ḥakam—Nuʿaym b. Ḥammād—(ʿAbd al-ʿAzīz b. Muḥammad) al-Darāwardī—ʿUthmān b. ʿUbaydallāh b. Abī Rāfiʿ—Saʿīd b. al-Musayyab: ʿUmar b. al-Khaṭṭāb convened the people and asked them, "From what day shall we start using a new Islamic dating system?" ʿAlī answered, "From the day the Messenger of God embarked upon the Hijrah leaving the land of polytheism behind." ʿUmar followed this suggestion.

According to ʿAbd al-Raḥmān—Yaʿqūb b. Isḥāq b. Abī ʿAttāb—Muḥammad b. Muslim al-Ṭāʾifī—ʿAmr b. Dīnār—Ibn ʿAbbās: The (Islamic) dating system was (taken as beginning in) the year in which the Messenger of God traveled to Medina and in which ʿAbdallāh b. al-Zubayr was born.

(Ṭabarī says:) In this year, ʿUmar b. al-Khaṭṭāb led the people on the pilgrimage. According to al-Wāqidī, he had left Zayd b. Thābit in control of Medina. That year ʿAttāb b. Asīd was ʿUmar's gover- [2481]
nor in Mecca, ʿUthmān b. Abī al-ʿĀṣ in al-Ṭāʾif, Yaʿlā b. Umayyah in Yemen, al-ʿAlāʾ b. al-Ḥaḍramī over al-Yamāmah and al-Baḥrayn,[198] Ḥudhayfah b. Miḥṣan in ʿUmān. Abū ʿUbaydah b. al-Jarrāḥ governed all of Syria for ʿUmar and Saʿd b. Abī Waqqāṣ was stationed in al-Kūfah. In charge of the judiciary of al-Kūfah was Abū Qurrah, while al-Mughīrah b. Shuʿbah governed al-Baṣrah and the surrounding territory. Ribʿī b. al-Afkal commanded the military operations (still to be carried out) in al-Mawṣil, while

196. The Baqīʿ is an area in Medina in which their dead were buried.

197. The first day of the Islamic calendar is July 16, 622, the day when the Hijrah from Mecca to Medina is said to have begun.

198. Contrary to today, when Baḥrayn is just the island in the Gulf, in those days the name denoted the entire coastal area along the Gulf between al-Baṣrah and ʿUmān, as it says in Yāqūt, *Muʿjam*, I, 506. Al-Yamāmah is the region between al-Baḥrayn and Mecca.

ʿArfajah b. Harthamah was in charge of the collecting of its *kharāj*. That is what some experts say; others claim that both military operations as well as *kharāj* were the responsibility of ʿUtbah b. Farqad; another opinion has it that all this was in the hands of ʿAbdallāh b. al-Muʿtamm. Finally, ʿIyāḍ b. Ghanm al-Fihrī[199] was governor in al-Jazīrah.

---

199. The Arabic text has al-Ashʿarī, but see *Glossarium*, p. DCXX, and Ibn Ḥajar, *Iṣābah*, IV, 757.

The Events of the Year 17

(January 23, 638–January 11, 639)

In this year the founding[200] of al-Kūfah took place and Sa'd moved there with his people from al-Madā'in, all this according to the account and the transmitted material of Sayf b. 'Umar.

The Reason Why Those Muslims Who Moved from al-Madā'in to al-Kūfah Did So, and the Reason for Their Planning of al-Kūfah, According to Sayf

According to al-Sarī—Shu'ayb—Sayf—Muḥammad, Ṭalḥah, al-Muhallab, 'Amr and Sa'īd: After the conquest of Jalūlā' and Ḥulwān, after al-Qa'qā' b. 'Amr's settling in the latter with his men, after the conquest of Takrīt and the twin fortresses (i.e., Nīnawā and al-Mawṣil), and after 'Abdallāh b. al-Mu'tamm and Ibn al- [2482]
Afkal had arrived there with their men, messengers brought all that news to 'Umar.[201] When 'Umar had seen them, he exclaimed,

200. In Arabic, *ikhtiṭāṭ*.

201. The Arabic original has the nonstructure of an anacoluthon. By disregarding the "and" preceding "approached" (the *wa-* of *qadimat*, l. 2), the sentence is straightened out.

"By God, how different you look from when you set out! Messengers carrying the news of al-Qādisiyyah and al-Madā'in came to me looking exactly the same as at their departure. But you look worn out. What caused that?" "The unhealthiness of that region," they answered. So ʿUmar looked into their needs and dismissed them as quickly as possible. Among the messengers of ʿAbdallāh b. al-Muʿtamm there were ʿUtbah b. al-Waʿl, Dhū al-Qurṭ, Ibn Dhī al-Sunayna, Ibn al-Ḥujayr and Bishr. All of these drew up a treaty with ʿUmar on behalf of the Banū Taghlib. ʿUmar agreed with them that those who converted to Islam would have the same privileges and duties as the Muslims. Those who refused to embrace Islam were to pay the *jizā'*. Pressure to accept Islam was to be exerted by the Arab tribesmen only on those tribesmen living in the peninsula itself. The messengers said, "(If that is your condition) then they might flee, cut themselves off (from their kinsmen) and become like Persians; would it not be better if they were to pay the Islamic alms tax (i.e. the *ṣadaqah*)?" "No," ʿUmar replied, "nothing other than the *jizā'* (will be levied from them)." "Then, please, make the rate of their *jizā'* the same as the alms tax paid by Muslims, that would be their only wish," they suggested. ʿUmar agreed to this on the condition that they would not bring up in a Christian way children whose parents had embraced Islam. They said, "We promise you that." So these Taghlibīs, and those of the Banū al-Namir and Banū Iyād who accepted their leadership, attached themselves to Saʿd[202] in al-Madā'in and, a little later, assisted him in the planning of al-Kūfah, while those who wanted, be they *dhimmī* or Muslim,[203] stayed on in their own lands on the conditions set by ʿUmar and concluded for them (by their representatives).

[2483] According to al-Sarī—Shuʿayb—Sayf—Ibn Shubrumah—al-Shaʿbī: Ḥudhayfah (b. al-Yamān) wrote to ʿUmar telling him that the Arab tribesmen were getting fatter,[204] while their vigor was

202. The technical term for "attach" used here is *hājara*.

203. For a detailed analysis of the conditions of the pact concluded with these Christian Arabs, see A. Noth, "Die literarisch überlieferten Verträge," *BOS*, N.S. 27/1.

204. This does not imply that they were in a state of well-being, but rather the opposite.

on the decline and their complexions sallow. Ḥudhayfah was at the time staying with Saʿd.

According to al-Sarī—Shuʿayb—Sayf—Muḥammad, Ṭalḥah and their authorities: ʿUmar wrote to Saʿd, "Enlighten me as to what caused the complexion of the Arab tribesmen to change and their flesh (to become flabby)." So Saʿd wrote back, "The unhealthiness of al-Madā'in and the Tigris region has made the tribesmen become flaccid and has definitively changed their complexion." ʿUmar replied, "No land suits Arab tribesmen except that which suits their camels. Therefore, dispatch Salmān and also Ḥudhayfah—the two principal scouts of the Muslim army—to reconnoitre; let them look for a suitable place to settle on the edge of the desert and (not entirely surrounded by, but with easy access to) the water,[205] so that no major river or bridge separates you from us here."

There was nothing to do with the army but that Saʿd entrusted it to a special man.[206] So he sent Salmān and Ḥudhayfah away (to survey the area). Salmān went off finally ending up in al-Anbār. He wandered around west of the Euphrates without ever chancing upon a spot with which he was really satisfied, until he came to a place called al-Kūfah. Ḥudhayfah went off, too, wandering around east of the Euphrates, similarly dissatisfied with everything he saw, until he also arrived at this place al-Kūfah. Al-Kūfah was (so called because its soil was) gravel, everywhere the sand was reddish of the sort called "coarse,"[207] mixed with the gravel. A piece of land like that is called a *kūfah*.[208] The two scouts arrived there and found three Christian monasteries, Dayr Ḥurqah, Dayr Umm ʿAmr and Dayr Silsilah,[209] with huts made of reeds scattered in [2484]

205. This is the—perhaps somewhat wordy—rendering of the words *barriyyan baḥriyyan*; in *Glossarium*, p. CXXX, it is suggested that the words mean respectively "bordering on the desert, on a river."

206. As so often is the case, this not altogether unambiguous sentence is lacking in Ibn al-Athīr's account which, as a rule, only faithfully follows Ṭabarī's when the interpretation of the text is straightforward and unproblematic.

207. In Arabic, *sihlah*, which also means "gravel."

208. Cf. *WKAS*, I, 439 f.; also Yāqūt, *Muʿjam*, IV, 322. From this last source it appears that the etymology is dubious, however.

209. Nothing else seems to be known about these; this is the only occurrence in Ṭabarī, while Yāqūt does not list them in his *Muʿjam*.

between. The site pleased them both. They alighted and performed a prayer ritual, each of them reciting:

O God, Lord of heaven and what it covers
Lord of the earth and what it carries
By the wind and what it scatters
By the stars and what they topple
By the seas and what they drown
By the demons and what they delude
By the spirits[210] and what they possess

Bless us in this gravelly site and make it an abode of firmnéss.[211]

Thereupon they wrote a report to Saʿd.

According to Muḥammad b. ʿAbdallāh b. Ṣafwān—Umayyah b. Khālid—Abū ʿAwānah—Ḥuṣayn b. ʿAbd al-Raḥmān: When, on the day of Jalūlā', the enemy had been defeated, Saʿd recalled the army.[212] When ʿAmmār (b. Yāsir) had arrived,[213] he left with the forces for al-Madā'in. But they did not like it there. ʿAmmār asked, "Do the camels thrive in this place?" "No," was the answer, "because of the mosquitoes." ʿAmmār commented, "ʿUmar once said that Arab tribesmen won't be healthy in a region in which their camels do not thrive." He went on: Therefore ʿAmmār departed with the army and in the end settled in al-Kūfah.

According to al-Sarī—Shuʿayb—Sayf—Makhlad b. Qays (al-ʿIjlī)—his father—al-Yusr b. Thawr:[214] After[215] we had alighted there, the Muslims found al-Madā'in to be insalubrious, being irritated by dust and flies. ʿUmar wrote to Saʿd ordering him to send scouts to select a (suitable) site on firm ground but with easy

---

210. I read *khiṣṣān* ("familiars") instead of *khiṣṣāṣ* ("huts").

211. The cripple rhyme "possess—firmnéss" is meant to resemble the equally cripple rhyme in the Arabic *ajannat-thabāt*. See also n. 180 above, and Appendix I.

212. Literally, it says, "he returned with the army," but that does not fit the known circumstances.

213. This ʿAmmār, a stalwart Muslim from the Aws tribe and a confederate of the Makhzūm clan, had been sent by ʿUmar to Iraq to give the Arab leaders there a helping hand.

214. This name should probably read (see *Glossarium*, p. DCXX) al-Nusayr b. Daysam b. Thawr al-ʿIjlī.

215. Here I have broken up a very long sentence into a number of short ones.

access to the water,[216] ". . . . for Arab tribesmen only thrive in regions where their camels and sheep are doing well." Then [2485] 'Umar asked someone on the spot[217] what the area looked like where the Muslim warriors were operating. So a certain leading Arab tribesman, who had seen (with his own eyes what the situation in) Iraq was like, drew 'Umar's attention to al-Lisān. The elevated site planned for al-Kūfah is called the "Tongue,"[218] because it (is a tongue-shaped stretch of land which) lies between two river arms of the Euphrates (stretching out) all the way to a certain well, namely that of the Banū Ḥadhdhā'. Arab tribesmen used to say, the land "sticks out its tongue in the countryside." What borders on the Euphrates of that tongue of land is called al-Milṭāṭ, and what is alongside al-Ṭīn[219] is called al-Nijāf.[220] Thus 'Umar wrote to Sa'd ordering him to go ahead with the founding of al-Kūfah.

According to al-Sarī—Shu'ayb—Sayf—Muḥammad, Ṭalḥah, al-Muhallab, 'Amr and Sa'īd: When Salmān and Ḥudhayfah approached Sa'd informing him about the site of al-Kūfah and, at the same time, a letter from 'Umar containing the same information had arrived, Sa'd wrote to al-Qa'qā' b. 'Amr saying, "Leave Qubādh in charge of the warriors at Jalūlā', along with those who initially followed you to join those of the Ḥamrā' who had been with him all the time." Al-Qa'qā' obeyed, and he presently made his way to Sa'd amidst his forces. Sa'd also wrote to 'Abdallāh b. al-Mu'tamm saying, "Leave in charge of al-Mawṣil that Muslim b. 'Abdallāh who was captured in the course of the battle of al-Qādisiyyah and was one of the Asāwirah[221] who responded to your call to embrace Islam, along with those Asāwirah who are with you." He obeyed and soon made his way among his troops to Sa'd. Sa'd (himself) departed with his forces from al-Madā'in. Finally, in the month Muḥarram of the year 17 (January–February 638),[222] he set up camp at al-Kūfah, fourteen lunar months having elapsed since

216. Again the expression *barrī baḥrī* is used, see n. 205 above.
217. That is, "available in Medina."
218. See above, pp. 1–2.
219. The reading is doubtful; Yāqūt, *Mu'jam*, III, 571, lists a fortress near al-Ḥīrah with that name.
220. This place name could not be traced.
221. See n. 147 above.

the battle of al-Madā'in. From the start of 'Umar's rule until the
[2486] foundation of al-Kūfah was a period of three years and eight months. It was in the fourth year of his rule in the month Muḥarram of the year 17 of the Muslim calendar that the foundation of al-Kūfah began. The warriors had been given their stipends in al-Madā'in in that same month, before they set out, (while the previous time they had received stipends was) in Muḥarram of the year 16[223] at Bahurasīr.

In Muḥarram of the year 17 the present-day settlement of the Baṣrans was established, that being after three previous temporary camps,[224] from each of which they had departed.[225] Their settling in al-Baṣrah came about in the same month in which the people of al-Kūfah settled.

According to al-Wāqidī—al-Qāsim b. Ma'n: The people settled in al-Kūfah at the end of the year 17/638. He went on: Ibn Abī al-Ruqqād informed me from his father: They settled there, when the year 18 (639) had just begun.

The Account Is Resumed Once More by Sayf

They continued: 'Umar wrote to Sa'd b. (Abī Waqqāṣ) Mālik and 'Utbah b. Ghazwān ordering that they, together with their people, should, every spring season, pasture their animals on the best of the lands under their control, and he ordered that the people be given supplementary allocations[226] in the month Rabī'[227] of every year and their stipends every Muḥarram. They should, furthermore, receive their share in the *fay'* every time when Sirius rises[228] and the revenues are forthcoming. Before settling in al-Kūfah, the people had been paid a stipend twice.

---

222. That is, between January 23 and February 21, 638.

223. That is, between February 2 and March 3, 637.

224. The Arabic word mentioned here is *nazalāt*, which I took to be the plural of *nazlah*, the *nomen vicis* of *nuzūl*, mentioned in *Lisān*.

225. In the following sentence, I have departed from the Ṭabarī text, because that does not seem to make sense. Instead I have opted for the text as preserved in Ibn al-Athīr, II, 411: *wa 'staqarra manziluhum fīhā fī al-shahri alladhī nazala ahlu al-Kūfah.*

226. See *EI*[2], s.v. *ma'ūna* (Crone).

227. It is indeed somewhat confusing that, in this year 17 (638), spring (which is *rabī'* in Arabic) coincided with the months al-Rabī' I and al-Rabī' II.

228. That is, in the middle of July, see Lane, 1560. The rising of Sirius, also called the Dog Star, still marks a new season for the Marsh Arabs described by Wilfred Thesiger (*The Marsh Arabs*, Penguin edition, Harmondsworth, 174).

According to al-Sarī—Shuʿayb—Sayf—Makhlad b. Qays—someone from the Banū Asad called al-Maghrūr:[229] When Saʿd had settled in al-Kūfah, he wrote to ʿUmar saying, "I have taken up residence on a site covered with pebbles;[230] it is situated between al-Ḥīrah and the Euphrates, one side borders on dry land, the other borders on the water.[231] Dry as well as tender thistles[232] abound [2487] there. I have left a free choice to the Muslims in al-Madā'in; those who have preferred to stay on in the latter, I have left behind there as a garrison. Thus a number of people from different clans have remained (in al-Madā'in), the majority of them being from the Banū ʿAbs." According to al-Sarī—Shuʿayb—Sayf—Muḥammad, Ṭalḥah, ʿAmr, Saʿīd and al-Muhallab: When the people destined for al-Kūfah had arrived there, and the people destined to populate al-Baṣrah had settled there, they formed themselves into *ʿirāfāt*[233] (to find out who was missing) and whoever[234] they had lost track of was thus returned to them.

Then the people of al-Kūfah asked permission to use reeds as building material. The people of al-Baṣrah put in the same request, whereupon ʿUmar said, "Living in an army camp is easier for you to mount your military operations from and is more convenient, but I do not like to disagree with you; what is this reed anyway?" They answered, "It is like *ʿikrish* (i.e. flax), when it is watered it puts forth stems and produces reeds." ʿUmar replied, "You do what you think best." Thus the people of the two garrison cities used reeds as building material. Then fires occurred in al-Kūfah, as well as in al-Baṣrah, the most vehement one occurring in the former. Eighty roof structures[235] were destroyed, not a single stem of reed being spared. That was in the month Shawwāl,[236] the people never stopped talking about it. Saʿd dispatched a few of the victims of those fires to ʿUmar to try and obtain the

229. *Glossarium*, p. DCXX: al-Maʿrūr b. Suwayd al-Asadī.

230. In Arabic, *kūfah*.

231. The Arabic expression used here is again *barriyyan baḥriyyan*, see n. 205 above.

232. Presumably making excellent camel fodder.

233. For the units called *ʿirāfāt* or *ʿarāfāt*, see Hinds, "Alignments," 347, 349, 351, and *EI*² s.v. *ʿArīf* (Cahen).

234. I interpret *mā* (lit. "what") as referring to people, rather than to inanimate objects; this constitutes one of the peculiarities of Sayf's usage.

235. This seems the best rendering of *ʿarīsh*.

236. That is, October–November.

latter's permission to use bricks for building. Thus they approached ʿUmar with the news about the fire and what losses they had incurred. No detail was left unmentioned; they did not touch on anything without asking his advice. ʿUmar said, "Go ahead,
[2488] but let nobody build more than three rooms for himself and do not let one build higher houses than the other. If you adhere to what is generally recognized as proper,[237] you will thrive." With that advice, the delegation returned to al-Kūfah. ʿUmar wrote a letter containing similar advice to ʿUtbah and the people of al-Baṣrah. The supervision over the settling of the inhabitants of al-Kūfah lay in the hands of Abū al-Hayyāj b. Mālik, while the same task in respect of the inhabitants of al-Baṣrah was undertaken by ʿĀṣim b. al-Dulaf Abū al-Jarbāʾ.

They continued: ʿUmar had enjoined the delegation to carry out what he had said, and he ordered the people (in Iraq) not to construct buildings that were higher than the "norm." "But what is this 'norm'?" they had asked. "The 'norm,'" ʿUmar said, "is that which keeps you well away from wastefulness but, at the same time, won't make you lose sight of what you are aiming at."

According to al-Sarī—Shuʿayb—Sayf—Muḥammad, Ṭalḥah, al-Muhallab, ʿAmr and Saʿīd: When they had agreed on the building plan of al-Kūfah, Saʿd sent a message to Abū al-Hayyāj and informed him of ʿUmar's letter containing instructions for the roads. ʿUmar had ordered that (main) thoroughfares of forty cubits (in width) be planned.[238] In between these[239] there should be (other) roads each thirty cubits wide, and between the former and the latter (again others) twenty cubits wide; finally, the side alleys should be seven cubits wide, no passageway should be narrower than that. The plots of land[240] had to measure sixty cubits (square?) except the one assigned to the Banū Ḍabbah.[241] The people who had insight in those matters assembled to carry out measurements, until Abū al-Hayyāj divided up all the available space among them, when they had decided on a certain plot.

237. The Arabic has here the major technical term *al-sunna.*

238. That may have been well over twenty meters, see n. 103 above, where the cubit measured a little over fifty centimeters.

239. Or conceivably, "parallel with."

240. The Arabic word used here is *qaṭāʾiʿ*.

241. See *EI*², s.v. Ḍabba (Caskel).

The first thing to be marked out in al-Kūfah and that was subsequently erected, when they had finally decided to make a beginning with building, was the mosque. It was situated in what is now the market area of the soap manufacturers and date sellers. [2489] Its ground plan was traced out. Then a man stationed himself in the center of this ground plan. He was an archer of prodigious strength. He shot (one arrow) to his right and ordered that anyone who wanted could start building for his own beyond where the arrow had landed. (Then he did the same with an arrow that he shot to the left.[242]) Next he shot an arrow straight ahead of him and one in the opposite direction and ordered that anyone who wanted could start building for himself beyond where these two arrows had landed. Thus they left a square for the mosque that the people could enter from all sides.[243] Over its front part,[244] a roof structure was built, that had no (walls at) either side, nor at the front or back. The whole square was meant for the people to congregate in, but in a way that they (need) not stand packed. In the same manner, other mosques were laid out, except the *masjid al-ḥarām;*[245] in those days they did not try to emulate that out of respect for its holiness. The roof structure of al-Kūfah's mosque measured two hundred cubits in width supported by columns of marble. Its ceiling, resembling the ceilings in Byzantine churches, was (taken from a palace formerly belonging) to the Persian kings.[246] They marked (the outer perimeter of) the congregation area by means of a ditch, lest anyone should inadvertently and boldly embark on building inside that perimeter for his own. They built a house for Saʿd, separated from the mosque by a nar-

---

242. Although this sentence is lacking in the Arabic original, Prym thinks, probably rightly, that it must have been part of the text originally, see Yāqūt, *Muʿjam*, IV, 323. Its inadvertently having been omitted in the manuscripts from which Prym worked constitutes in my opinion a clear case of *homoioteleuton.*

243. What follows is riddled with what appear to be architectural terms not explained in the standard dictionaries; while doing this translation I benefitted from O. Grabar, *The formation of Islamic art*, New Haven 1973, esp. 113, and the ground plan of the mosque of al-Kūfah, fig. 35.

244. We will see later (see also Grabar, illustration no. 35) that that is its part facing southwest.

245. That is, the mosque that houses the Kaʿbah in Mecca.

246. This interpretation is tentative, but in the equivalent passage in Ibn al-Athīr, II, 412, it is implied that the marble pillars once stood in a Persian royal palace in al-Ḥīrah.

row alley of two hundred cubits (in length).[247] The treasure chambers were incorporated in this house. It is the present-day citadel of al-Kūfah. Rūzbih (b. Buzurgumihr) built it for Saʿd out of baked bricks previously used in buildings of the Persian kings in al-Ḥīrah.

North of the congregation area five main thoroughfares branched out, from the south side four such thoroughfares branched out, while from the east and the west (sides) three such roads were planned. All these roads were marked out (by Saʿd). North of the congregation area, adjacent to it, he settled Sulaym and Thaqīf along two roads, Hamdān along another road, Bajīlah along an-
[2490] other and Taym al-Lāt as well as Taghlib along yet another road. South of the congregation area he settled Banū Asad along one road, with another road separating them from Nakhaʿ, who in turn were separated from Kindah by another, while the latter were separated from al-Azd by yet another road. East of the congregation area he settled the Anṣār and Muzaynah along one road, Tamīm and Muḥārib along another, and Asad and ʿĀmir along yet another. Finally, west of the congregation area he settled Bajālah and Bajlah along one road, Jadīlah as well as various groups of mixed origin along another, and Juhaynah as well as other groups of mixed origin along yet another. Thus, all those who lived right next to the congregation area as well as all the other people were housed between (the main thoroughfares) and beyond them, the entire territory having been divided up into plots.[248] These, then, were the main thoroughfares; they also built narrower ones that sometimes would run parallel with the former, then merge with them, and yet others that did not merge with the main roads. These last-mentioned roads, however, were less wide. The dwelling places were found in the space beyond and in between these roads. All the roads and paths[249] began at the congregation area and, right there, he settled the "tenths",[250] into which the veterans of the battles

247. That is how this sentence is translated in *Glossarium*, p. DXXVI, but the grammatical structure remains obscure.

248. For a reconstruction of this ground plan, see L. Massignon, in *Mélanges Maspéro*, III, 336–60.

249. This is how I render the secondary plural *ṭuruqāt*.

250. The "tenths" comprised ten subdivisions originally created by Saʿd at Sharāf before the battle of al-Qādisiyyah, see Ṭabarī, I, 2224, and G. M. Hinds, *The early history of Islamic schism in Iraq*, unpubl. PhD thesis, London 1969, 30 f.

preceding al-Qādisiyyah and those of al-Qādisiyyah and its aftermath[251] had earlier been divided. For those warriors who were at the time manning the border garrisons and that of al-Mawṣil, he held various plots ready until they themselves might come to them. When the first and second waves[252] of newcomers[253] joined the Arab warriors (in al-Kūfah) and swamped them, the people found their plots too cramped. Those groups whose newcomers were particularly numerous, went out and joined them (i.e. outside al-Kūfah), vacating the plots they had occupied, while those groups whose newcomers were few in number, settled those—since they were only few in number—in the homesteads of those who had gone to join their newcomers (i.e. outside al-Kūfah) if the latter had been living next door. If that had not been the case, those staying behind chose for themselves more cramped quarters, thus accommodating their newcomers. The congregation area remained in [2491]
this state during the entire period of ʿUmar's reign, the tribesmen not coveting it. There was nothing there but the mosque, the citadel and the markets, which were devoid of buildings or even markings (for buildings). ʿUmar had said, "Markets are to be organized on the basis of the norms valid for mosques: he who gets to a certain place first, has sole rights to it, until he vacates it to go home or as the case may be until he has sold all his wares." For every newcomer they prepared "reception" camps,[254] everyone arriving there being treated on a basis of equality. Those quarters today are the dwelling places of the Banū al-Bakkā'. (The newcomers stayed there) until they came to Abū al-Hayyāj so that he might attend to them by assigning plots to them where they wanted.

In the plot destined for that purpose, Saʿd built a citadel facing the spot where the *miḥrāb*[255] of the mosque of al-Kūfah is today. He built it and incorporated the treasury in it. He himself lived right next to it. Then, (somewhat later, robbers) dug a tunnel to the

---

251. See nn. 43 and 114 above.

252. For this rendering, see *Glossarium*, p. CLV.

253. This is, perhaps, the best rendering of *rawādif*, a term that indicates the nomads who came to join their clansmen—relatives or otherwise—in the conquered territories. *Glossarium*, p. CCLXI, calls them "new conscripts." See Hinds, "Alignments," 352 ff; Donner, 231 ff; Morony, *Iraq*, 242.

254. The word used is *munākh* "a place where one's camel is made to kneel down."

255. This is the niche that indicates the direction toward Mecca.

treasure chamber and stole from its contents. Sa'd notified 'Umar of this by letter describing to him the layout of the governor's residence and the treasure chambers vis-à-vis the congregation area as situated north of the building. 'Umar replied, "Move the spot where you actually perform the prayer ritual[256] to a place as close as possible to the building housing the treasure chambers; in so doing, you make it the direction for prayer.[257] For in the mosque there are always people present,[258] day and night, they will act as guards of what is also their treasure." Thus the place where the prayer ritual was performed was brought closer (facing the treasure chambers[259]) and then Sa'd set about building it.[260] A dihqān from the people of Hamadhān, called Rūzbih b. Buzurgumihr, said to him, "I shall build it for you, and I shall also build a citadel for you; I shall make some sort of connection between the one and the other so that they constitute one and the same building." Thus he planned the citadel of al-Kūfah according to a well-considered design. Then Rūzbih commenced building it from baked bricks taken from the ruin of a citadel the Persian kings used to have in
[2492] the neighborhood of al-Ḥīrah,[261] which today is still in its place.[262] Sa'd did not allow this to continue, however. He built the mosque facing the treasure chambers, with the entire length of the citadel being situated to the right of that side of the mosque facing south.[263] Then he extended it to the right, up to the far end of the Square of 'Alī b. Abī Ṭālib with this square as the prayer direction. Then he extended it yet some more so that the prayer direction of the mosque encompassed the whole square as well as the right side of the citadel.

---

256. The Arabic reads *al-masjid,* but my—admittedly wordy—translation is meant to convey the original meaning of the word, which happens to suit the context best.

257. Or rather, ". . . . in so doing you make sure that the building lies in the direction in which the people would look when they pray."

258. It is conceivable that with these people some sort of mosque personnel is meant.

259. Presumably this was done *before* the roof structure on the marble pillars was built.

260. A textual variant admits of the interpretation "and then he looked for someone, an architect, to build it."

261. This ancient city, mentioned a few times before, lay three miles to the west of al-Kūfah.

262. Rendition tentative.

263. That is, the direction of prayer.

The building[264] was supported by pillars made of marble originally from Christian churches[265] belonging to the king. (This roof structure) had no walls, a situation that lasted until the building (complete with walls), as it is today, was constructed in the time of Muʿāwiyah b. Abī Sufyān at the hands of Ziyād (his adopted brother and governor of Iraq). When Ziyād set out to construct it, he invited several architects who were born in the Jāhiliyyah to come to him. He described to them the location of the mosque, its size and how high he wanted it to reach up into the air, saying, "I want something higher than anything I have ever heard described." Then a certain architect, who had previously been in the service of the king, said to him, "This can only be done when supported by pillars made from blocks of stone quarried at Ahwāz; these blocks have to be pierced and hollowed out, then filled with lead and (held together by) iron bars, so as to enable you to raise the pillars made of these blocks thirty cubits into the air. Then you build a roof over them and, to grant (the whole structure) extra solidity, you build walls on all sides (i.e., supporting the edges of that roof structure)." Ziyād answered, "This is a description of a structure about which I used to have inward discussions that I have never been able to settle."[266]

Saʿd provided the gate of the citadel with a lock. The reason for this was that the markets used to be held nearby right in front of Saʿd's living quarters, the tumult being so deafening as to prevent Saʿd from conducting a normal conversation. When the citadel was built, people began to ascribe things to him he had never said. [2493]
Thus they alleged that Saʿd had said (on one occasion), "Stop that terrible noise!"[267] News of this reached ʿUmar, and also that the people were calling it "Saʿd's citadel." So he called Muḥammad b. Maslamah[268] and sent him to al-Kūfah, saying, "Make for the citadel and burn down that gate, then return to me forthwith." Muḥammad b. Maslamah departed and journeyed until he arrived

264. Sc. the roof structure over the southern part of the mosque.

265. For the relationship of the king with the Christian church, see Morony, *Iraq*, 332–42.

266. After this digression dealing with an event from Ziyād b. Abīhi's governorship of Iraq, some time between the years 661 and 680, the narrative goes back once more to the time of Saʿd, that is, 638.

267. The word for "noise" here is *ṣuwayt*, a diminutive expressing enhancement, *li 't-taʿẓīm*, see Wright, I, 166.

268. For more on this man, see Ibn Ḥajar, *Iṣābah*, VI, 33–5.

in al-Kūfah. He bought some firewood, brought it to the citadel and burned down its gate. Someone went to Sa'd and told him what had happened. Sa'd said, "This must be a messenger sent here for this very purpose."[269] So he dispatched someone to find out who it was. It was none but Muḥammad b. Maslamah! Immediately, Sa'd sent a message inviting him inside. But he refused. Then Sa'd came outside and invited him in, offering him hospitality. But he refused again. Next Sa'd offered to bear the expenses of the man's staying on in al-Kūfah, but he would not hear of it. Instead he handed Sa'd a letter from 'Umar that read, "It has come to my notice that you have built a citadel and that you have taken possession of it as your personal fortress, it being called 'Sa'd's citadel.' You have even made a gate separating you from the people! However, it is not your property; have you gone insane?[270] Go and find yourself a place to live near the treasure chambers and lock that (if you insist), but don't have a gate in the citadel preventing the people from entering it and depriving them of their right to sit freely with you in counsel even at the time when you choose to leave your quarters." Sa'd swore to Muḥammad b. Maslamah that he had not said what the people had imputed to him. So, instantly, Muḥammad b. Maslamah set out on his return journey. When, in the vicinity of Medina, his provisions had run out, he had to still his hunger with what bark of trees he could find. Suffering from indigestion, he finally approached 'Umar and told him all that had happened. 'Umar asked, "Did you not take anything from Sa'd for me?" Muḥammad answered, "If you had
[2494] wanted that, you should have (said so in the) letter you gave me for him, or you should have given me leave to use my own judgment in this matter." Whereupon 'Umar said, "The most sagacious man is he who displays his own initiative, when he has no directives from his superior to fall back on, or who, without holding back, gives expression to his own views." Then Muḥammad b. Maslamah told 'Umar of the oath Sa'd had sworn and what he had said (on that occasion). Believing Sa'd to be sincere, 'Umar

269. In my translation I disregard the preposition *min*, which is lacking in manuscript Co.

270. Literally, "it is the citadel of insanity (or wickedness)," or as *Glossarium* suggests "the palace of perversity." I suspect that the reading *khabāl* here is dubious.

said, "He is surely more veracious than those who informed on him or those who told me (all about this)."

According to al-Sarī—Shuʿayb—Sayf—ʿAṭāʾ Abū Muḥammad, the freedman of Isḥāq b. Ṭalḥah: I used to sit in the great mosque before Ziyād built (the extensions that he added); at that time, (the roof structure) had no walls (i.e. to support it on any side), so that I could see from the mosque the monastery of Hind as well as the gate leading to the bridge.

According to al-Sarī—Shuʿayb—Sayf—Ibn Shubrumah—al-Shaʿbī: When someone was seated in the mosque, one could see from it the gate leading to the bridge.

According to al-Sarī—Shuʿayb—Sayf—ʿUmar b. ʿAyyāsh, the brother of Abū Bakr b. ʿAyyāsh—Abū Kathīr: Rūzbih b. Buzurgumihr b. Sāsān came from Hamadhān. He had had control over one of the approaches to the territory of the Byzantines, to whom he sometimes brought arms. The Persian kings made threats against him, so he joined the Byzantines. But he was never sure of his life, until Saʿd b. (Abī Waqqāṣ) Mālik had come (i.e., to Iraq). For him Rūzbih built the citadel and the mosque. Then Saʿd sent him with a letter to ʿUmar in which he gave the particulars of the situation. (When he had arrived in Medina), Rūzbih embraced Islam. ʿUmar entered his name in the register of stipends and sent him back to Saʿd with a group of professional camel drivers. Professional camel drivers in those days were (from that class of people called) *ʿibād*.[271] Rūzbih set out until, when at a place later called Qabr al-ʿIbādī,[272] he suddenly died. So the camel drivers dug a grave for him and then they sat down and waited beside the corpse for someone to pass by that route whom they could prevail upon to testify to Rūzbih's having died (a natural death). And, indeed, a group of Bedouins passed along that route, right after they had [2495]
finished digging a grave for him at the roadside. So they showed the corpse to those Bedouins, so that they would declare them innocent from having shed Rūzbih's blood and would bear witness to that effect. They named that place the Grave of the ʿIbādī; it was called that on account of these camel drivers (who hailed

271. ʿIbād is the term by which the Christian Arabs of al-Ḥīrah are designated, see Morony, *Iraq*, index s.v. *ʿibād*.

272. Literally "the grave of the ʿIbādī."

from the class of the *'ibād*[273]). Abū Kathīr added: "That man, this Rūzbih, was my father, by God." Then I[274] said, "Did you not tell anybody about him?" "No," said Abū Kathīr.

According to al-Sarī—Shu'ayb—Sayf—Muḥammad, Ṭalḥah, al-Muhallab, 'Amr, Sa'īd and Ziyād: The "tenths"[275] became greatly imbalanced in numbers. Sa'd wrote to 'Umar regarding the possibility of dividing the army up into a more appropriate number of contingents. So 'Umar wrote back, "Yes, by all means." Then Sa'd sent for a number of experts in tribal genealogy, and some clever and sagacious men, among whom were Sa'īd b. Nimrān and Mash'alah b. Nu'aym. These experts redivided the Muslim army into "sevenths," creating seven contingents. Kinānah, with its confederates from among the Aḥābīsh[276] and others, as well as Jadīlah, that is the Banū 'Amr b. Qays 'Aylān, formed one so-called *sub'*.[277] Quḍā'ah, among whom in those days were Ghassān b. Shibām, as well as Bajīlah, Khath'am, Kindah, Ḥaḍramawt and Azd formed (another) *sub'*. Madhḥij, Ḥimyar, Hamdān as well as their confederates formed a (third) *sub'*. Tamīm and all of Ribāb and Hawāzin formed a (fourth) *sub'*. Asad, Ghaṭafān, Muḥārib, al-Namir, Ḍubay'ah and Taghlib formed a (fifth) one. Iyād, 'Akk, 'Abd al-Qays, the people of Hajar[278] and the Ḥamrā'[279] formed a (sixth) *sub'*.[280] This subdivision into seven contingents was maintained during the entire period of the reigns of 'Umar, 'Uthmān, 'Alī as well as the better part of that of Mu'āwiyah. Then Ziyād redivided the army into "fourths."

---

273. Yāqūt, *Mu'jam*, IV, 28, penult, adds a remark to the effect that the place was called by this name because ". . . it was thought that Rūzbih had been one of those *'ibād*."

274. This is presumably the transmitter of Abū Kathīr, Abū Bakr b. 'Ayyāsh, see p. 2494 above.

275. See n. 250 above.

276. See *EI*[2], s.v. *Ḥabash, Ḥabasha*, final part (Watt).

277. Literally, "one-seventh."

278. The city in the coastal region of al-Baḥrayn is meant, see Yāqūt, *Mu'jam*, IV, 953.

279. See n. 147 above.

280. A seventh group is lacking. Is that due to a scribal mistake/omission of the manuscript(s) Prym worked from, or should we insert anywhere in this enumeration the words *sub'an wa-ṣārat*, thus creating a seventh one? According to Caskel (*EI*[2], s.v. *Ḍabba*), the seventh group was made up of Ḍabbah, Bakr and Ṭayyi'. For more speculations, see Morony, *Iraq*, 243.

The Redivision of the People into ʿIrāfahs[281] [2496]

The people were divided into units, *ʿirāfah*s, each of which was entitled to 100,000 dirhams. Every unit consisting especially of veterans of al-Qādisiyyah, comprising forty-three men, forty-three women and fifty children, had 100,000 dirhams (to be distributed among them). Every *ʿirāfah* of the *ahl al-ayyām*[282] was similarly entitled to 100,000 dirhams, twenty men receiving 3,000 dirhams and twenty women, as well as every child receiving one hundred dirhams each. Every *ʿirāfah* of the first immigration wave,[283] consisting of sixty men, sixty women and forty children, whose fighting members(?) were each entitled to (?) 1,500, had similarly 100,000 dirhams to divide between them. A similar calculation was applied to other *ʿirāfah*s. ʿAṭiyyah b. al-Ḥārith said: I personally met one hundred *ʿarīf*s.[284] The people of al-Baṣrah were organized and administered according to the same principles. The stipends were handed out to the commanders of the *subʿ*s[285] and the standard bearers, all standards being carried by pure-blooded tribesmen. These passed the stipends on to the *ʿarīf*s, (other) leaders and chiefs who duly distributed them among the people in their respective dwelling places.

The Conquest of al-Madāʾin before the Founding of al-Kūfah

According to al-Sarī—Shuʿayb—Sayf—Muḥammad, Ṭalḥah, al-Muhallab, ʿAmr and Saʿīd: The conquests of al-Madāʾin comprised the Sawād, Ḥulwān, Māsabadhān and Qarqīsiyāʾ. The frontier ways of access of al-Kūfah were the following four: Ḥulwān under the command of al-Qaʿqāʿ b. ʿAmr, Māsabadhān under the command of Ḍirār b. al-Khaṭṭāb al-Fihrī, Qarqīsiyāʾ under the com- [2497]

281. For more information on the unit called *ʿirāfah* and the function of its administrator (*ʿarīf*), mainly responsible for the distribution of state stipends among its members, see *EI*[2] s.v. *ʿArīf*, and Hinds, "Alignments," 349.

282. That is, the veterans of the battles preceding that of al-Qādisiyyah, see n. 43 above.

283. This comprised the first contingents of *rawādif* to join the Muslim warriors in al-Kūfah, see above p. 71, especially n. 253.

284. See. n. 281 above.

285. See p. 76 above.

mand of ʿUmar b. Mālik or ʿAmr b. ʿUtbah b. Nawfal b. ʿAbd Manāf, and finally al-Mawṣil under the command of ʿAbdallāh b. al-Muʿtamm. That situation lasted for some time.[286] Then, after that, Saʿd moved out (sc. of al-Madāʾin) to found al-Kūfah and with part of the inhabitants staying behind in al-Madāʾin, he ordered the abovementioned people[287] to come and join him in al-Kūfah, after they had appointed those men who were willing to stay behind and assume control as successors commanding the ways of access. Thus al-Qaʿqāʿ's successor over Ḥulwān was Qubādh b. ʿAbdallāh, ʿAbdallāh b. al-Muʿtamm's successor over al-Mawṣil was Muslim b. ʿAbdallāh, Ḍirār's successor was Rāfiʿ b. ʿAbdallāh and finally ʿUmar's was ʿAshannaq b. ʿAbdallāh.[288] ʿUmar (b. al-Khaṭṭāb) wrote to them instructing them to call in the help of the Asāwirah,[289] as many as they needed, and to exempt them from paying the *jizā*ʾ. Thus they did. When the ground plan of al-Kūfah had been laid out, and the people had obtained permission to start building their dwelling places, they carried their doors with them from al-Madāʾin to al-Kūfah and hung them in their new homes. In this way, they made al-Kūfah their base and those (four frontier towns mentioned above) were their ways of access, while they had no control over the adjoining countryside.

[2498] According to al-Sarī—Shuʿayb—Sayf—Mujālid—ʿĀmir: In other words, the conquests of al-Madāʾin comprised the acquisition of al-Kūfah and its surrounding agricultural area as well as the conquest of the border areas Ḥulwān, al-Mawṣil, Māsabadhān and Qarqīsiyāʾ. ʿAmr b. al- Rayyān—Mūsā b. ʿĪsā al-Hamdānī, told a similar report, in which ʿUmar b. al-Khaṭṭāb forbade the people of al-Kūfah to venture outside those areas, not allowing them to penetrate further into enemy-held territory.[290]

They all said: Saʿd b. (Abī Waqqāṣ) Mālik ruled over al-Kūfah for

286. I have divided the following very long sentence into a number of shorter ones, changing the order somewhat.

287. Sc. of those four border towns.

288. This enumeration of four successive "fathers" all being called ʿAbdallāh is one more clear example of how the commonest Muslim names were regularly used *either* to conceal someone's unknown parentage *or* to conceal the non-Muslim origin of someone's ancestors. See further Juynboll, *Muslim tradition*, 145 f.

289. See n. 147 above.

290. See p. 45 above.

three and a half years after it had been founded, in addition to the period he had previously spent in al-Madā'in and the period he was 'Umar's governor in the entire area comprising al-Kūfah, Ḥulwān, al-Mawṣil, Māsabadhān and Qarqīsiyā', all the way to (i.e., but not including) al-Baṣrah. While ruling over al-Baṣrah, and while Sa'd ruled al-Kūfah, 'Utbah b. Ghazwān died. He had found his office distressing.[291] In 'Utbah's place 'Umar appointed Abū Sabrah (b. Abī Ruhm al-'Āmirī); then he dismissed Abū Sabrah from al-Baṣrah and employed al-Mughīrah (b. Shu'bah) as his governor. After he had also dismissed al-Mughīrah, he installed Abū Mūsā al-Ash'arī in that position.

The Story of Ḥimṣ When the Byzantine Commander Marched on Its Muslim Occupants

In this year, the Byzantines marched on Abū 'Ubaydah b. al-Jarrāḥ and those warriors from the Muslim army who were with him in Ḥimṣ to make war on them. What happened to the Byzantines and the Muslims, as related in Abū 'Ubaydah's own words, is according to al-Sarī—Shu'ayb—Sayf—Muḥammad, Ṭalḥah, 'Amr and Sa'īd: The first time 'Umar allowed the troops in al-Kūfah to venture outside (i.e. to penetrate into enemy-held territory[292]) was when the Byzantines, after having exchanged messages with the inhabitants of al-Jazīrah, marched out heading for Abū [2499]
'Ubaydah and the Muslims in Ḥimṣ. So Abū 'Ubaydah gathered his armed units around him ordering them to make camp in the city square of Ḥimṣ. Khālid also approached from Qinnasrīn. He joined them (sc. in Ḥimṣ) amidst other commanders of armed units. Then Abū 'Ubaydah sought their advice: should they prepare to wage battle or should they fortify themselves inside the city until help might come? It was Khālid who suggested to him to fight the Byzantines, whilst the other Muslim commanders advised him to dig himself in and write to 'Umar.[293] Abū 'Ubaydah took the latter's advice and discarded Khālid's. Then he wrote to 'Umar informing him of the Byzantines' offensive

291. Why he may have done so can be gleaned from Ibn Sa'd, VII 1/3, 10 ff.
292. See n. 289 above.
293. Presumably in order to ask for help and obtain fresh orders.

against him and their keeping the Muslim troops in Syria fully occupied, so that they could not help him.

Of late, ʿUmar had concentrated cavalry in every city, in each a contingent commensurate with its size. The horses had been left behind by the Muslim forces to be held ready for some unforeseen contingency. Thus there were in al-Kūfah four thousand horses. So when the news (sc. from Ḥimṣ) reached ʿUmar, he wrote to Saʿd b. (Abī Waqqāṣ) Mālik, "Detail the cavalry under the command of al-Qaʿqāʿ b. ʿAmr and dispatch them forthwith to Ḥimṣ the moment my letter reaches you, for Abū ʿUbaydah is under siege there. Therefore, march on them with the utmost speed." Furthermore, he wrote to him saying, "Dispatch Suhayl b. ʿAdī with an armed force to al-Jazīrah; let him make for al-Raqqah, for it is the inhabitants of al-Jazīrah who incited the Byzantines to take up arms against the people of Ḥimṣ. The people of Qarqīsiyā' have a good record. But send ʿAbdallāh b. ʿItbān to Naṣībīn.[294] Let both
[2500] these men also find out more about Ḥarrān and al-Ruhā'.[295] Then dispatch al-Walīd b. ʿUqbah at the head of the tribesmen of al-Jazīrah, viz. Rabīʿah and Tanūkh, and send ʿIyāḍ too, for if there is any fighting to be done, I have placed the command over all the forces in the hands of ʿIyāḍ b. Ghanm. ʿIyāḍ was originally one of the Muslim warriors in Iraq who had marched out with Khālid b. al-Walīd to help the Muslims fighting in Syria, and he was also one of those who came along when the Iraqi forces left (Syria again) to aid the forces at al-Qādisiyyah; he used to be Abū ʿUbaydah's personal aide.

So on the day ʿUmar's letter arrived, al-Qaʿqāʿ, at the head of four thousand men, set out toward Ḥimṣ. ʿIyāḍ b. Ghanm and the commanders of the al-Jazīrah forces marched out too, taking the road to al-Jazīrah sometimes along the frontier garrisons, at other times bypassing them. Each commander headed toward the district over which he was appointed. Suhayl went to al-Raqqah and ʿUmar left Medina in aid of Abū ʿUbaydah, heading for Ḥimṣ until

294. The edition here repeats the preceding sentence, but Prym points out that it is lacking in the two main manuscripts, and I have accordingly decided to leave it untranslated.

295. The verb used for "to find out more about" is *nafaḍa*, see Lane, 2830, right column, but the reading is dubious; Ibn al-Athīr has the verb *qaṣada* "to go."

he alighted at al-Jābiyah.[296] At first,[297] the people of al-Jazīrah helped the Byzantines and incited them against the Muslims in Ḥimṣ, remaining in close contact with them. But then, when they heard the rumor from those who were scattered in al-Jazīrah[298] that those (mounted) forces had pulled out of al-Kūfah, they[299] did not know whether those Kūfan troops were marching on al-Jazīrah or on Ḥimṣ. So they dispersed to their regions and their brethren and they deserted the Byzantines. After this dispersal, Abū ʿUbaydah viewed the situation no longer as he had done at first, and he again sought Khālid's advice as to whether or not they should venture a sortie. Khālid thought they should. So God granted Abū ʿUbaydah and his men victory over the besiegers.

[Translator's note [2501]

Now follows in the edition an insert covering three pages, which Prym found in the Ibn Ḥubaysh manuscripts, and of which there was no trace in the other manuscripts from which he worked. At first he thought it best to leave it out altogether, but then he decided against that because, as he argued, the information contained in this insert gives details found nowhere else, and he inferred the likelihood of a lacuna in the Ṭabarī manuscript of which C and Co (sc. Prym's principal manuscripts) are (in)direct copies. I see no reason why I should not follow Prym's example, and therefore I insert the translation of these pages forthwith.]

According to Sayf with his *isnād*—Rajā' b. Ḥaywah and others: Heraklius sent an expeditionary force by sea against Ḥimṣ. (Some time ago the Muslim forces[300]) had formed armed units.[301] While ʿAlqamah b. Mujazziz and ʿAlqamah b. Ḥakīm had entrenched themselves in al-Ramlah and ʿAsqalān and their respective environs, Yazīd (b. Abī Sufyān) and Shuraḥbīl (b. Ḥasanah) having

---

296. A town near Damascus, see Yāqūt, *Muʿjam*, II, 3f. For its importance, see *EI*2, s.v. *Djābiya* (Lammens).

297. I have broken a convoluted sentence into several manageable, shorter ones.

298. In order to make this sentence convey any sense at all, I read *ḥadīthu* instead of *ʿan ḥadīthi*, a suggestion of M. Hinds.

299. I read *lam* with one manuscript, and not *wa-lam*, as it says in the edition.

300. This translation is based on a marginal gloss in one Ibn Ḥubaysh manuscript.

301. Or "strong points."

done likewise, Heraklius asked the people of al-Jazīrah for help and sought to rouse the inhabitants of Ḥimṣ. But those latter (in Ḥimṣ) sent him a message that read, "We have made a pact with them[302] and we fear that we will not win (if we do as you suggest)." Then Heraklius marched on Abū ʿUbaydah amidst a mighty cavalry force.[303] Abū ʿUbaydah asked Khālid to come and help him, so the latter came with every man he had, not leaving anyone behind. After Khālid had left, the inhabitants of Qinnasrīn went back on their promises made to the Muslims and sided with Heraklius. Most of the people who lived there were sedentary Tanūkh. Nonetheless, every Muslim leader held on to his own district. That shows how courageous the Muslims were.[304] Heraklius closed in on Ḥimṣ, made camp and sent spies (to reconnoiter). The Muslims were unanimous in digging themselves in and writing to ʿUmar, except Khālid, who maintained that they should prepare to fight. So they dug themselves in at Ḥimṣ and wrote to ʿUmar imploring him to help them. The Byzantines and those who aided them drew nearer and nearer until they alighted close by and surrounded them. The forces from al-Jazīrah (rallying with Heraklius) numbered 30,000, this apart from the Tanūkh and others from Qinnasrīn. Thus they created a truly desperate situation for the Muslims.

The letter reached ʿUmar while he was on his way to Mecca for the pilgrimage. He proceeded on his journey but sent the following message to Saʿd: "Abū ʿUbaydah is under siege, forced to stay
[2502] entrenched. (Please) send your Muslim warriors all over al-Jazīrah and harass the Byzantines with your cavalry so that they cannot address themselves properly to the people in Ḥimṣ and their protégés. Help Abū ʿUbaydah with al-Qaʿqāʿ b. ʿAmr and (further) manpower." So al-Qaʿqāʿ went forth in aid of Abū ʿUbaydah and the cavalry squadrons marched on al-Raqqah, Ḥarrān and Naṣībīn. When they arrived in al-Jazīrah and news of that reached the enemy, while they were (laying siege) to Ḥimṣ, they scurried back to their (respective) cities, which they tried to reach before

302. Presumably the Muslim Arabs who had control over much of the northern part of Syria are meant.

303. That is what I think that *ḥalbah* means in this context; it is not found anywhere in the dictionaries.

304. The translation is dubious, but so is the Arabic text.

the (pursuing) Muslims. Then they dug themselves in, and the Muslims descended upon them in their fortifications. When al-Qaʿqāʿ moved nearer to Ḥimṣ, the members of a certain clan from Tanūkh wrote a letter to Khālid in which they cajoled him and informed him about the situation. Khālid sent a message back saying, "By God, had it not been for the fact that I am under somebody else's orders, I would not have cared whether you had been few or many, whether you would have stayed or whether you would have departed. If you are sincere, you had better disperse, as all the other people of al-Jazīrah have done." They suggested this to the others of Tanūkh, who agreed. Then they sent a message to Khālid, "This is what we propose to you: If you want (us to do as you said), we will do it. But if you want to march against us, then we will flee with the Byzantines." They gave him assurances. But Khālid said, "No, stay, only if we march out against you, then you will flee with the Byzantines." In the meantime, the Muslims said to Abū ʿUbaydah, "The inhabitants of al-Jazīrah have dispersed in all directions, but the people of Qinnasrīn are contrite and have offered to meet us out of their own free will. After all they are Arab tribesmen. Come with us." Meanwhile, Khālid remained silent. So Abū ʿUbaydah said, "Khālid, why do you not say anything?" Khālid answered, "You have always known what I think about this matter, but you did not listen to what I said." Then Abū ʿUbaydah said, "Speak now, I will listen to you and do as you suggest." So Khālid said, "March out with the Muslims. God may have decreased their numbers, while the enemy is still at full combat strength. (But we may not forget that) since we embraced Islam, we only fought to win in the end, so do not be vexed by the enemy's superior forces."

According to ʿAlqamah b. al-Naḍr and others: Abū ʿUbaydah assembled the people, praised God and extolled Him and said, "Listen, you men, this is a day that will decide the future.[305]
Those of you who will survive this day, your possessions and [2503]
homesteads will be undisturbed and, on the other hand, those of you who will die will achieve martyr status. So hold your God in the highest esteem and let nothing, short of polytheism, that is, committed by anyone of you, induce you to abhor death. But turn

305. See n. 122 above.

to God again and offer yourselves up to martyrdom. I testify—and this is no time for lies—that I heard the Messenger of God say: 'He who dies without ever having worshiped other deities but God, will surely enter Paradise.' " Then there was a general rustle among the men as they untied their camels. They marched out, led by Abū 'Ubaydah, who commanded the main body of the army, with Khālid over its right wing and 'Iyāḍ[306] over its left wing, while Mu'ādh b. Jabal stayed behind guarding the gate of the city. Thus they became engaged in combat there, never giving way, when suddenly al-Qa'qā' hurriedly approached with one hundred (horsemen). Then the people of Qinnasrīn began to flee with the Byzantines. The main body of the Muslim army and the right wing grappled with the main body of the enemy's army, one of whose wings had been crushed. The reinforcements joined the Muslim troops which resulted in not a single enemy warrior escaping to tell what had happened. The enemy's left wing all fled in one direction, the last straggler being caught at Marj al-Dībāj.[307] This was where they finally ended up, having broken their weapons and thrown down their furred coats to be less encumbered. But they were overtaken and their belongings were confiscated as spoils of war. When the Muslims had achieved this victory, Abū 'Ubaydah assembled them and delivered the following speech, "Do not flinch now, do not even consider receding in stages from this military operation; for if I had known beforehand that just one of us would survive, I would not have told you this story."[308] The last of the Kūfan horsemen to arrive did so three full days after the battle.[309]

[2500–
Al-Qa'qā' b. 'Amr arrived with the troops from al-Kūfah three
2503] days after the battle (sc. of Ḥimṣ) and 'Umar came and made camp
in al-Jābiyah. They[310] wrote to 'Umar telling him about the victo-
[2504] ry and the arrival of the reinforcements three days later and ask-
ing him for a decision in this affair. So 'Umar wrote back saying,

306. This, instead of 'Abbās, is the reading proposed in the errata in *Glossarium*, p. DCXX.

307. According to Yāqūt, *Mu'jam*, IV, 488, this was a river bed ten miles from al-Maṣṣīṣah, commanding spectacular views.

308. Sc. the tradition ascribed to the Prophet mentioned above.

309. This is the end of the insert from Ibn Ḥubaysh. After this, Ṭabarī's account is resumed.

310. Presumably, Abū 'Ubaydah and Khālid.

"Give them a share in the booty. May God reward the Kūfans with His bounty; they protect their own territory but they also give aid to the inhabitants of other garrison cities."

According to al-Sarī—Shuʿayb—Sayf—Zakariyyā' b. Siyāh—al-Shaʿbī: Abū ʿUbaydah asked ʿUmar for reinforcements. The Byzantines, followed by the Christians[311] had marched on him and besieged him (sc. in Ḥimṣ). Thereupon ʿUmar left (Medina) and wrote to the people of al-Kūfah. So, on an early morning, 4,000 men on mules leading horses by their sides,[312] hurriedly made their way toward the besieged Muslims. Three days after the battle between Abū ʿUbaydah and his besiegers they arrived (sc. at Ḥimṣ). Abū ʿUbaydah wrote about this to ʿUmar who had finally reached al-Jābiyah. ʿUmar wrote back, "Let them share in the booty, for they rushed out in aid of you and on account of them your enemy dispersed."

According to al-Sarī—Shuʿayb—Sayf—Ṭalḥah—Māhān: ʿUmar had 4,000 horses at his disposal, held ready for an emergency, which he caused to pass the winter tethered (in the square) south and left of the citadel in al-Kūfah. Hence that spot is called al-Ārī,[313] until this very day. ʿUmar also had them pasture on fresh grazing land between the Euphrates and the built-up area of al-Kūfah alongside the river bend.[314] The Persians called this stretch of land Ākhur al-Shāhijān,[315] which means "the place where the princes have their horses foddered." Its commander was Salmān b. Rabīʿah al-Bāhilī at the head of a group of people from al-Kūfah, who organized races for the horses and made them exercise all year round. In al-Baṣrah there was a similar number of horses, whose commander was Jaz' b. Muʿāwiyah. In fact, the eight garrison cities, each according to its size, (had a similar cavalry squadron). And when something unforeseen came to pass, a group of horsemen would ride out and grapple with the situation, until [2505]
the main body of fighting forces was brought into readiness.

311. Presumably, from among the Arab tribes living in al-Jazīrah.

312. Thus the horses were spared until the moment when speed was required in military action. Then the horses were exchanged for the mules. All this seems to be implied in the Arabic verb used in this context, see Lane, 464, right column.

313. Sc. a stable, or a post to which an animal is tethered.

314. The Arabic word for "bend" used here is *ʿāqūl*. It is also the name of a certain monastery, see Dayr al-ʿĀqūl in Ṭabarī's index.

315. Literally "the stable of the nobles."

Al-Sarī—Shuʿayb—Sayf—Ḥallām—Shahr b. Mālik gave a similar report (adding): . . . and when they had finished (clearing up matters), they would return.

In this year, I mean the year 17 (638), the conquest of al-Jazīrah took place.

The Conquest of al-Jazīrah

The conquest of al-Jazīrah took place according to the account of Sayf (in the year 17 (638)), but Ibn Isḥāq mentioned that it was conquered in the year 19 (640) of the Hijrah. He related among the causes leading to the conquest: According to Ibn Ḥumayd—Salamah—Ibn Isḥāq: ʿUmar wrote to Saʿd b. Abī Waqqāṣ, "God has conquered Syria and Iraq for the Muslims. So from where you are dispatch an army to al-Jazīrah and put one of the following three, Khālid b. ʿUrfuṭah or Hāshim b. ʿUtbah or ʿIyāḍ b. Ghanm in command." When this letter finally reached Saʿd, he said, "The Commander of the Faithful mentioned ʿIyāḍ b. Ghanm's name only as the last possible choice for commander because he harbors a secret wish that I put him in charge. Therefore I shall put him in charge." So he dispatched ʿIyāḍ and an armed force with him. On the same mission he also sent Abū Mūsā al-Ashʿarī, his own son ʿUmar b. Saʿd, a young lad without experience in leadership, and ʿUthmān b. Abī al-ʿĀṣ b. Bishr al-Thaqafī. That was in the year 19 (640). ʿIyāḍ marched on al-Jazīrah and descended with his troops on al-Ruhā' whose inhabitants concluded a peace treaty with him on the condition that they pay the *jizyah*. Ḥarrān also
[2506] concluded a treaty when al-Ruhā' did, its inhabitants committing themselves to pay the *jizyah*. Then Saʿd sent Abū Mūsā al-Ashʿarī to Naṣībīn and his son ʿUmar to Ra's al-ʿAyn among a contingent of cavalry as reinforcements for the Muslims. Saʿd himself moved with the remainder of the Muslim warriors to Dārā and went against it until he had conquered it. Abū Mūsā conquered Naṣībīn; that was in the year 19 (640). Then Saʿd dispatched ʿUthmān b. Abī al-ʿĀṣ to southern Armenia,[316] where some fight-

316. The southernmost part of Armīniyā or Armenia, or the fourth part as it is called in Arabic; it is the region due west of Naṣībīn and due north of al-Raqqah. The emperor Justinian (527–65) had divided Armenia into four parts, see Vasiliev, I, 196.

ing occurred in which Ṣafwān b. al-Muʿaṭṭal al-Sulamī died a martyr's death. Then the people of the region concluded a peace treaty with ʿUthmān b. Abī al-ʿĀṣ on the condition that they pay the *jizyah,* which amounted to one dīnār for each family (per year). After that the conquest of Qaysāriyyah in Palestine took place. Heraklius fled.

As for Sayf's account, that runs as follows: According to al-Sarī—Shuʿayb—Sayf—Muḥammad, al-Muhallab, Ṭalḥah, ʿAmr and Saʿīd: ʿIyāḍ followed in the traces of al-Qaʿqāʿ. The other commanders marched out. . . .[317] That was at the time when ʿUmar wrote to Saʿd instructing him to send al-Qaʿqāʿ with 4,000 troops as reinforcements for Abū ʿUbaydah, whom the Byzantines were marching upon while he was in Ḥimṣ. So the commanders took the road to al-Jazīrah via the border garrisons and other localities. Thus Suhayl b. ʿAdī and his army force followed the route along the border garrisons until they finally reached al-Raqqah. In the meantime the rebellious people of al-Jazīrah had dispersed from Ḥimṣ on their way back to their respective districts, when they heard of the impending arrival of the Kūfan forces. So he (sc. Suhayl) descended upon these people of al-Jazīrah and held them surrounded by his men until they were prepared to make peace with him. This whole process was precipitated, because they said to one another, "We are (caught) between (two fires: on the one hand there are) the Iraqi reinforcements and (on the other hand there are) the Muslim forces in Syria. How can we survive a war against the ones as well as against the others?" So they sent a message concerning that predicament to ʿIyāḍ who, at the time, had made his camp right in the middle of al-Jazīrah. ʿIyāḍ decided
to look favorably upon their submission, and they gave the oath [2507]
of allegiance to him, which he accepted. The man who actually concluded the treaty with them was Suhayl b. ʿAdī, acting on the order of ʿIyāḍ, because Suhayl was in charge of the actual fighting. They followed the same procedure in respect of the territories they had taken by force—after which the defeated side gave in—as they had used with *dhimmī*s.[318]

---

317. This last sentence is a well-nigh classic example of an anacoluthon. What these commanders did will be told as from the next sentence.

318. This is a technical term which, for reasons of expedience, I rather leave untranslated. It denotes the "people of protection," adherents of the other main

The second commander to leave (sc. to leave al-Kūfah) was ʿAbdallāh b. ʿAbdallāh b. ʿItbān. He traveled along the Tigris until he arrived at al-Mawṣil where he crossed to the other bank to a place called Balad.[319] Then he proceeded towards Naṣībīn. Its inhabitants came out to meet him to offer him peace, acting as the people of al-Raqqah had done. Indeed, harboring the same fears as the latter, they had written to ʿIyāḍ who saw fit to accept their capitulation. Thus ʿAbdallāh b. ʿAbdallāh concluded a treaty with them, following the same procedure in respect of the territories they had taken by force—after which the defeated side gave in—as followed in the case of *dhimmī*s.

Al-Walīd b. ʿUqbah also left (i.e. al-Kūfah) and marched until he reached the Taghlib and the Arab tribesmen living in al-Jazīrah. All of them, irrespective of whether or not they had become Muslims, threw in their lot with al-Walīd except the members of the Iyād b. Nizār tribe, for they departed with bag and baggage and penetrated into Byzantine territory. Al-Walīd reported all that to ʿUmar b. al-Khaṭṭāb by letter.

When the inhabitants of al-Raqqah and Naṣībīn had promised obedience, ʿIyāḍ joined the forces of Suhayl and ʿAbdallāh (b. ʿAbdallāh b. ʿItbān) with his own, marched with all these forces on Ḥarrān and conquered all the territory separating him from that city. When he finally was about to grapple with (the Ḥarrānians) themselves, they protected themselves against potential harm from him by consenting to pay the *jizyah*. ʿIyāḍ accepted this, following the same procedure with them as used with *dhimmī*s, after they had given in upon their defeat.

Then ʿIyāḍ dispatched Suhayl and ʿAbdallāh to al-Ruhā', whose inhabitants surrendered to them by consenting to pay the *jizyah*. All other people followed their example, al-Jazīrah thus being the simplest region to keep under control and the easiest to conquer. All this having been so easy was not only an ignominy for those

---

faiths (Jews, Christians, etc.), who yield to the authority of Islam in their region and pay *jizyah* in exchange for freedom of religion.

319. According to Yāqūt, *Muʿjam*, I, 715, an ancient city upstream from al-Mawṣil, also called Balaṭ.

conquered but also for those Muslims who stayed on among them. ʿIyāḍ b. Ghanm composed the following poem (in *kāmil*): [2508]

Who will tell the world that our forces together
have conquered Jazīrah in days of fierce battle?
They gathered those wanting to help from the region,
dispelling from Ḥimṣ the dark threat of besiegers.
Our warriors, the mighty and noble, have driven
the enemy away, leaving cleft skulls behind them.
Defeating the kings of Jazīrah, but failing
to conquer those people who made it to Syria.[320]

When ʿUmar arrived at al-Jābiyah and the people of Ḥimṣ were liberated, he sent Ḥabīb b. Maslamah to reinforce ʿIyāḍ b. Ghanm, and in that capacity he reached ʿIyāḍ. Abū ʿUbaydah wrote to ʿUmar, after his departure from al-Jābiyah, and asked him that ʿIyāḍ b. Ghanm be detailed to him, since Khālid was detailed to Medina. Hence ʿUmar sent ʿIyāḍ to him, but he dispatched Suhayl b. ʿAdī and ʿAbdallāh b. ʿAbdallāh (b. ʿItbān) to al-Kūfah in order to deploy them in the east. Over the non-Arabs of al-Jazīrah ʿUmar appointed Ḥabīb b. Maslamah as governor and military commander, and al-Walīd b. ʿUqbah he set over the Arab tribesmen there. Both remained in al-Jazīrah performing their duties.

They went on: When the letter from al-Walīd had reached him, ʿUmar wrote to the emperor of Byzantium, "It has come to my notice that a certain group of Arab tribesmen has left our territory and has sought residence in your territory; by God, if you do not drive them back, we will surely dissolve our covenants with the Christians living under Arab sovereignty, and expel them." Hereupon the emperor of Byzantium expelled the Arabs who duly left Byzantine territory. Thus 4,000 of them reimmigrated with Abū

320. The translation of this poem is a tentative one. There are many textual variants preserved, e.g. "tombstones" for "battle" in l. 2. Furthermore, the geographical name al-Jazīrah is repeated no less than four times in as many verses of two hemistichs each. In l. 2 I believe it indicates simply the region; in l. 3 it seems to refer to the Arabs of the region who remained loyal to the Muslim cause, while in ll. 6–7 those inhabitants of al-Jazīrah seem to have been meant who rebelled against that cause. The penultimate hemistich can also be interpreted as "to conquer Jazīrah they beat kings, but they failed (sc. stopped short. . .)."

ʿAdī b. Ziyād, while the rest lagged behind scattering all over the
[2509] border regions between Syria, al-Jazīrah and Byzantine territory. Every member of Iyād in the land of Arab tribesmen belonged to those 4,000. Al-Walīd b. ʿUqbah refused to accept anything from the Taghlib except complete submission to Islam. But they argued, "As for those who were made chiefs of their clans according to the treaty made with Saʿd, as well as those who have accepted this condition, for them you have the right to demand that; but as for those who did not see a chief appointed over them and who as a consequence did not walk in the footsteps of those who were placed under a chief, what are you going to do with them? So al-Walīd wrote to ʿUmar about them. ʿUmar replied, "That rule (which you want to impose upon the Taghlib) is only applicable to the Arabian peninsula; there nothing but strict surrender to Islam is acceptable. But leave those Taghlib be, on the condition that they do not bring up their (newborn) children in a Christian fashion and accept it when they do embrace Islam." Thus al-Walīd agreed with the Taghlib that they would not christen their (newborn) babies and that they would not prevent anyone from embracing Islam. Some Taghlibīs conceded this and adopted this rule; others only conceded to pay the *jizā*ʾ. So al-Walīd reached agreement with them on the same conditions as drawn up with the ʿIbād and Tanūkh.[321]

According to al-Sarī—Shuʿayb—Sayf—ʿAṭiyyah—Abū Sayf al-Taghlibī: The Messenger of God drew up a treaty with the delegation of the Taghlib that stipulated that they would not bring up their newborns as Christians. That was the condition imposed upon the delegation as well as on those who had sent them as a delegation, but it was not applicable to members of other tribes. When the time of ʿUmar had come, those Taghlib tribesmen who had become Muslims said, "Do not alienate them[322] by imposing the *kharāj* upon them, so that they go away, but double the amount they have to pay as alms tax, which you levy from their
[2510] wealth. In this way, it will have become *jizā*ʾ. For they resent it when *jizā*ʾ are mentioned in the context of the stipulation that they will not christen a newborn child, when its parents have

321. See A. Noth, "Die literarisch überlieferten Verträge," 306 f.
322. That is, the other non-Muslim tribesmen.

embraced Islam." So a Taghlib delegation traveled to ʿUmar concerning this matter. When al-Walīd had sent him the heads and leaders of the Christian tribesmen, ʿUmar said to them, "Pay the *jizyah*." But they said to him, "Send us to a place where we can be safe. By God, if you impose upon us the *jizā*ʾ, we will certainly enter Byzantine territory, for, by God, you have brought disgrace upon us among the other Arab tribesmen." Then ʿUmar said to them, "You yourselves have brought it upon you by holding points of view different from those of your own people among those camp-dwelling tribesmen who opposed Medinan sovereignty and as a consequence brought disgrace upon themselves. But, by God, I insist you pay it, you are contemptible nobodies. If you seek refuge with the Byzantines, I shall certainly write to them about you and I shall come and lead you away into captivity." They said, "Then take something from us, but do not call it *jizā*ʾ." Then ʿUmar replied, "As for us, we shall call it *jizā*ʾ; you call it whatever you want." "But, Commander of the Faithful," ʿAlī b. Abī Ṭālib said to him, "did Saʿd b. Mālik not double the amount they had to pay as alms?" "Yes," ʿUmar admitted, paying attention to what ʿAlī had said. So he contended himself with the *jizā*ʾ (which they were already paying), whereupon the Taghlib delegation returned (to where they were living) with tax matters drawn up in this way.

Nevertheless, among the Taghlib there were many proud and stubborn people who never stopped arguing with al-Walīd. Concerned as to how to deal with them, al-Walīd composed the line (in *ṭawīl*):

O Taghlib, when I shall fasten [2511]
The turban around my head,
You are, O daughter of Wāʾil,[323]
indeed as good as dead!

News of this reached ʿUmar, who feared that they might harass al-Walīd to the point where he would lose his patience and pounce on them. So he dismissed him and appointed Furāt b. Ḥayyān and Hind b. ʿAmr al-Jamalī over them as governors. Al-Walīd left, having entrusted the camel herd he had to one

323. The tribe of Taghlib is called Taghlib b. Wāʾil, see Caskel, II, 541. In Arabic, a tribe is usually a feminine concept, see Wright, I, 181, hence "daughter of Wāʾil."

Ḥurayth b. al-Nuʿmān of the clan of Kinānah b. Taym of the Taghlib tribe. There were one hundred camels in all, but after al-Walīd had departed, he (lost them as a result) of Ḥurayth's cheating.

The conquest of al-Jazīrah took place in the year 17 in Dhū al-Ḥijjah (December–January 638–9).

Also in this year, I mean the year 17 (638), ʿUmar left Medina for Syria (and traveled) until he reached Sargh,[324] as Ibn Isḥāq reports on whose authority it reached me via Salamah—Ibn Ḥumayd. I received this report also on the authority of al-Wāqidī.

ʿUmar's Journey to Syria

According to Ibn Ḥumayd—Salamah—Muḥammad b. Isḥāq: ʿUmar left (Medina) in the year 17 (638) for a campaign in Syria. Then, when he had arrived in Sargh, the commanders of the Muslim armies came to meet him. They told him that the country was diseased, so he returned to Medina with his retinue.

[2512] According to Ibn Ḥumayd—Salamah—Muḥammad b. Isḥāq—Ibn Shihāb al-Zuhrī—ʿAbd al-Ḥamīd b. ʿAbd al-Raḥmān b. Zayd b. al-Khaṭṭāb—ʿAbdallāh b. al-Ḥārith b. Nawfal—ʿAbdallāh b. ʿAbbās: ʿUmar left (Medina) to go on a campaign. The Muhājirs and the Anṣār left with him. All the people traveled in close formation until, when they had arrived at Sargh, they were met by the army commanders Abū ʿUbaydah b. al-Jarrāḥ, Yazīd b. Abī Sufyān and Shuraḥbīl b. Ḥasanah, who informed ʿUmar that the country was diseased. So ʿUmar said, "Assemble before me the first Muhājirs."[325]

He said: Thus I assembled the first Muhājirs for him. ʿUmar asked their opinion, but they were divided. Some said, "You set out in a direction in which you wanted to please God, seeking to obey His orders. We think that no tribulation which presents itself to you, should deter you from that purpose." But others said, "This is a veritable affliction that may bring about perdition; we are of the opinion that you should not draw any closer to

324. A place where the Ḥijāz ends and Syria begins, thirteen days traveling from Medina, see Yāqūt, *Muʿjam*, III, 77.

325. This appellative meant those of the Companions of the Prophet who converted to Islam *before* the Hijrah.

it." When they thus disagreed, he said, "Leave me." Then he ordered that the Muhājirat al-Anṣār[326] be assembled before him, so I convened them before him. ʿUmar asked their advice, but they reacted in the same way as the Muhājirs had done. It was as if they had heard what the latter had said and simply copied their remarks. When they thus disagreed, ʿUmar ordered them to leave him and said, "Bring me the Muhājirat al-fatḥ of Quraysh."[327] I assembled them before ʿUmar, who asked their advice. This time, no two men among them disagreed, but they all said, "Return (to Medina) with the men; this is an affliction that may bring about our ruin." He went on: ʿUmar said to me, "Ibn ʿAbbās, go amongst the men and cry out the following message: The Commander of the Faithful informs you that, tomorrow morning, he will be early in the saddle. Do you likewise!" He went on: So, the following morning, ʿUmar made ready to leave, as did all his men. When they were all gathered together, ʿUmar addressed them and said, "Men, I am going back; do likewise." Then Abū ʿUbaydah b. al-Jarrāḥ said to him, "Are you fleeing from God's providence?" "Yes," ʿUmar replied, "I flee from one divine ordinance to an- [2513]
other. Don't you see? Suppose a man goes down into a riverbed with two slopes, one fertile, the other barren, does the one who grazes his animals on the infertile slope not do so according to God's ordinance, and does the one who grazes his animals on the fertile one not do so according to God's ordinance?" ʿUmar went on, "If somebody other than you had said this, Abū ʿUbaydah, ..."[328] Then he went with him to a spot away from the people. While the men were thus busily readying themselves to depart, suddenly ʿAbd al-Raḥmān b. ʿAwf appeared on the scene. He had been following at a distance and had not been present yesterday. He exclaimed, "What on earth is the matter with the

326. This term presumably meant those Anṣār who, by converting to Islam, had made a *hijrah*, dissociating themselves from strictly tribal affiliations and committing themselves solely to the cause of Islam. In Mālik, II, 895, Bukhārī, IV, 59, and Muslim, IV, 1740, they are simply designated as Anṣār.

327. Literally, "the Muhājirs of the conquest" (that is, of Mecca). This appellative seems to encompass those Meccans who only embraced Islam when circumstances seemed to dictate this, immediately before and after the conquest of Mecca. See Ibn Ḥajar, *Fatḥ*, XII, 292.

328. Presumably he might have finished this sentence with words to the effect that he would have punished him. For other possibilities, see *ibid.*, XII, 293.

men?" So he was told. Then he said, "I know something about this which is relevant." ʿUmar said, "In our eyes you are a truthful and honest man; what can you tell us?" ʿAbd al-Raḥmān said, "I heard the Messenger of God say: 'When it comes to your notice that there is a pestilence in a certain country, do not go near it, and if it breaks out while you are in it, do not flee from it then.' Therefore," ʿAbd al-Raḥmān concluded "nothing should make you leave this place except those words." ʿUmar exclaimed, "God be praised, so leave, all you men!" Then he departed with them.

According to Ibn Ḥumayd—Salamah—Muḥammad b. Isḥāq—Ibn Shihāb al-Zuhrī—ʿAbdallāh b. ʿĀmir b. Rabīʿah and Sālim, ʿUmar's grandson, who related that ʿUmar, only on the strength of ʿAbd al-Raḥmān b. ʿAwf's tradition, decided to return with his men (to Medina). When ʿUmar returned, the governors[329] in their turn went back to their respective provinces.

As for Sayf, according to al-Sarī—Shuʿayb—Sayf—Abū Ḥārithah, Abū ʿUthmān and al-Rabīʿ: A plague broke out in Syria, Egypt, and Iraq. It was persistent in Syria, but making victims
[2514] among the inhabitants of all the garrison cities who had spent the months of al-Muḥarram and Ṣafar there. Then the plague disappeared. Letters describing this reached ʿUmar except from Syria. So ʿUmar set out and traveled until, when he was near to it,[330] news reached him that the plague there was more severe than it had ever been. So he said, "As the Companions say, the Messenger of God said: 'If there is a pestilence in a certain country, do not enter it and if it breaks out in a country while you happen to be in it, do not leave it.'" So ʿUmar returned (to Medina and stayed there), until the plague had disappeared and the people of Syria had written to him about it. They also wrote about various inheritance matters they were concerned with. ʿUmar convened the people in the month Jumādā I of 17 (May–June, 638), and sought their advice on the (conquered) territories, saying, "It seems a good idea to make an inspection trip along the Muslims in their conquered territories in order to see what influence they exert on their surroundings. May I have your advice?" Kaʿb al-

329. "Governors" is in Arabic *ʿummāl;* they are of course the same men as the "army commanders" (*umarāʾ*) mentioned above (p. 92). The use of both these titles permits us to draw inferences as to the duties that a "governor" had in early Islam. See further *EI*[2] s.v. *ʿĀmil* (Duri).

330. That is, the area where Syria proper was supposed to begin.

Aḥbār, who had become a Muslim in that very year of ʿUmar's reign and who happened to be present, said, "Where would you like to make a start, Commander of the Faithful?" "Iraq," was ʿUmar's reply. Kaʿb said, "Do not do that. Evil and good both consist of ten parts. But whereas the one part that is good lies in the east and nine in the west, the one part that is evil lies in the west while the nine other, evil parts lie in the east. The devil and every severe disease are linked with Iraq."

According to al-Sarī—Shuʿayb—Sayf—Saʿīd—al-Aṣbagh—ʿAlī: ʿAlī went up to him saying, "Commander of the Faithful, by God, al-Kūfah is a place to which one makes a *hijrah* after the Hijrah;[331] it is the 'dome' of Islam.[332] There will come a day when there is no believer left who does not go there out of longing. God will be made victorious through its inhabitants just as He overcame the people of Lot with stones."[333] [2515]

According to al-Sarī—Shuʿayb—Sayf—al-Muṭarraḥ—al-Qāsim—Abū Umāmah: Then ʿUthmān said, "Commander of the Faithful, the western part of the conquered territories is a land of wickedness; this wickedness is divided into one hundred parts, one part of which is seated in its people and the other parts in the land itself."

According to al-Sarī—Shuʿayb—Sayf—Yaḥyā al-Taymī—Abū Mājid: ʿUmar said, "Al-Kūfah is the spear of God and the dome of Islam. The tribal chieftains will protect their frontier ways of access and they will give military aid to the garrison cities. The estates[334] of the victims of the plague in ʿAmawās[335] are left untended[336] so I will begin (my tour of inspection) there."[337]

331. The first occurrence of the word *hijrah* is the technical term conveying that one embraces the cause of Islam by giving up one's links with one's tribe and throwing in one's lot with the Muslims. The second occurrence constitutes the emigration on June 22, 622, from Mecca to Medina.

332. The Arabic is *qubbah;* in Lane it is al-Baṣrah which is described by this vague honorific.

333. That is, the cities of Sodom and Gomorrah, see Q. LI, 33.

334. This is used here in the sense of that which is inherited by heirs. See next paragraph.

335. ʿAmawās (present day Imwas, the Biblical Emmaus) is a district six miles from al-Ramlah along the road to Jerusalem in central Palestine. It is alleged that the plague started there.

336. For this connotation of the Arabic verb *ḍāʿa,* see Lane, 1812, middle column.

337. That is, I shall begin my tour in Syria.

According to al-Sarī—Shuʿayb—Sayf—Abū ʿUthmān, Abū Ḥārithah and al-Rabīʿ b. al-Nuʿmān: ʿUmar said, "Since the estates of the people who recently died in Syria are left untended, I shall start my tour there. I shall properly divide the estates and I shall take measures for them as I think best. After that I shall return and travel all over the country, renouncing my previous orders to them."[338] (In all,) ʿUmar went to Syria four times, twice in the year 16 (637) and twice in 17 (638), but he did not set foot on Syrian soil on the first trip of the year 17 (638).

According to al-Sarī—Shuʿayb—Sayf—Bakr b. Wā'il—Muḥammad b. Muslim (al-Zuhrī): The Messenger of God said, "Taking care is divided into ten parts, nine of which are with the Turks,
[2516] one with all the other people. Miserliness is divided into ten parts, nine of which are found with the Persians, one with all the other people. Generosity is also divided into ten parts, nine of which are found with negroes, one with all the other people. Lechery is divided also into ten parts, nine of which are found with Indians, one with all the other people. Bashfulness is also divided into ten parts, nine of which are found in women, and one with all the other people. Envy is also divided into ten parts, nine of which are found with the Arabs and one with all the other people. Lastly, arrogance is divided into ten parts, nine of which are found in the Byzantines and one in all the other people.[339]

Variant Features of the Story of the Plague of ʿAmawās[340] *and the Uncertainty as to the Year That It Occurred*

According to Ibn Ḥumayd—Salamah—Ibn Isḥāq: Then the year 18 (639) began, in which the plague of ʿAmawās broke out. One after the other the people perished in it. Also Abū ʿUbaydah b. al-

338. The Arabic reads *anbidhu* "I give up, forswear." Since this does not seem to be in keeping with ʿUmar's usual emphasis on the centralization of government, and since the reading is dubious in any case, it is tempting, as Hinds suggests, to read *unaffidhu ilayhim amrī* "I shall transmit my orders to them."

339. This catalogue of popular generalizations is not found in any of the canonical *ḥadīth* collections.

340. For an interesting study on this plague and other epidemics in early Islamic history, as well as a detailed analysis of the technical terms used for describing such calamities, see L. I. Conrad, "*Ṭāʿūn* and *wabā'*. Conceptions of plague and

Jarrāḥ died, the supreme commander (of Syria), as well as Muʿādh b. Jabal, Yazīd b. Abī Sufyān, al-Ḥārith b. Hishām, Suhayl b. ʿAmr, ʿUtbah b. Suhayl and (many more) noble people.

According to Aḥmad b. Thābit—Isḥāq b. ʿĪsā—Abū Maʿshar: The plague of ʿAmawās and al-Jābiyah was in the year 18 (639).

According to Ibn Ḥumayd—Salamah—Muḥammad b. Isḥāq—Shuʿbah b. al-Ḥajjāj—al-Mukhāriq b. ʿAbdallāh al-Bajalī—Ṭāriq b. Shihāb al-Bajalī: We went to Abū Mūsā (al-Ashʿarī), who was in [2517] his home in al-Kūfah, to talk to him. When we were seated, he said, "I am not asking from you that you make light of this matter, for in this house someone succumbed to this disease, but neither do you need to keep away from this town, leaving for the wide and wholesome open spaces of your land until this pestilence abates. I shall tell you what ideas are frowned upon, with which one might try to protect oneself in this respect: that someone who does leave town thinks that, if he had stayed, he would have died, and that someone who does *not* leave and does contract the disease thinks that, if he had left, he would not have been infected. If the veritable Muslim does not think this, then there is no real need for him to leave town or to keep far away from it. I was with Abū ʿUbaydah b. al-Jarrāḥ in Syria in the year when the plague of ʿAmawās broke out. When the disease had become widespread and news of that had reached ʿUmar, he wrote to Abū ʿUbaydah in an attempt at inducing him to leave the contaminated area, saying, "Peace be upon you. Listen; a problem has presented itself to me that I urgently need to discuss with you. I implore you that, when you set eyes on this letter from me, you will not put it down until you are actually on your way back to me."

He went on: Abū ʿUbaydah realized only too well that all ʿUmar [2518] wanted was to get him out of (this) plague-(stricken country). "May God forgive the Commander of the Faithful," he thought. Then he wrote to ʿUmar, "I understand your need for me, Commander of the Faithful, but the fact is that I am surrounded here by an army of Muslim warriors for whom I could not possibly

---

pestilence in early Islam," in *JESHO*, XXV (1982): 268–307; idem, "Arabic plague chronologies and treatises: social and historical factors in the formation of a literary genre," in *Studia Islamica*, LIV (1981):51–93.

muster the slightest dislike. I do not want to separate myself from them until God has carried out His divine plan in respect of me and them. Please, absolve me from my duty toward you, Commander of the Faithful, and let me stay here among my soldiers." When ʿUmar read this letter, he burst into tears. The people (around him) asked, "Has Abū ʿUbaydah died, Commander of the Faithful?" "No," he replied, "but it is as if he had."

Then ʿUmar wrote to him saying, "Peace be upon you. Listen; you have let your men settle in a country that is diseased. (I beg of you), make them depart to more elevated and wholesome surroundings." When this letter had reached Abū ʿUbaydah, he called me to him and said, "Abū Mūsā, I just received this letter from the Commander of the Faithful; see for yourself what he orders. Go and scout around for a suitable site for the army to make camp. I shall follow you later with the troops." So I returned to where I was living in order to get ready for my journey. There I found that the woman I was living with had contracted the disease. I returned to Abū ʿUbaydah immediately and said to him, "By God, in my own household there is a casualty." "Is it perhaps the woman you are living with?" he asked. "Yes," I answered.

He went on: Thereupon Abū ʿUbaydah ordered his camel to be saddled for him and just as he placed his foot in the stirrup, he suffered (an acute attack of) the plague. "By God," he exclaimed, "now I have contracted it." But even so, he himself traveled with his men all the way to al-Jābiyah. Eventually the pestilence abated.

According to Ibn Ḥumayd—Salamah—Muḥammad b. Isḥāq—Abān b. Ṣāliḥ—Shahr b. Ḥawshab al-Ashʿarī—someone from his
[2519] clan who, after his father had died, was left behind to take care of his mother and an eyewitness of the plague of ʿAmawās, (in other words Shahr's) stepfather:[341] When the disease became wide-

341. The Ṭabarī text has Rābah, as if that is the name of a man. In his edition of Ibn Ḥanbal's *Musnad*, Aḥmad Shākir (in III, no. 1697) proposes that, instead of *ʿan rābata rajulin min qawmihi*, we read *ʿan rābbihi rajulin min qawmihi*. The connotation "stepfather" is also listed in Lane, 1005, right column. The following story is also found in a few other sources such as Ibn Kathīr, *Bidāyah*, VII, 78 f; Ibn Ḥajar, *Iṣābah*, VII, 455. The common link in the different *isnād*s is Muḥammad b. Isḥāq. Whether it is he who is responsible for the story, or just for (part of) the wording, cannot be established. The transmitter Shahr b. Ḥawshab (d. between 110–12/728–30), who figures also in the *isnād*, a man of Syrian background who spread many stories of his own making in Iraq, is a far likelier candidate.

spread, Abū ʿUbaydah stood up among his men and delivered the following speech, "Men, this sickness is a mercy from your Lord, a request from your Prophet Muḥammad and it has caused the death of the pious who died before you; I, Abū ʿUbaydah, ask God that He assign to me my share thereof." Suddenly he suffered (an acute attack of) the disease, as a result of which he died. Muʿādh b. Jabal was appointed as his successor over the people.

He went on: Then, after that, (Muʿādh) delivered a speech in which he said, "Truly, men, this sickness constitutes a mercy from your Lord, a request from your Prophet and it has caused the death of the pious who died before you; I, Muʿādh, ask God that He assign thereof a share to my family." Then his son, ʿAbd al-Raḥmān b. Muʿādh, suffered (a sudden attack of) the plague as a result of which he died. Then Muʿādh stood up and prayed for a share of the disease for himself, after which it smote him in the palm of his hand. Indeed, I saw him looking at his palm, then he kissed the back of his hand and said, "I prefer not to have anything of this world (together) with what (I have) in you (sc. my hand)." When he had died, ʿAmr b. al-ʿĀṣī was made his successor over the people. ʿAmr stood up to address the people and said, "Men, when this sickness strikes, it spreads like wildfire, so let us run away from it to the mountains." Then Abū Wāthilah al-Hudhalī said, "By God, you are known to us as a liar. While you were still no better than the donkey I sit on, I had already become a Companion of the Prophet. But," he went on, "by God, this time I will not reject what you say. I swear by God, we should not stay here!" Then he departed and the people went with him and scattered in all directions. Eventually God took the plague away from them. He went on: News of this opinion of ʿAmr b. al-ʿĀṣī's
reached ʿUmar b. al-Khaṭṭāb and, by God, he did not raise objec- [2520]
tions to it.

According to Ibn Ḥumayd—Salamah—Ibn Isḥāq—someone anonymous—Abū Qilābah ʿAbdallāh b. Zayd al-Jarmī: From among the words spoken by Abū ʿUbaydah and Muʿādh b. Jabal it came to my notice that they said, Verily, this sickness constitutes a mercy from your Lord, a request from your Prophet and it has caused the death of the pious who died before you. At this point I used to say, How can the Messenger of God pray for such (a calamity to befall) his community! Someone whose veracity I do not suspect even related to me that he had heard it from the

Prophet's own mouth and also that Gabriel once came to the Messenger of God and said to him, "The perdition of your community will occur as the result of a spear thrust or the plague."[342] Then the Messenger of God began to intone, "O my God, death through the plague!", and so I realized that those were the same words spoken by Abū ʿUbaydah and Muʿādh.

According to Ibn Ḥumayd—Salamah—Muḥammad b. Isḥāq: When news of the deaths of Abū ʿUbaydah and Yazīd b. Abī Sufyān finally reached ʿUmar, he put Muʿāwiyah b. Abī Sufyān in charge of the forces in Damascus and its *kharāj* and Shuraḥbīl b. Ḥasanah in charge of the forces in al-Urdunn[343] and its *kharāj*. As for Sayf, he claims that the plague of ʿAmawās occurred in the year 17 (638).

According to al-Sarī—Shuʿayb—Sayf—Abū ʿUthmān, Abū Ḥārithah and al-Rabīʿ via their (respective) *isnād*s: That plague, that is the plague of ʿAmawās, was so devastating[344] that nothing resembling it had ever been seen. The enemy ardently wished the Muslims to succumb to it, the hearts of the latter being filled with terror. The death toll was enormous and it persisted a long
[2521] time, so long—months in fact—that the people talked about nothing else.

According to al-Sarī—Shuʿayb—Sayf—ʿAbdallāh b. Saʿīd—Abū Saʿīd: As a result of this pestilence a rapidly spreading, fatal sickness struck al-Baṣrah. A certain man from Tamīm ordered a Persian servant of his to put his young son—his only child—on a donkey and to bring him to Safawān,[345] where he would shortly join them. The servant left just before daybreak, in time followed by his master, who soon reached a spot overlooking Safawān. As

342. Both "spear thrust" and "plague" are words derived from the same root *ṭ-ʿ-n*. The message conveyed seems to be, "Your community will perish as a result of warfare and disease."

343. This was a large district (see Yāqūt, *Muʿjam*, I, 200 f.) comprising at the time, among other places, Ṣūr, ʿAkkā and Ṭabariyyah (present day Tyre, Acre and Tiberias). Al-Urdunn has given rise to the name Jordan.

344. The Arabic word used here is *mūtān*, a word used to indicate a mortal disease that destroys entire herds of sheep or camels.

345. This is a watering place at one day's journeying from al-Baṣrah, see Yāqūt, *Muʿjam*, III, 98 f; the name is said to mean "dust" raised by the prevailing winds there, or "earth" causing the water there to be muddy.

he came closer to his son under the care of his servant, the latter suddenly raised his voice reciting loudly (in *rajaz*):

They 'll never see God outstripped by a donkey,
Or even a thoroughbred spurred on to fly,
For death may surprise the night traveler at dawn.

The man was not quite sure (whether or not he did see his son with his servant) until he had come quite close. But then he saw it was they. He exclaimed, "Curse you, what were you reciting?" "I do not know," the servant replied. Then the master said, "Go back now." Thus the father returned with his son, realizing that he had been made to hear as well as see a sign from God.[346]

He went on: Another man intended to leave for a country in which a plague had broken out. After he had departed, he was overcome by doubt. Suddenly he heard a Persian servant of his, urging the camels with the following song (in *rajaz*):

O you, who are fraught with anxiety, don't fret!
If fever is writ for you, that's what you'll get!

In this year, I mean 17 (638), ʿUmar made his last trip to Syria, never to set foot there again, as Sayf has it. As for Ibn Isḥāq's account, that has been mentioned above.

Sayf's Account of ʿUmar's Last Trip to Syria and How He Introduced New Ideas for the Well-Being of the Muslims [2522]

According to al-Sarī—Shuʿayb—Sayf—Abū ʿUthmān, Abū Ḥārithah and al-Rabīʿ: Having left ʿAlī in charge of Medina, ʿUmar departed, taking a group of Companions with him. They made good time, taking the road to Aylah.[347] Finally, when he was near Aylah, he left the track, followed by his servant, and alighted in order to pass water. Then he went back to the track and mounted his servant's camel. A pelt turned upside down was placed on its

346. This is the second time in this translation that someone is introduced who is heard speaking a language he is not supposed to know. Is this a coincidence or do we have here a *topos*? See above, pp. 11 f.

347. This is present day Elat.

saddle. ʿUmar gave his servant his own camel to ride. When an advance party of the local population met him, they asked, "Where is the Commander of the Faithful?" "In front of you," ʿUmar answered, meaning that he himself was facing them. They went on ahead[348] passing him. Finally ʿUmar arrived at Aylah and dismounted. The advance party was told, "The Commander of the Faithful entered Aylah some time ago and dismounted." So at last they made their way to him.

According to al-Sarī—Shuʿayb—Sayf—Hishām b. ʿUrwah—his father (ʿUrwah b. al-Zubayr): When ʿUmar b. al-Khaṭṭāb had arrived in Aylah with his following of Muhājirs and Anṣār, he gave a cotton *qamīṣ*[349] of his, which had a tear in the backside as a result of the long journey, to the (local) bishop[350] saying, "Have this cleaned and mended." So the bishop left with ʿUmar's *qamīṣ* and had it mended. He also had another one just like it sewn for him, which he brought to ʿUmar, who said, "What is all this?" "As for this one here," the bishop answered, "that is the *qamīṣ* you gave me that I had washed and mended; as for the other one, that is a garment[351] I hereby give you as a present." ʿUmar in-
[2523] spected it and rubbed its fabric. Then he donned his own *qamīs*, but returned the other to the bishop saying, "The one I am wearing is better in that it absorbs more sweat."

According to al-Sarī—Shuʿayb—Sayf—ʿAṭiyyah and Hilāl—Rāfiʿ b. ʿUmar: I heard al-ʿAbbās in al-Jābiyah say to ʿUmar, "If you practice the following four customs, you deserve the title 'righteous': honesty in money matters, equality in dividing up,[352] keeping your promise and steering clear of disgrace; purify yourself and your people."

According to al-Sarī—Shuʿayb—Sayf—Abū ʿUthmān, al-Rabīʿ and Abū Ḥārithah each with his own *isnād:* ʿUmar divided the allowances and ordained the winter and summer campaigns. He

348. "Ahead," in Arabic *ilā amāmikum*, and "in front of you" or "facing you," in Arabic *amāmakum*, can easily be confused.

349. A *qamīṣ* is a shirtlike, sleeved garment reaching down almost to the ground.

350. See H. Busse, "ʿOmar b. al-Ḫaṭṭāb in Jerusalem," in *JSAI*, V(1984):109 f., who sees in this an association with the story of the investiture of Joshua.

351. The Arabic word used here is the noncommittal *kiswah*.

352. That is, for instance when dividing booty.

manned[353] the frontier roads and observation posts at the border of Syria and he began to make inspection tours in the country, ordaining those measures in every district. He made ʿAbdallāh b. Qays governor over the coastal plains of every district; he dismissed Shuraḥbīl (b. Ḥasanah) and appointed Muʿāwiyah (b. Abī Sufyān) as governor in his place. Abū ʿUbaydah and Khālid (b. al-Walīd) were given high commands in the army under the authority of Muʿāwiyah. Shuraḥbīl asked ʿUmar, "Did you sack me out of discontent, Commander of the Faithful?" "No," was the reply, "I appreciate you as you are, but I really want a more forceful man."[354] "All right," Shuraḥbīl said, "but, please, clear my name in public, lest I be criticized for a shortcoming (which I do not have)." So ʿUmar addressed the congregation and said, "(Listen, you) people, by God, I did not relieve Shuraḥbīl of his functions out of discontent, but I just wanted a more forceful man." He placed the granaries under the supervision of ʿAmr b. ʿAbasah and ordained all those measures. Then he addressed the people (in a meeting) to say goodbye.

According to al-Sarī—Shuʿayb—Sayf—Abū Ḍamrah and Abū ʿAmr—al-Mustawrid—ʿAdī b. Suhayl: When ʿUmar had finished seeing to the access routes (to the Ḥijāz) and his other business, he divided the estates of persons recently deceased, letting various heirs who were still alive inherit from various others, and
then he presented the estates to the living heirs of every man [2524]
(deceased) among them.

According to al-Sarī—Shuʿayb—Sayf—Mujālid—al-Shaʿbī: Al-Ḥārith b. Hishām departed (for Syria) amidst seventy of his relatives of whom only four eventually returned. Al-Muhājir b. Khālid b. al-Walīd recited the following lines (in *sarīʿ*):

Who settles in Syria goes surely to rest there!
    For ev'n if we can't be destroyed by calamities,
It's Syria that killed off the children of Rayṭah,[355]
    Those twenty young knights, their lips' down still
    untrimmed,

353. That is what I think is meant by the verb *sadda* which usually means "to block," "obstruct."

354. Literally, it says, I want a man stronger than a man.

355. She seems to be al-Ḥārith b. Hishām's grandmother.

And likewise their equally noble young cousins!
At such a disaster th' onlooker's perplexed:
Their deaths were all caused by spear wounds and the plague;[356]
That's what we were told by the military scribe.[357]

He went on: ʿUmar returned from Syria to Medina in the month of Dhū al-Ḥijja. When he was about to depart, he addressed the people in congregation, praised God and extolled Him, and said, "I have been put in charge over you and I have carried out what I had to do in respect of those matters concerning you, which God has entrusted to me. If He wills, we will justly distribute among you the revenues of your *fay*ʾ lands, your living quarters and your raiding assignments.[358] We have given you your due. We have mobilized armed forces for you, we have put your access routes in order. We have indicated places for you to settle. We have extended the revenues of your *fay*ʾ lands for you and of that part of Syria you fought for. We have ordained your foodstuffs for you[359] and we have given orders that you will be given your stipends, allowances and supplementary allocations. He who possesses
[2525] information[360] on a certain issue, should act upon it. Let anyone inform me[361] (about something special he knows), then I myself shall put that into practice, God willing. There is no power except with God."

The hour for the prayer ritual had struck and the people asked ʿUmar, "Could you please order Bilāl to call us to prayer?" So

356. Again the Arabic expression *ṭaʿn wa-ṭāʿūn* is used; see above, p. 100.

357. Is this the function referred to by Morony, *Iraq*, 54?

358. To be ordered to go on a raid was a privilege in view of the anticipated booty. See above, p. 43, where raiding was temporarily suspended.

359. I have opted for *aṭʿimātikum* from the apparatus rather than *aṭmāʿakum* in the text.

360. The "information" alluded to, in Arabic *ʿilm*, is knowledge of how one should behave in certain circumstances. According to the ancient *sunnah* principle, which dates back to the Jāhiliyyah, one had only to follow the exemplary behavior of a revered ancestor to be certain that one had taken the right course of action. But "knowledge" of these "precedents" was not universal. So, if someone "knew" some solution to a problem, his "knowledge" served others as guiding principle. We find in this Ṭabarī passage the ancient *sunnah* principle alluded to still without a reference to, or an association with, (prophetic) *ḥadīth*. See Juynboll, *Muslim tradition*, 26–30.

361. I have opted for the variant *falyuʿlimnā* listed in the apparatus. Surely, the contrast *ʿilm—ʿamal* is also apparent in the second sentence, in which verbs, rather than nouns, are used.

ʿUmar issued the order and Bilāl sang out the call to prayer. There was no one, whose lifetime reached back to the lifetime of the Messenger of God, who did not weep, moistening his beard, when Bilāl's call rang out. ʿUmar wept most copiously of all and everyone too young to have seen the Prophet with his own eyes wept all the same, moved by the weeping of the others, with memories of the Messenger of God coming back to him.[362]

According to al-Sarī—Shuʿayb—Sayf—Abū ʿUthmān and Abū Ḥārithah: Khālid remained in control of Qinnasrīn, until he went on that campaign in which he was so successful; he distributed among the others that part of the booty which he had gained for himself.

According to al-Sarī—Shuʿayb—Sayf—Abū al-Mujālid: a similar report. They said: The news reached ʿUmar that Khālid once entered the bathhouse where, after he had removed the depilatory agent, he rubbed himself with a thick mixture of safflower[363] and wine. So he wrote to him, saying, "It has reached me that you rubbed your body with wine; but God has forbidden the drinking of wine or its use in any other way just as He has forbidden sins[364] committed in a direct or indirect manner. He has even forbidden the touching of wine unless you cleanse yourself of it immediately, just as He has forbidden you to drink it. So make sure it will not touch your body, for it is filth.[365] And if you are actually still practicing this, (stop doing it immediately and) do not do it again!" Thereupon Khālid wrote to ʿUmar, "We have diluted the wine with so much water[366] that it is no longer wine but has become (ordinary) washing water." Then ʿUmar wrote to him, "Methinks the descendants of al-Mughīrah[367] have picked up some bad manners, but I pray that God will not destroy you for this." This last letter finally reached Khālid.

---

362. For the *topoi* discernible in this story, see H. Busse, *op. cit.*, 106.

363. *Carthamus tinctorius*, a dye used to achieve an orange-red color.

364. The Arabic word used is *ithm*, which also means "wine" as well as "game of hazard." Perhaps a double entendre is intended here.

365. The use of "filth" in this context seems to imply that touching it causes a person to incur a state of ritual impurity.

366. For "diluting wine" Arabic uses the verb "to kill."

367. That is, al-Mughīrah b. ʿAbdallāh b. ʿUmar, who was Khālid's grandfather and the eponym of a major subclan of the Makhzūm clan of Quraysh. Caskel, pedigrees 22, 23. See also *EI*², s.v. *Makhzūm* (Hinds).

In this same year, I mean the year 17 (638), Khālid b. al-Walīd and ʿIyāḍ b. Ghanm went on a military campaign according to Sayf—his authorities.

An Account of the Campaign of Khālid and ʿIyāḍ

[2526] According to al-Sarī—Shuʿayb—Sayf—Abū ʿUthmān, Abū Ḥārithah and al-Muhallab: In the year 17 (638), Khālid and ʿIyāḍ went on a campaign in enemy territory. They journeyed and came upon huge riches. They had set out from al-Jābiyah, from where ʿUmar returned to Medina. Abū ʿUbaydah was in charge of Ḥimṣ with Khālid under his command in Qinnasrīn. Yazīd b. Abī Sufyān was in control of Damascus, Muʿāwiyah in al-Urdunn, ʿAlqamah b. Mujazziz administered Palestine. ʿAmr b. ʿAbasah was in charge of the granaries and ʿAbdallāh b. Qays had the coastal plains under his control. Over every administrative area a governor was appointed. The strong points of Syria, Egypt and Iraq have remained thus until today. It was no longer the case that a community passed from its own administrative area into another's without these forces pouncing on them after the (first) default.[368] For in that case the troops would be sent in. This state of equilibrium was achieved in the year 17/638.

According to al-Sarī—Shuʿayb—Sayf—Abū al-Mujālid, Abū ʿUthmān, al-Rabīʿ and Abū Ḥārithah: When Khālid had returned and the rumor had reached the general public how much that summer expedition had brought in, people were drawn toward him. Thus people from near and far flocked to Khālid. Among those who did so was al-Ashʿath b. Qays, who went to seek out Khālid in Qinnasrīn. The latter gave him an allowance of ten thousand dirhams. Nothing that went on in Khālid's province remained hidden from ʿUmar, who was informed in writing by someone from Iraq about those who departed, while someone

368. The Arabic text has the word *kufr*, literally "unbelief." Not obeying the law of Islam, even in matters such as the paying of taxes, in the eyes of early Muslims constituted an act of "unbelief." Closely associated with this is the appellative of the so-called apostasy wars, in Arabic *riddah*. Just before, and on a larger scale immediately after, the Prophet's death, various Arab tribes started to refuse (*radda*) to pay the alms tax imposed by Muḥammad and, in doing so, became *murtadd* ("apostate"), a word like *riddah* derived from the same root *r-d-d*.

from Syria wrote to him about those who had received an allowance (i.e. from Khālid). Then ʿUmar called a courier and dispatched a message with him for Abū ʿUbaydah ordering him to summon Khālid to appear in front of him, to tie him up with his own turban and to take off his cap,[369] until he disclosed to them from what source he had taken the allowance for al-Ashʿath, from his own wealth or from loot that he had acquired. If Khālid stated that it was part of the loot, then thereby it would have been established that he had cheated, and if he claimed that it was part of his own wealth, then he would be earmarked as a squanderer. "Dismiss him from his post in either case and add his administrative area to your own," ʿUmar concluded. Abū ʿUbaydah wrote a message to Khālid who promptly made his way to him. Then Abū ʿUbaydah assembled the people and sat in front of them on the pulpit. The courier stood up and said, "Khālid, did you give this ten thousand dirhams allowance out of your own pocket or did you take it from loot acquired during a campaign?" Khālid did not reply even when the courier insisted, while all the time Abū ʿUbaydah remained silent, not speaking a word. Then Bilāl went to him and said, "The Commander of the Faithful has ordered that you be dealt with in the following manner." Then Bilāl took off Khālid's cap and bound him with his own turban, whereupon he said, "Speak up, was it from your own pocket or from loot?" "No," Khālid answered finally, "from my own pocket." Then Bilāl released him, returned his cap to him and, with his own hands, wound the turban around Khālid's head again. This finished, he said, "We hark unto our governors and obey them, and we honor and serve our masters."

[2527]

They went on: For a time, Khālid remained bewildered, not knowing whether or not he had been dismissed. Initially, Abū ʿUbaydah did not inform him until, when ʿUmar was becoming impatient for Khālid to show up, he pondered the things that had happened. He wrote to Khālid to come to him. So the latter went to Abū ʿUbaydah and said, "May God have mercy upon you, what

369. This was probably in order to humiliate him. The Arabic word is *qalansuwah*, a headdress that the Arabs copied from the Persians. In this early age we have to visualize a skull cap rather than the pointed bonnet, the usual shape of the *qalansuwah* in ʿAbbāsid times. See *EI*[2] s.v. *Libās* (Y. K. Stillman); Morony, *Iraq*, 259.

do you want now with me in addition to what you have already done to me! You have always kept something hidden from me that I have wanted to know for so long." Then Abū ʿUbaydah said, "By God, I am not the sort of man to scare you as long as I can avoid it, but now I know that what I have got to tell you is going to scare you."

They continued: Khālid returned to Qinnasrīn, addressed the people of his province in a speech, and took his leave of them. Then he packed and started off to Ḥimṣ, where he gave a speech to the people in which he said goodbye to them. After that he departed in the direction of Medina. Finally, he approached ʿUmar and muttered to him, "I complained about you to the Muslims. So help me God, ʿUmar, you have treated me like dirt!" "Where did you get all that money?" ʿUmar asked. "From the booty that was freely distributed and from sharing in the loot handed out in strictly equal portions; everything over sixty thousand is for you," Khālid answered. So ʿUmar assessed the value of Khālid's possessions. The outcome was that twenty thousand (dirhams) were singled out for ʿUmar, which he deposited in the treasury. Hereupon ʿUmar said, "By God, Khālid, you are a truly honorable man in my esteem, and you are dear to me; after today you will
[2528] never have occasion to blame me for anything."

According to al-Sarī—Shuʿayb—Sayf—ʿAbdallāh b. al-Mustawrid—his father—ʿAdī b. Suhayl: ʿUmar wrote to the garrison cities, "I have not relieved Khālid from his post because he has caused me displeasure or because of deceit on his part. But the people were captivated by illusions on account of him, so I was afraid that they would confer too much trust upon him and would consequently be tested. I wanted them to realize that it is God who is the creator of all things and I did not want them to be subject to an illusion."

According to al-Sarī—Shuʿayb—Sayf—Mubashshir—Sālim: When Khālid came to him, ʿUmar quoted a verse (in *ṭawīl*) alluding (to Khālid):

Although you have done things that no one can do,
Remember it's God who creates and not you![370]

370. Literally "mankind."

Then ʿUmar obliged Khālid to pay a certain sum of money and gave him compensation for this. He wrote a letter to the people concerning Khālid in order to absolve him from guilt so that they knew exactly what had happened.

In this year, I mean the year 17 (638), ʿUmar performed a *ʿumrah*.[371] He built the Masjid al-Ḥarām,[372] as al-Wāqidī asserts, and widened it. In all, he stayed in Mecca for twenty days. He demolished the properties of those who refused to sell their homes and he deposited the compensation thereof in the treasury, where it remained until they came and collected it.

Al-Wāqidī continued: The month in which ʿUmar performed that *ʿumrah* was Rajab (July–August 638). He had left Zayd b. Thābit in charge of Medina.

Al-Wāqidī continued: Also in (the course of) this *ʿumrah*, he ordered the renewal of the boundary markers of the Ḥaram[373] to be carried out by Makhramah b. Nawfal, al-Azhar b. ʿAbd ʿAwf, Ḥuwayṭib b. ʿAbd al-ʿUzzā and Saʿīd b. Yarbūʿ.

Al-Wāqidī continued: According to Kathīr b. ʿAbdallāh al- [2529]
Muzanī—his father—his grandfather: In the year 17 (638) we approached Mecca in the company of ʿUmar (who was on his way to perform) a *ʿumrah*. He passed the track[374] where he was addressed by the overseers of the wells, who asked him whether they were allowed to build road stations between Mecca and Medina, where hitherto there had not been structures of any sort. ʿUmar gave his consent, and stipulated that the wayfarer[375] was even more entitled to shelter and water (than pilgrims).

Al-Wāqidī said: Also in this year, ʿUmar b. al-Khaṭṭāb married Umm Kulthūm, the daughter of Fāṭimah (the daughter of the

---

371. The Arabic term for the lesser pilgrimage consisting mainly of a visit to, including circumambulations of, the Kaʿbah.

372. Islam's holiest sanctuary, the great mosque in Mecca housing the Kaʿbah.

373. This is the entire area of Mecca and surroundings closed to non-Muslims.

374. Perhaps this "track" refers to the route generally taken by travelers from Medina to Mecca.

375. The "wayfarer," in Arabic *ibn al-sabīl* ("son of the road"), in Arabian society used to form a special class of people, the preservation of whose well-being was a sacred duty of the (partially) settled. In Islam the *ibn al-sabīl* received his own special share from the fifth set aside from the booty acquired in battle. For an analysis of the connotations of *ibn al-sabīl* in the Jāhiliyyah and early Islam, see Puin, 43–57, and Abū ʿUbayd, *Amwāl*, 416–19.

Messenger of God) and ʿAlī b. Abī Ṭālib. ʿUmar consummated the marriage in Dhū al-Qaʿdah (November–December 638).

Al-Wāqidī continued: In this year, ʿUmar put Abū Mūsā al-Ashʿarī in charge of al-Baṣrah and ordered him to send al-Mughīrah (b. Shuʿbah) back to him in Rabīʿ I (March–April 638). According to Maʿmar (b. Rāshid)—al-Zuhrī—Saʿīd b. al-Musayyab: Abū Bakrah, Shibl b. Maʿbad al-Bajalī, Nāfiʿ b. (al-Ḥārith b.) Kaladah and Ziyād (b. Abīhi) bore witness against him.[376]

Al-Wāqidī went on: According to Muḥammad b. Yaʿqūb b. ʿUtbah—his father: (Al-Mughīrah) used to visit Umm Jamīl, a woman from Hilāl. She had had a husband from Thaqīf, called al-Ḥajjāj b. ʿUbayd,[377] but he had died some time back. So al-Mughīrah started having an affair with her. The people of al-Baṣrah got wind of this and were shocked. One day al-Mughīrah left (his house) and entered her house, which the people had kept under close observation. The men, who were to testify against him, went together (to this house) and tore away the curtain.
[2530] There he was, making love to her! Abū Bakrah wrote about this to ʿUmar (and consequently went to him in Medina to discuss matters).[378] ʿUmar heard his voice, (but could not see him for) there was a curtain between him and his visitor. ʿUmar asked, "Is it you, Abū Bakrah?" "Yes," the latter said, "Have you come because of something bad having happened?" asked ʿUmar. "It is really al-Mughīrah who caused me to come to you," Abū Bakrah answered, and he told ʿUmar the whole story. Then ʿUmar dispatched Abū Mūsā al-Ashʿarī (to al-Baṣrah) as the new governor and ordered him to send al-Mughīrah back to him (in Medina). (After Abū Mūsā had arrived in al-Baṣrah), al-Mughīrah presented him with (a servant girl of his called) ʿAqīlah saying, "I have chosen her especially for you." Then Abū Mūsā sent al-Mughīrah back to ʿUmar.

Al-Wāqidī continued: According to ʿAbd al-Raḥmān b. Muḥam-

376. In respect of what legal matter will become clear in what follows.

377. In Yaʿqūbī, II, 166, ʿAtīk.

378. Prym states in the apparatus that, apparently, something from the Ṭabarī text is missing and draws attention to a similar version of this story in Yaʿqūbī, *loc. cit.*, showing a considerable textual overlap but containing a seemingly more complete account. This last sentence, added in brackets, is distilled from that account.

mad b. Abī Bakr b. Muḥammad b. ʿAmr b. Ḥazm—his father—Mālik b. Aws b. al-Ḥadathān: I was present when al-Mughīrah was brought before ʿUmar; al-Mughīrah had a proper wife from the tribe of Murrah. ʿUmar said to him, "You have taken leave of your senses, you randy old goat." Then I heard him interrogate al-Mughīrah about the woman with whom he was supposed to have had illicit relations. Mālik b. Aws said: She was called al-Raqṭā', she was from Hilāl, and her late husband had been from Thaqīf.

Ṭabarī said: The reason for what occurred to Abū Bakrah and the testimony he gave against al-Mughīrah is according to al-Sarī—Shuʿayb—Sayf—Muḥammad, al-Muhallab, Ṭalḥah and ʿAmr, supported by their respective *isnād*s: What happened in actual fact between Abū Bakrah and al-Mughīrah b. Shuʿbah was that al-Mughīrah made it his custom to start conversations with Abū Bakrah, but the latter avoided him every time the former did so. At the time, both lived in al-Baṣrah; they were each other's neighbors, with a road separating their houses. Both used to spend time sitting behind their latticed windows[379] opposite one another in their respective houses. Both lattices were fitted with peepholes, the one exactly opposite the other. One day, some people came together in Abū Bakrah's house for a chat at his lattice, when a [2531]
(sudden) gust of wind opened the peephole. Abū Bakrah stood up in order to close it. Then—the wind having also opened the peephole of the lattice window opposite—he saw al-Mughīrah lying between the legs of a woman. He said to his visitors, "Come and look!" They got up and looked. Then Abū Bakrah said, "Bear witness!" "Who is she, anyway?" they asked. "Umm Jamīl, the daughter of al-Afqam," Abū Bakrah replied. Umm Jamīl was one of the ʿĀmir b. Ṣaʿṣaʿah tribe; she was al-Mughīrah's mistress, making it her business to offer her services to governors and tribal nobles (*ashrāf*) as some other women did in those days. The men ex-

---

379. In Arabic *mashrabah*, in modern Arabic *mashrabiyyah*. These latticed windows have for centuries been characterized by woodwork through which the people inside can see what is going on outside, but passersby cannot distinguish what is going on inside the house. Whether or not the same applies to these supposedly seventh-century Baṣran latticed windows mentioned here is hard to establish. But why not? Thesiger describes latticed windows in the *muḍīf*s of the Marsh Arabs in southern Iraq that have the same properties as the oriel-shaped *mashrabiyyah*s found elsewhere. *Muḍīf*s are guesthouses made of bundles of reed according to allegedly age-old designs, see Thesiger, ch. 23.

claimed, "We only saw buttocks, we do not know what she looks like." They kept staring when she stood up. When al-Mughīrah left the house to go to the *ṣalāt,* Abū Bakrah stopped him and said, "You may not perform the prayer ritual with us." Thereupon, they wrote about the affair to ʿUmar and exchanged letters with him. ʿUmar sent for Abū Mūsā and said to him, "Abū Mūsā, I am going to employ you as governor, I shall send you to a land where the devil has taken up residence, spreading his evil.[380] Stick to what you know is proper and do not change, lest God wreak a change in you!" Abū Mūsā replied, Commander of the Faithful, then help me with a number of Companions of the Messenger of God, Muhājirs as well as Anṣārīs, for I have found them, in this community as well as in those outlying administrative areas, to be like the salt without which no food tastes good."[381] ʿUmar informed him, "Seek the help of anyone you care for." So Abū Mūsā asked for twenty-nine men, among whom were Anas b. Mālik, ʿImrān b. Ḥuṣayn and Hishām b. ʿĀmir. Then he departed in their company and journeyed until he came to the Mirbad.[382] (The news) reached al-Mughīrah that Abū Mūsā had alighted at the Mirbad and he
[2532] thought, "By God, Abū Mūsā has not come simply to pay a visit or even for trade purposes, but he has come here in his function of commander." People were going about their business there, when suddenly Abū Mūsā came and approached them. He handed a letter from ʿUmar to al-Mughīrah. It was truly the most concise letter ever written by anyone, just four statements with which ʿUmar dismissed, censured and ordered the immediate return of one person, and installed another as governor. (It read:)

"Listen. A shocking rumor has reached me. I have sent Abū Mūsā to be governor. Hand all authority over to him. Hurry hither."

ʿUmar wrote to the inhabitants of al-Baṣrah:

"Listen. I have sent Abū Mūsā to be your governor. He is to

380. The Arabic has here the expression "the devil has laid eggs and produced young."

381. One is perhaps justified in being reminded of Matthew v, 13, in which the apostles are addressed with the words, "Thou art the salt of the earth." Christians were found everywhere in Iraq of the seventh century and it is feasible that expressions used by them also caught on with adherents of different faiths.

382. Al-Mirbad was the commercial center of al-Baṣrah where caravans stopped, see *EI*² s.v. (Pellat).

take away from the affluent among you to give to the poor. Together with you he will fight your enemy. He is to defend your security and to count the revenues of your *fay'* lands. Then he will distribute those among you. Finally, he will rid your roads (of unwanted elements) for you."

Al-Mughīrah presented Abū Mūsā with a slave girl from al-Ṭā'if[383] called ʿAqīlah, saying, "I have chosen her especially for you." She was very attractive. Then al-Mughīrah, and also Abū Bakrah, Nāfiʿ (b. al-Ḥārith) b. Kaladah, Ziyād (b. Abīhi) and Shibl b. Maʿbad al-Bajalī departed and journeyed until they came to ʿUmar. ʿUmar confronted them with al-Mughīrah who said, "Ask these nobodies[384] how they saw me; was I facing them or did I have my back toward them? And how did they see the woman, or how could they recognize her? For if they were facing me, how was it that I was not hidden (i.e. from their sight, because the woman was between me and them)? And if I had my back toward them, on what grounds did they permit themselves to spy on me in my own home, making love to my own wife? God in heaven, I have never bedded anyone except my own wife. This Umm Jamīl woman must have looked like her."

Then ʿUmar started by asking Abū Bakrah, who testified against al-Mughīrah that he had seen him lying between the legs [2533] of Umm Jamīl, heaving up and down like a kohl[385] stick in its phial. ʿUmar asked, "In what position did you see them?" "From behind," he replied. "But how did you establish her identity?" pursued ʿUmar. "Standing on my toes, I stretched out my neck,"[386] was the answer. Then ʿUmar summoned Shibl b. Maʿbad who testified to the same effect. ʿUmar asked him, "Did they have their backs toward you, or did they face you?" "No, they faced me," Shibl answered. Then Nāfiʿ testified, giving the same testimony as Abū Bakrah. Ziyād, however, did not offer the same testimony saying, "I saw him sitting between the legs of a

383. The Arabic technical term used here is *muwallad(ah),* which indicates a slave boy or slave girl of foreign background but born and reared among Arabs.

384. Literally, "serfs."

385. Webster: a cosmetic preparation, usually powdered antimony sulfide, used . . . to darken the eyelids.

386. This is how I render the verb *taḥāmaltu;* this connotation was suggested by *Glossarium.* I think the reading is dubious, but the message seems clear.

woman; I saw two painted feet[387] tapping on the floor and two bare buttocks and I heard heavy panting." ʿUmar asked, "Did you notice a heaving up and down like a kohl stick in its phial?" "No," Ziyād said. "And did you recognize the woman?" "No, I did not, I must have confused her with somebody else." ʿUmar told him, "Step aside." Then he ordered the other three to be flogged according to the Qur'ānic punishment[388] and he recited: "And when they cannot produce witnesses, then they are liars in God's view."[389] Then al-Mughīrah spoke, "Rid me of these nobodies," but ʿUmar said, "Be silent, may God strike you dumb, for by God, if their testimony had turned out to be valid, then I would have stoned you with your own stones."[390]

In that year, I mean 17 (638), the conquest of Sūq al-Ahwāz,
[2534] Manādhir and Nahr Tīrā[391] took place according to some; according to others, that was in the year 16 (637) after the Hijrah.

An Account of the Circumstances Leading to the Conquest of al-Ahwāz and of Him Who Carried It Out

According to al-Sarī—Shuʿayb—Sayf—Muḥammad, Ṭalḥah, al-Muhallab and ʿAmr: Al-Hurmuzān was one of the seven noble families among the Persians.[392] His territory was comprised of

387. Women painted their fingers and toes with henna, an ancient custom that persists to this day.

388. The Qur'ānic, fixed penalty for *qadhf*, that is, an unproven, and therefore slanderous, accusation of illicit sexual relations, is eighty stripes for a free person. Proof of fornication is only established on the testimony of at least four male witnesses. If their testimony turns out to be valid and is, subsequently, accepted, the Qur'ānic fixed punishment for *zinā'* (stoning, or one hundred lashes plus in some cases one year of banishment) is meted out to the guilty couple. *Qadhf* is succinctly dealt with in Q. XXIV, 4, "Those who accuse honorable women (of adultery) and then cannot produce four witnesses, give them eighty lashes and never accept their testimony again; those are the evildoers."

389. Q. XXIV, 13.

390. He means probably, ". . . with the stones you then would have coming to you."

391. All three are districts (in Arabic, *kuwar*) in al-Ahwāz, which is the Arabicized name of Khūzistān. The main city in the region of al-Ahwāz is called Sūq al-Ahwāz, which literally means "Market of al-Ahwāz," see Yāqūt, *Muʿjam*, I, 410 f.

392. See Morony, *Iraq*, 186, for more details on the *ahl al-buyūtāt*, as they are called.

Mihrijān Qadhaq and the districts of al-Ahwāz. These were families who were higher in rank[393] than anybody in Fārs. When al-Hurmuzān was routed at the battle of al-Qādisiyyah, he headed for his territory in the abovementioned region.[394] He went on governing his subjects and fought with them those who attacked them. Al-Hurmuzān used to make raids on the people of Maysān and Dastimaysān[395] from two directions, Manādhir and Nahr Tīrā.[396] ʿUtbah b. Ghazwān asked Saʿd for reinforcements, so the latter sent him Nuʿaym b. Muqarrin and Nuʿaym b. Masʿūd, ordering them to go to the highest point overlooking Maysān and Dastimaysān until they had reached a position between where al-Hurmuzān (and his people) were and Nahr Tīrā. ʿUtbah b. Ghazwān sent Sulmā b. al-Qayn and Ḥarmalah b. Muraytah out on a certain mission. They were two of the Companions of the Messenger of God, who had made the Hijrah with him; both were from the ʿAdawiyyah clan of Ḥanẓalah. They arrived at the border of the land of Maysān and Dastimaysān, at a point between al-Hurmuzān and Manādhir. There they called upon the Banū al-ʿAmi.[397] So Ghālib al-Wāʾilī and Kulayb b. Wāʾil al-Kulaybī [2535]
responded.[398] They had separated from Nuʿaym (b. Muqarrin) and Nuʿaym (b. Masʿūd) and turned away from them. Now they went to Sulmā and Ḥarmalah. After they had arrived there, the latter

393. The term "high in rank" is expressed by the Arabic preposition *dūna*, which usually means the opposite "lower," "baser." This seems an example of a *ḍidd*, that is the phenomenon in Arabic that a word has two diametrically opposed connotations, one of which is used most of the time, its opposite rarely. That *dūna* is such a *ḍidd* is confirmed in Lane.

394. In this passage the word *ummah*, usually rendered as "community," occurs twice; I opted here for "territory." See also pp. 3–4 above.

395. These are districts north of al-Baṣrah and west of al-Ahwāz.

396. These are two more districts of al-Ahwāz, see Yāqūt, *Muʿjam*, IV, 644, 837.

397. A clan affiliated to Tamīm that had been living among the Persians for some time. See the next note and further down for an explanation of how that came to pass.

398. Literally "they went out" (*kharaja*). In the edition, a pedigree is given allegedly indicating how these two men fitted in their clan and, subsequently, in Tamīm. When compared with Caskel (nos. 59 ff.), this pedigree is not substantiated. But in no. 212 of Caskel, a man, Murrah b. Wāʾil, is mentioned who is the reputed ancestor of the Banū al-ʿAmm or al-ʿAmi and who is listed as having descended from Azd. Whether or not the Banū al-ʿAmm, or al-ʿAmi, were originally Tamīmīs, or only became affiliated to Tamīm by "adopting" Mālik b. Ḥanẓalah as 'forefather' is anybody's guess.

said, "You are from the same tribe[399] therefore you may not desert us. When the day such-and-such has come, rise against al-Hurmuzān. One of us will attack Manādhir, the other Nahr Tīrā and we will kill al-Hurmuzān's fighters. Then we will come to you again. God willing, there is no other enemy than al-Hurmuzān." After the two men from the ʿAmi b. Mālik clan had promised their cooperation, they returned to their clansmen who, in their turn, also agreed to help.

Sayf went on: There is a story explaining how this man called al-ʿAmi[400] came by his name. This al-ʿAmi was Murrah[401] b. Mālik b. Ḥanẓalah b. Mālik b. Zayd Manāt b. Tamīm, with whom, as well as with al-Uṣayyah b. Imriʾ al-Qays, there settled a mixed bunch of people from Maʿadd.[402] Those people who were of the opinion that he should not give support to the Persians in controlling al-Ardawān[403] had believed him to be blind[404] to what was
[2536] the proper course of action. Concerning this attitude, Kaʿb b. Mālik, his brother—sometimes it is Ṣudayy (b. Mālik) who is mentioned—composed the following verses (in *ṭawīl*):

(Though) once a good man, now our Murrah is blind,
and, deaf to his kinsmen's pleas, he has set out

---

399. That is to say, the two of you are descended from the same woman as we, namely al-ʿAdawiyyah who, according to Caskel, II, 136, is al-Ḥarām bt. Khuzaymah b. Tamīm.

400. In the following story, two forms of the name alternate: al-ʿAmi, with a short *i*, a poetic license for *ʿamiya* "he was blind," occurring in the poem that follows shortly, and al-ʿAmī, with long *ī*, as if it is a regular *nisbah*. Caskel (II, 166) lists the clan as the Banū al-ʿAmm. In Abū al-Faraj al-Iṣfahānī, *Kitāb al-Aghānī* (Cairo 1323–), III, 257, the name is interpreted as "cousins," conveying that the members of the Banū al-ʿAmm clan are as "dear to us as our own cousins." Whether the clan was, or had become, part of Tamīm, as is suggested in this story, is a matter of controversy. Other sources claim that they originated from Azd, see *Tāj*, VIII, 410; also Caskel, no. 212, and Kaḥḥālah, II, 820 f. See also Juda, 77.

401. Murrah was allegedly the grandfather of Ghālib and the great-grandfather of Kulayb, the two persons mentioned in the pedigree of Prym's apparatus.

402. Maʿadd is a collective name for the northern Arab tribes, see *EI²*, s.v. *Maʿadd* (Watt).

403. This is another name for Khūzistān, the Persian name of the Ahwāz district; see Yāqūt, *Muʿjam*, I, 204.

404. In Arabic *ʿammā*, form II of *ʿamiya* mentioned in n. 400 above. It is also possible to interpret this verb as meaning "they made him blind to the proper course of action." Although the second form of this verb may be used to convey "to consider someone to be blind," neither Lane nor *Glossarium* confirm this.

To settle away from us, spurning his land,
and seek with the Persian lords[405] power and fame.

Because of the first line he, Murrah, was called al-ʿAmi, and the saying became current: the Banū al-ʿAmi have deemed him blind[406] to the right course of action because of[407] the support that he gave to the Persians. The Qur'ānic expression, "They have become blind and deaf,"[408] is to be taken in a similar vein. Yarbūʿ b. Mālik[409] composed the following poem (in *ṭawīl*):

The best of Maʿadd realize that it's we
who'll be in the contest the stars of the race[410]
In spite of the enemies[411] we settled ourselves,
Though none of Tamīm did[412] nor any big tribe.
We drove out the lowly,[413] so nothing remained
Which the Persians begrudged us, not even a pin.
If the lands of the noblest of nomads are rich,[414]
we boast of lands richer in water than theirs.

Ayyūb b. al-ʿUṣayyah b. Imri' al-Qays recited the following lines (in *ṭawīl*):

Of (all) the tribes we were the first here to settle,
On purpose we did so where large groups would gather.

---

405. The term used is Asāwirah, see n. 147 above.

406. Or conceivably "have made him blind to . . ."

407. Or conceivably "through."

408. Q. V, 71; "they" refers to the Jews and Christians.

409. He is another alleged brother of Murrah al-ʿAmi.

410. Probably a reference to one of the big fairs organized in various places in the peninsula, during which members of different tribes, by entering various contests, tried to outdo one another to the glory of the winner's tribe and the detriment of the loser's.

411. Probably a reference to those former inhabitants of the area who were forced to make room for the Arab settlers.

412. *Glossarium*, p. DCXXI, suggests that we read *wa-lam nunikh* or *yanakh* for *wa-lam yutnakh*. This does not affect the translation given here and is, in fact, required by the meter.

413. The word used is *nabīṭ*, which initially stood for Nabateans, and was later applied to people of mixed origin who settled in southern Iraq, north of al-Baḥrayn, reviled for their lifestyle as petty agriculturalists in small villages scattered over the swampy area known as al-Baṭā'iḥ and also in the Sawād.

414. Rich in water.

While ruling them, those who came first we did honor,
Henceforth at all times we ruled over all neighbors.

[2537] When that particular night had come, agreed on by Sulmā, Ḥarmalah, Ghālib and Kulayb, al-Hurmuzān being at the time between Nahr Tīrā and Duluth,[415] Sulmā and Ḥarmalah left, very early the following morning, with a fully equipped armed force, and roused Nuʿaym (b. Muqarrin) and Nuʿaym (b. Masʿūd). All of these and al-Hurmuzān came face to face at a spot between Duluth and Nahr Tīrā, Sulmā b. al-Qayn at the head of the warriors from al-Baṣrah and Nuʿaym b. Muqarrin in command of those from al-Kūfah. Then fighting broke out. While they were thus engaged, the reinforcements recruited by Ghālib and Kulayb approached. Then the news that Manādhir and Nahr Tīrā had been taken reached al-Hurmuzān. So God broke his strength[416] and that of his army and defeated him and his troops. The Muslims killed and captured as many as they wanted from them and they pursued them until they came to a halt on the bank of the Dujayl,[417] having occupied all the land this side (i.e. that is west) of the river. They encamped opposite Sūq al-Ahwāz. In the meantime, al-Hurmuzān had crossed the bridge to Sūq al-Ahwāz and taken up residence there. So the Dujayl became the line of demarcation between al-Hurmuzān on the one hand and Sulmā, Ḥarmalah, Nuʿaym (b. Muqarrin), Nuʿaym (b. Masʿūd), Ghālib and Kulayb on the other.

According to al-Sarī—Shuʿayb—Sayf—ʿAbdallāh b. al-Mughīrah al-ʿAbdī—a man from ʿAbd al-Qays called Ṣuḥār: I went to Harim b. Ḥayyān in the region between al-Dulūth and the Dujayl with baskets of dates, for which he could hardly wait. Most of his
[2538] provisions, when stocked up, consisted of dates. When (the regular provisions) ran out, he chose for himself from some of those baskets that he used as provision bags, while his comrades were already on their way. Then he carried these bags and ate from

415. Also spelled Dulūth, see Yāqūt, *Muʿjam*, II, 583, and a few lines down.

416. The unusual combination in the text of *kasara* "to break" and the preposition *fī* "in" looks dubious; see Lane, 961, middle column, ad finem, where *fī* is replaced by *min*; see also *WKAS*, I, 179, right column, l. 38. The meaning seems clear, however.

417. The Dujayl is a river in Khūzistān-al-Ahwāz, see Le Strange, *Lands*, 232. Nowadays it is called Kārūn.

them, giving also to others, wherever he happened to be, in the plains or in the mountains.

They said: When the Muslim warriors invaded al-Hurmuzān's territory and set up their camp close to where he was in al-Ahwāz, he realized that he lacked the manpower to overcome them. So he begged for peace, whereupon they wrote about that proposal to 'Utbah, asking him for directives in this matter. Al-Hurmuzān sent a letter to 'Utbah who, while accepting the proposed peace treaty, answered that al-Hurmuzān was to remain in control of all of al-Ahwāz and Mihrijān Qadhaq with the exception of Nahr Tīrā and Manādhir and that area of Sūq al-Ahwāz that the Muslims had already conquered. What we had liberated from Persian rule would not be returned to them. Sulmā b. al-Qayn placed a garrison[418] in Manādhir under the command of Ghālib, and Ḥarmalah placed one in Nahr Tīrā under the command of Kulayb. They had formerly commanded the forces of al-Baṣrah.

Meanwhile, groups of the Banū al-'Ami left their former dwelling places and took up residence in al-Baṣrah, one group after another. 'Utbah wrote about that to 'Umar and sent a delegation (i.e. from them to 'Umar). Among these were Sulmā, who had been ordered to leave someone in control of his district, as well as Ḥarmalah—both had been Companions of the Prophet—furthermore, Ghālib and Kulayb. Also, other delegations from al-Baṣrah traveled in those days (i.e., to Medina). Upon their arrival, 'Umar[419] ordered them to voice their needs, whereupon each of them said, "As far as the common people are concerned, you are their lord;[420] the only ones (who have demands to make) are our élite." So they voiced their demands beyond those raised by al-Aḥnaf b. Qays,[421] who said:

"Commander of the Faithful, you are the sort of man as they have described; but there is perhaps something that eludes you, [2539]
that is our duty to bring to your attention, something that is

418. Or "set up an army camp."

419. The text in Ṭabarī admits also of 'Utbah being the one who gives the order, but the text of Ibn al-Athīr, II, 424, implies clearly that it was 'Umar.

420. Presumably this means "you are directly responsible for their well-being."

421. Al-Aḥnaf b. Qays was a leader of Tamīm in al-Baṣrah, see *EI²*, s.v. *al-Aḥnaf b. Ḳays* (Pellat). The parallel passage in Ibn al-Athīr, II, 424, leaves out the words *illā mā kāna min*, which means that they asked that al-Aḥnaf be heard as their spokesman. The text in Ṭabarī can conceivably be interpreted in this way too.

connected with the well-being of the common people. But, then, a ruler looks into matters (happening in a spot) from which he is far removed with the eyes and the ears of his informants. We kept on moving from one place to another, until we arrived at a piece of open country. Well, our brothers among the inhabitants of al-Kūfah have settled in a place rich in vegetation,[422] overflowing with sweet springs and lush palm groves; in a never-ceasing flow its fruit produce reaches them. But we, the people of al-Baṣrah, we have settled in a soggy swamp, which does not produce anything. One side faces the desert and the other side gives on to a brackish river. Supplies reach this region like a trickle from an ostrich's gullet. Our houses are crammed, our daily rations poor. Our numbers are large, but our nobles are few in number. Many of us have fought vigorously, but our finances are straitened, while our plots of land are small. In the past God enriched us and increased our land. So may you now enrich us, Commander of the Faithful, and increase the daily rations assigned to us so that we may survive!"

So ʿUmar reviewed their dwelling places which they had occupied until they moved out into the desert. Then he gave them the region as their share in the booty and allotted plots to them, also taken from what used to belong to the Persian royal family. Thus all the land between the Tigris and the desert became *fay'*
[2540] land. They divided it among themselves. The other properties of the royal family in the land around al-Baṣrah were thus dealt with in the same manner as the land of al-Kūfah was dealt with: they let those who were interested settle there and divide it up among themselves—where no preference was given to the first or second wave of settlers—after they had singled out one fifth of its revenues for the governor.

The land occupied by the people of al-Baṣrah consisted of two halves, one was divided up into plots; the other was left for the benefit of the armed forces and the community. The *aṣḥāb al-alfayn,*[423] from those who had been present at the battle of al-

422. Literally, it says "in a camel's eye," as Lane (532, middle column, line 1) asserts ". . . a tract abounding with herbage; likened to the *ḥadaqah* 'the black of the eye' of the camel because this is plentifully supplied with moisture."

423. Literally, "the people of two thousand," that is, the people who received annual stipends of two thousand dirhams. In Ṭabarī, I, 2412, l. 14, the veterans of al-Qādisiyyah and Syria are singled out for this amount. See vol. XII of this series.

Qādisiyyah and then had gone to al-Baṣrah together with ʿUtbah, were five thousand in number, while in al-Kūfah they numbered thirty thousand. ʿUmar increased the numbers of the veterans of al-Baṣrah from those who had displayed valor among the stipendiaries of two thousand dirhams by so many that their numbers became the same as those of al-Kūfah, by adding all those who (had fought) in al-Ahwāz. Then ʿUmar decreed, "This young man[424] is to be the leader of the people of al-Baṣrah," and he wrote to ʿUtbah in respect of him that he listen to him and make use of his counsel. Then ʿUmar sent Sulmā, Ḥarmalah, Ghālib and Kulayb back to Manādhir and Nahr Tīrā, where they had to keep themselves prepared for any eventuality and where they had to set apart the *kharāj*.

According to al-Sarī—Shuʿayb—Sayf—Muḥammad, Ṭalḥah, al-Muhallab and ʿAmr: While the people of al-Baṣrah and those who were living under their protection were thus engaged, a controversy flared up, each side putting forth contradictory claims concerning the boundaries of their lands, between al-Hurmuzān on the one hand and Ghālib and Kulayb on the other. Sulmā and Ḥarmalah went there to see what was going on among them and found Ghālib and Kulayb to be in the right and al-Hurmuzān to be wrong. So they separated the quarreling parties. Moreover, al-Hurmuzān went back on his word and withheld what he had accepted to pay. Then he called upon the Kurds to help him, whereupon his army grew in strength. Sulmā, Ḥarmalah, Ghālib [2541]
and Kulayb wrote about the designs of al-Hurmuzān, as well as about his unfairness and his broken promise, to ʿUtbah b. Ghazwān who, in turn, notified ʿUmar about this. ʿUmar wrote back, giving him his orders and sent them Ḥurqūṣ b. Zuhayr al-Saʿdī, one of the Prophet's Companions, as reinforcement. ʿUmar put him in command of all military operations and of all the land conquered (sc. in al-Ahwāz). Al-Hurmuzān, together with those who were with him, went forth to wage war; Sulmā, Ḥarmalah, Ghālib and Kulayb did likewise until, when they had reached the bridge to Sūq al-Ahwāz, they sent a message to al-Hurmuzān that ran, "Either you cross over to our side, or we to yours."[425] Al-

424. That is, al-Aḥnaf b. Qays.
425. Noth, 121, identifies such phrases as a *topos*.

Hurmuzān answered, "You may cross over to our side of the water." So, when they crossed over the bridge to the other side, fighting broke out while they were still on that part directly facing Sūq al-Ahwāz. In the end, al-Hurmuzān was beaten. He set out in the direction of Rāmhurmuz,[426] took a village called al-Shaghar[427] on the dam of Arbuk[428] and finally alighted at Rāmhurmuz.

Ḥurqūs conquered Sūq al-Ahwāz and took up residence there. Then he entered the mountain region, and the administration of the whole region from Sūq al-Ahwāz all the way to Tustar[429] became well organized. He imposed the *jizyah,* wrote the news about the conquest to ʿUmar and sent the fifth parts of the booty acquired in the different areas, dispatching a delegation to carry this to him. ʿUmar praised God and asked Him to confer stability upon Ḥurqūs and grant him territorial expansion.

The Companion al-Aswad b. Sarīʿ[430] on this occasion composed the following lines (in *wāfir*):

The sons of our father[431] have not been neglectful,
 But have remained firm among those who obeyed,
Listening to their Lord, while th' enemy revolted
 Against Him, with others who heed no command.
[2542] The Magians who'd never been bound to a Scripture
 Thus joined in a struggle from which they retreated.
Al-Hurmuzān fled on a steed at a gallop,
 Relentlessly hunted by all of our warriors,
Reluctantly leaving the area's capital[432]
 On the Day of the Bridge,[433] just as springtime[434] set in.

---

426. A city some eighty kilometers due east of Sūq al-Ahwāz; see also Yāqūt, *Muʿjam,* II, 738.

427. The name of this village, not identified as such in *ibid.,* III, 303, where the term al-Shughr is dealt with, indicates that it was deserted by its inhabitants and left defenseless. See further down.

428. The name of a region in al-Ahwāz, see *ibid.,* I, 185 f.

429. Present-day Shushtar, a city some eighty kilometers due north of Sūq al-Ahwāz.

430. Al-Baṣrah's first storyteller and a well-known poet, see Ibn Ḥajar, *Iṣābah,* I, 74.

431. This expression is meant to convey that he is proud of his fellow tribesmen from Tamīm.

432. Literally, "the navel of al-Ahwāz."

433. That is, the day of the battle on the bridge.

434. The Arabic word *rabīʿ* used here may in actual fact refer to a number of

As for Ḥurqūṣ, he recited the following lines (in *wāfir*):

We wrested from al-Hurmuzān a whole area
so rich in provisions in every district!
Its dry land and water supply well in balance,
when excellent groves come to early fruition.
This land has a turbulent stream into which pour
tributaries from both sides, always overflowing.

In the same year, I mean the year 17 (638), Tustar was conquered according to Sayf and the report he transmits. Other historians say it was conquered in 16 (637), still others say it was as late as the year 19 (640).

The Conquest of Tustar

According to al-Sarī—Shu'ayb—Sayf—Muḥammad, Ṭalḥah, al-Muhallab and 'Amr: When al-Hurmuzān had been defeated on the day (of the battle) of Sūq al-Ahwāz, and after Ḥurqūṣ b. Zuhayr had conquered that city, the latter took up residence there. He dispatched Jaz' b. Mu'āwiyah to Surraq[435] in pursuit of al-Hurmuzān, as 'Umar had ordered. 'Umar had charged Ḥurqūṣ, should God conquer the area for them, to send Jaz' after al-Hurmuzān in pursuit, and also to take the direction to Surraq. So Jaz' left on the heels of al-Hurmuzān who, on the run, had taken the direction to Rāmhurmuz. Jaz' ruthlessly killed those enemies (who crossed his path) until he arrived at the village of al-Shaghar, where al- [2543]
Hurmuzān was not able to withstand him. Since al-Shaghar was abandoned by its inhabitants[436] because of its poverty, Jaz' set out for Dawraq, the administrative center of the district of Surraq.[437] The people who lived there were not able to defend the city, so Jaz' took possession of it as "special property"[438] and wrote about it to 'Umar and to 'Utbah. He also mentioned that he had invited those who had fled to pay the *jizā'* and in exchange to accept

different seasons of the year as well as to two months of the Muslim calendar (see Lane, 1018 f.); in other words, the interpretation of this term as indication of time is vague.

435. A district in al-Ahwāz province.

436. See n. 427 above.

437. A place of some importance, see Yāqūt, *Mu'jam*, II, 618 ff.

438. In Arabic, *ṣāfiyah*, the singular of *ṣawāfī*, a term dealt with in n. 167 above.

protection, terms that they accepted. Then ʿUmar wrote to Jazʾ b. Muʿāwiyah and Ḥurqūṣ b. Zuhayr to hold on to the territory they had conquered and to take up residence there, until orders from him reached them. ʿUmar wrote about this to Jazʾ[439] in a letter addressed to ʿUtbah. Jazʾ and Ḥurqūṣ did as they were told. Moreover, Jazʾ asked ʿUmar's permission to colonize his territory, a request ʿUmar granted. So Jazʾ had the waterways opened up and the uncultivated land cultivated.

When al-Hurmuzān had arrived in Rāmhurmuz and the province of al-Ahwāz had become crammed full of the Muslims settling in it, even right in front of him, he sought a peace agreement and sent messages to Ḥurqūṣ and Jazʾ asking for this. Then Ḥurqūṣ wrote to ʿUmar about him. ʿUmar in turn replied to him and ʿUtbah, ordering the latter to accept al-Hurmuzān's peace proposal on the condition that that territory, which the Muslims had not yet conquered, to wit, Rāmhurmuz, Tustar, al-Sūs, Jundaysābūr, al-Bunyān and Mihrijān Qadhaq[440] (would come under Muslim control). Al-Hurmuzān told them that he accepted these conditions. The commanders of al-Ahwāz set up the administration of the regions assigned to them and al-Hurmuzān complied with the conditions of the peace treaty, gathering taxes for the Muslim commanders while the latter defended him; in case the Kurds of Fārs were to make raids on him, they would help and defend him.

[2544] ʿUmar wrote to ʿUtbah, "Send me a delegation of ten God-fearing men from the garrison at al-Baṣrah." Thus the men traveled to ʿUmar. Among them was al-Aḥnaf who, when he approached ʿUmar, was addressed by the latter with the following words, "You are in my eyes someone worthy of my faith in you. I have seen that you have comported yourself like a man; tell me, is it true that the protection granted to the conquered people has been violated? Have they run away because of an injustice done to them, or was there another reason for this?" Al-Aḥnaf answered, "No, on the contrary, it was not because of an injustice; besides,

---

439. Or should we translate "to them" and substitute *ilayhimā* for *ilayhi* in l. 6? The dual of *faʿalā* that follows seems to indicate that.

440. All these towns lie roughly at the same distance in a semicircle around Sūq al-Ahwāz. Only the place called al-Bunyān is not clearly defined, see Yāqūt, *Muʿjam*, I, 749.

the people are now living in conditions you would approve of." "Allright then," ʿUmar said, "you may return to your camels."[441]

The party went back to the camels. ʿUmar looked over their luggage and found a garment, its hem sticking out from a clothes bundle. He smelled it and said, "Which one of you is the owner of this garment?" "I am," al-Aḥnaf replied. Then ʿUmar asked him, "How much did you pay for this?" Al-Aḥnaf mentioned a low price, eight dirhams or something like that, lowering the real figure for which he had bought it, which was twelve dirhams. "Could you not have acquired something for less?" ʿUmar said, "then you might have spent the remainder in a way that might have benefitted a fellow Muslim! Take pains[442] and spend what you do not need in a proper manner, then you will set your conscience at ease and you will have spent your money well.[443] And do not squander it, so that you will lose your peace of mind as well as your money. If a man only looks after his own desires and indulges them, he will have to face the consequences in the hereafter."[444] Then ʿUmar wrote to ʿUtbah, "Keep the people far from injustice, fear God[445] and take care lest fortune turn against you because of an act of treachery or concupiscence committed by one of you. For through God you have attained what you have, on the basis of a covenant that He has concluded with you, and He has shown you His grace in matters He reproached you for. So fulfill the covenant with God and carry out His commands; then He will give you help and victory."

News reached ʿUmar that Ḥurqūṣ had invaded the mountainous region of al-Ahwāz, while the people kept seeking refuge with him. These mountains are well-nigh impassable, causing those who want to climb them great hardship. Thus ʿUmar wrote to him, saying, "It has come to my notice that you have ventured into an impassable region where you cannot be attacked except with difficulty. But take it easy, and do not cause one Muslim or [2545]

441. Literally, "saddles."

442. I take *ḥaṣṣa* to mean the same as *ḥaṣḥaṣa*; this is confirmed in Lane.

443. The intentional double entendre in the Arabic verb *arāḥa* does not seem to be translatable with one English verb.

444. Literally, "he will be compensated (by God)."

445. In Arabic, *wa'ttaqū*, which is a conjecture of Prym; in the apparatus he lists from the Leiden Ibn Ḥubaysh *wa'nqaw* "be pure," which makes equally good sense.

one confederate any hardship. But if you handle your affairs with firmness and caution,[446] you will attain the hereafter, while this material world will be untroubled for you. And let not indifference or hastiness determine your behavior, so that your life on earth is spoiled, and your chances of attaining the afterlife disappear." Then, at Ṣiffīn,[447] Ḥurqūṣ joined those who went off to Ḥarūrā'.[448] He did not change his mind and was killed in the battle of al-Nahrawān[449] on the side of the Ḥarūriyyah.

In that year, I mean 17 (638), the Muslims raided the land of Fārs opposite al-Baḥrayn,[450] as Sayf has asserted and reported.

The Raid into Fārs

According to al-Sarī—Shu'ayb—Sayf—Muḥammad, al-Muhallab and 'Amr: In al-Baṣrah and its environs, comprising in those days the adjacent Sawād and al-Ahwāz, the Muslims had been living in circumstances prevailing until that day:[451] what they had conquered was fully under their control, and the region with which they had concluded a peace treaty was under the control of its inhabitants, who duly paid the *kharāj*, with the understanding that they would not be invaded, enjoying full protection and with al-Hurmuzān being responsible for the terms of the treaty to be observed. 'Umar had said, "With the adjacent cultivated area and al-Ahwāz, the people of al-Baṣrah should be content; I wish there were between us and the people of Fārs a mountain of fire, through which they cannot reach us, nor we them." In the same

---

446. This translation is suggested in *Glossarium*, p. CCLX.

447. The battle in 37 (657) in which Mu'āwiyah and 'Alī faced one another, and which ended, more or less undecided, with the mutal acceptance of arbitration, a move on the part of 'Alī that led to the desertion of a sizable part of his following, people who first grouped themselves in the village of Ḥarūrā' (hence the name Ḥarūriyyah) and later became generally known as the Khārijites or Khawārij. For more details, see *EI*², s.v. *Ḥarūrā'* (L. Veccia Vaglieri).

448. In Arabic, *Taḥarrara;* this rendering is suggested in *Glossarium*, p. CLXXXVI.

449. This is the battle at which 'Alī dealt the rebelling Khārijites a death blow in 38 (658).

450. For this region, see n. 198 above. For a detailed study of this raid, see M. Hinds, "The first Arab conquests in Fārs," in *Iran*, XXII (1984):39–53.

451. Presumably this means that these circumstances were about to change shortly.

manner he had expressed himself concerning the people of al-Kūfah, "I wish there were a mountain of fire between them and the Jabal region, through which the people of al-Jabal cannot get at us, nor we at them."

During the reign of Abū Bakr, al-ʿAlāʾ b. al-Ḥaḍramī[452] was [2546]
administrator of al-Baḥrayn. ʿUmar dismissed him and nominated Qudāmah b. al-Maẓʿūn[453] in his place. Then he dismissed Qudāmah and returned al-ʿAlāʾ (to al-Baḥrayn). Al-ʿAlāʾ used to feel rivalry for Saʿd, caused by a rift that Fate had struck between them. Al-ʿAlāʾ had had very much the upperhand as a result of his exploits in the apostasy wars. However, when Saʿd was victorious at al-Qādisiyyah, had removed the Persian royal family from its palace, had established boundaries of the adjacent cultivated area, had grown in social position and submitted more booty (to Medina) than al-ʿAlāʾ had done, the latter was filled with desire to achieve something himself in territory held by the Persians, in the happy expectation that his fortune would take a turn for the better, as had been the case with Saʿd. But al-ʿAlāʾ failed to assess the situation properly, for he did not distinguish diligently between the merit of obedience and that of disobedience.

Abū Bakr had made use of his services as governor and had given him permission to fight the people who had apostatized. Then ʿUmar employed him in the same function while forbidding him to venture out overseas. But al-ʿAlāʾ did not appreciate the difference between obedience and disobedience and their respective consequences, for he ordered the people of al-Baḥrayn to go on a raid into Fārs. The people jumped at the occasion. Al-ʿAlāʾ divided them into several contingents, one commanded by al-Jārūd b. al-Muʿallā, another by al-Sawwār b. Hammām, yet another one by Khulayd b. al-Mundhir b. Sāwī, while the latter was also in charge of the whole fighting force. He ordered them to put out to Fārs without ʿUmar's consent. ʿUmar never used to allow anyone to go on a raid by ship, objecting to the risk for the fighters, in so doing following the example of the Prophet and Abū Bakr, both of whom never put out to sea for a raid.

---

452. For more information about this man, see Ibn Saʿd, IV/2, 76–9.

453. One of the first men to be converted to Islam. Once he was flogged for drinking wine, as Ibn Ḥajar, *Iṣābah*, V, 423–6, has it.

However, those fighting forces crossed from al-Baḥrayn to Fārs and headed for Iṣṭakhr,[454] where they met the people of Fārs face to face under the command of their Hirbadh,[455] under whose
[2547] leadership they had assembled. Then they cut the Muslims off from their ships. Thereupon Khulayd stood up among his people and said, "Listen. When God decrees something, the fate of the people runs parallel with it, until that comes to pass. Through what they have done, they have really not done more than challenge you to fight them. But you have come here with the single purpose of waging war against them. The ships and the land will belong to him who is victorious." (And then he recited,) "Therefore, ask endurance and the prayer ritual to help you, for the (situation) is grave except for those who humble themselves."[456] The people reacted positively to his suggestion and performed the noon *ṣalāt*. Then they moved in the direction of the enemy and fought a hard battle at a place called Ṭāwūs. On that day, al-Sawwār began to declaim a poem in *rajaz* in which he praised his warriors, saying,

O people of ʿAbd al-Qays, on to the struggle!
  Reserve troops have gathered apace in the plains,
Each one of them, skilled in the art of armed battle,
  Rains hefty blows on enemy (heads) with their swords.

(He recited these lines) until he was slain. Then al-Jārūd started to declaim verses in *rajaz*, saying,

If it had been a thing near at hand, I'd have eaten it,
  If it had been a well clogged with mud, I'd have cleared it!
But I shrink from this ocean that's come over us!

(He recited these lines) until he got killed. On that day, ʿAbdallāh b. al-Sawwār and al-Mundhir b. al-Jārūd hung on to dear life,[457]

---

454. The ancient capital of Fārs, in Greek: Persepolis, see Le Strange, *Lands*, 257 f.

455. A functionary of the Zoroastrian fire temple, see Christensen, *L'Iran*, 114.

456. Q. II, 45, this verse can also be interpreted as pointing to the *ṣalāt* being described as a demanding duty except for those who perform it faithfully. My rendering is based upon R. Paret's interpretation (*Der Koran. Kommentar und Konkordanz*, Stuttgart, 1971, 18). See also Ṭabarī, *Tafsīr*, 2nd impression, Cairo, 1954, I, 261.

457. Rendition tentative. I have not found corroboration for my interpretation of the expression *waliya ḥayātahumā*. Or should we translate "they fought to their last drop of blood?"

until they died. That same day Khulayd began to recite the following verses in *rajaz*, saying,

O tribe of Tamīm, tell your clans to assemble![458] [2548]
The army of ʿUmar has virtually perished.
And each of you should know (the weight) of my words!

(He went on to shout,) "Come hither!" So they did and the armies fought. The people of Fārs were killed in a bloodbath such as they had never before experienced. Then the Arabs moved away, heading for al-Baṣrah, but their ships had been scuttled. So they had no means of transport to return by sea. After that they found that (a Persian named) Shahrak had blockaded the roads against the Muslims,[459] so they had to make camp and defend themselves in the isolated location in which they were.[460] When ʿUmar was brought the news of what al-ʿAlāʾ had done by sending that army overseas, an idea of what that desperate situation might be like occurred to him, and he was furious with al-ʿAlāʾ. He wrote to him to dismiss him from his function, he uttered threats and he ordered him to do something most painful and to take a step most odious: he had to place himself under the command of Saʿd. "Go," ʿUmar told him, "join Saʿd b. Abī Waqqāṣ accompanied by your entourage." So, amid his entourage, al-ʿAlāʾ left for Saʿd.

ʿUmar wrote to ʿUtbah b. Ghazwān: "Al-ʿAlāʾ b. al-Ḥaḍramī compelled an armed force of Muslims to go overseas, consequently, the inhabitants of Fārs cut them off from returning in their ships. Al-ʿAlāʾ has disobeyed me, I do not think he was seeking God's approval with this. Moreover, if they do not get help, I fear that those men marooned in Fārs will be defeated, cut off from help as they are. Therefore, before they are wiped out, send them reinforcements and, once rescued, place them under your supervision."

ʿUtbah dispatched the reinforcements and told them what ʿUmar had written. Those detailed were ʿĀṣim b. ʿAmr, ʿArfajah b. Harthamah, Ḥudhayfah b. Miḥṣan, Majzaʾah b. Thawr, Nahār b. [2549] al-Ḥārith, al-Tarjumān b. Fulān,[461] al-Ḥuṣayn b. Abī al-Ḥurr, al-Aḥnaf b. Qays, Saʿd b. Abī al-ʿArjāʾ, ʿAbd al-Raḥmān b. Sahl and

458. Or "tell (everybody) to come hither together."
459. Presumably, preventing them from finding their way back home over land.
460. For this rendering of *nushūb*, see *Glossarium*, p. DXII.

Ṣaʿṣaʿah b. Muʿāwiyah. They marched out among twelve thousand men, riding mules leading horses on their sides. Abū Sabrah b. Abī Ruhm, one of the Mālik b. Ḥisl b. ʿĀmir b. Lu'ayy was in command. Life in the garrisons, meant to assist raiding parties and the sedentary population alike,[462] as well as among the conquered people in al-Ahwāz, was as usual. Thus Abū Sabrah marched out with his men, taking a route along the coast. On the way, he was not met, or resisted by, anyone. Finally, Abū Sabrah came face to face with Khulayd in exactly the same spot as the latter found himself when the enemy, after the battle at Ṭāwūs, had manned the roads against the Muslims. Only the inhabitants of Iṣṭakhr and a few more people from other areas had undertaken to fight them. After they had cut the Muslims off from taking the overland route, thus isolating them, the inhabitants of Iṣṭakhr had asked all the other people of Fārs for military support against them. In this way the Muslims suffered attacks from every region and district.

Then they were joined by Abū Sabrah after the battle of Ṭāwūs, the Muslims thus receiving reinforcements just as the unbelievers, who were under the command of Shahrak, had received theirs. Then they fought, God granting the Muslims victory and killing the unbelievers. The Muslims acquired as much booty from them as they wanted. This was the raid during which the newly conscripted warriors of al-Baṣrah distinguished themselves. They were the best new conscripts of all the garrison cities, the recruits of al-Baṣrah being even better than those of al-
[2550] Kūfah.[463] Then they returned with what they had acquired, for ʿUtbah had sent them his orders. He had written to them to come to him in haste, and not to tarry. So they joined him in al-Baṣrah. Warriors originally hailing from al-Baṣrah returned to their Baṣran quarters, and those of the people of Hajar[464] who had been

461. *Tarjumān* means "interpreter," this man's real name was probably something else.

462. I take *-hum* in l. 6 to refer to *masāliḥ* in l. 5 rather than to the preceding *al-dhimmah,* which is used here in the connotation *ahl al-dhimmah,* see Lane, 976, right column, l. 9.

463. This admittedly free rendition is tentative.

464. See n. 278 above.

rescued in Fārs scattered over their tribes, while those from the ʿAbd al-Qays clan spread to a place (called) Sūq al-Baḥrayn.[465]

When ʿUtbah held al-Ahwāz under control and had subdued Fārs, he asked ʿUmar permission to go on the pilgrimage, which was granted. When he had completed the rites, he asked ʿUmar to be relieved of his duties, but the latter refused to let him go and he adjured him to return to his governorate. Then ʿUtbah offered up a prayer, departed and died in Baṭn Nakhlah,[466] where he was buried. When his news reached ʿUmar, he went by that place to pay a visit to ʿUtbah's grave, where he said, "It is I who killed you, were it not for the fact that death is set at a fixed hour and described in a 'written book'."[467] Then he praised him for his merits. ʿUtbah had not assigned special living quarters to himself as the (other) Muhājirs had done, but his children inherited their quarters from Fākhitah, a daughter of Ghazwān. She was a wife of ʿUthmān b. ʿAffān. Khabbāb, ʿUtbah's client, had adopted his master's conduct and had never sought special living quarters for himself.

ʿUtbah b. Ghazwān died exactly three and a half years after Saʿd had departed for[468] al-Madā'in. He had left Abū Sabrah b. Abī Ruhm as his successor to govern the people, while his officials were retained in their functions. He left garrisons in Nahr Tīrā, Manādhir, Sūq al-Ahwāz and Surraq, al-Hurmuzān under the conditions of a peace agreement being left in Rāmhurmuz. He also left garrisons in al-Sūs, al-Bunyān, Jundaysābūr and Mihrijān Qadhaq. These were organized after the rescue of those whom al-ʿAlā' had forced to put out to sea to Fārs and after their settling in al-Baṣrah. They used to be called "the people of Ṭāwūs" after the battle that goes by the same name.

ʿUmar retained Abū Sabrah b. Abī Ruhm in al-Baṣrah for the [2551]
rest of the year. Then he employed al-Mughīrah b. Shuʿbah in the second year after ʿUtbah's death. Al-Mughīrah remained governor

465. This geographical name is not found in Yāqūt's *Muʿjam.* Does it refer to the spot where the seasonal fairs were held, and can it be considered as the center of al-Baḥrayn, just as Sūq al-Ahwāz is the center of al-Ahwāz?

466. According to Yāqūt, *Muʿjam,* I, 667, this is a village near Medina along the route to al-Baṣrah.

467. An allusion to Q. LXXXIII, 9, 20.

468. Rendition tentative. The preposition preceding al-Madā'in is *bi* "at," rather than a preposition we would have expected like *min* "from" or *ilā* "toward."

for the rest of that year and the next one, with no one rebelling against him during his governorate. He was endowed with integrity and he committed no outrage except that which occurred to him and Abū Bakrah.[469] Then ʿUmar employed Abū Mūsā to command al-Baṣrah, after which he was transferred to al-Kūfah. Next ʿUmar appointed ʿUmar b. Surāqah (al-Makhzūmī) governor (i.e. of al-Baṣrah) after which he was also transferred to al-Kūfah, while Abū Mūsā was sent back to al-Baṣrah to administer it for a second time.

In this year, I mean 17 (638), the conquests of Rāmhurmuz, al-Sūs and Tustar took place and, according to what Sayf transmits, al-Hurmuzān was taken prisoner in it.

The Conquest of Rāmhurmuz, al-Sūs, and Tustar

According to al-Sarī—Shuʿayb—Sayf—Muḥammad, Ṭalḥah, al-Muhallab and ʿAmr: Meanwhile, Yazdajird never gave up rousing the people of Fārs, regretting the fiascos for which they had been responsible. While he was in Marw, he wrote to them reminding them of the rancor he bore them and upbraiding them saying, "Have you resigned yourselves, people of Fārs, to the fact that the Arabs have wrested from you the Sawād and the adjacent region and al-Ahwāz! However, they will not be satisfied with that and will go on until they have descended upon you in your own country, and even inside your very houses." Thereupon they stirred and started exchanging letters with the people of al-Ahwāz. They concluded a pact and gave each other promises and pledges to help one another.

Rumors (of this) reached Ḥurqūṣ b. Zuhayr, while Jazʾ, Sulmā
[2552] and Ḥarmalah were notified by a rumor passed on by Ghālib and Kulayb. Sulmā and Ḥarmalah wrote to ʿUmar and to the Muslims in al-Baṣrah, the letter sent by those two being the first to arrive. Thereupon ʿUmar wrote to Saʿd saying, "Mount a large expedition to al-Ahwāz under the command of al-Nuʿmān b. Muqarrin. Hurry and dispatch Suwayd b. Muqarrin, ʿAbdallāh b. Dhī al-Sahmayn, Jarīr b. ʿAbdallāh al-Ḥimyarī and Jarīr b. ʿAbdallāh al-Bajalī and let them set up camp right across from where al-Hur-

469. See above, pp. 110–14.

muzān is presently, so that they can get a clear picture of what he is up to." Then 'Umar wrote to Abū Mūsā, "Send a large army into al-Ahwāz and put Sahl b. 'Adī, Suhayl's brother,[470] in charge, and dispatch al-Barā' b. Mālik, 'Āṣim b. 'Amr, Majza'ah b. Thawr, Ka'b b. Sūr, 'Arfajah b. Harthamah, Ḥudhayfah b. Miḥṣan, 'Abd al-Raḥmān b. Sahl and al-Ḥuṣayn b. Ma'bad with him. Abū Sabrah b. Abī Ruhm is to be commander-in-chief of the forces from al-Kūfah and al-Baṣrah; everybody who comes to him is to give him support." So al-Nu'mān b. Muqarrin marched out amidst his warriors from al-Kūfah, cutting right through the Sawād, until he crossed the Tigris near Maysān. Then he traveled over dry land to al-Ahwāz on mules with horses at their sides, until he came to Nahr Tīrā. He passed through it and then through Manādhir from where he passed on to Sūq al-Ahwāz. He left Ḥurqūs, Sulmā and Ḥarmalah behind and made his way to al-Hurmuzān who, at the time, was in Rāmhurmuz.

When al-Hurmuzān heard that al-Nu'mān was heading toward him, he hastened to organize a counterattack against him, hoping he would cut short (the other's) offensive. Al-Hurmuzān had been anxious to enlist the help of the people of Fārs. They had come to him and the first units of their reinforcements had reached Tustar. Al-Nu'mān and al-Hurmuzān came face to face in Arbuk and fierce fighting broke out. Then God routed al-Hurmuzān for [2553]
al-Nu'mān. The former vacated Rāmhurmuz and left it to go to Tustar. Al-Nu'mān moved out of the Arbuk area until he arrived at Rāmhurmuz. Then he went up to Īdhaj,[471] where Tīrawayh[472] offered him a peace agreement, which he accepted. Then he left Tīrawayh, returned to Rāmhurmuz and stayed there.

They said: When 'Umar had written to Sa'd and Abū Mūsā, and al-Nu'mān and Sahl had marched out, al-Nu'mān, amidst the troops from al-Kūfah, outstripped Sahl with his forces from al-Baṣrah and drove out al-Hurmuzān (i.e. from Rāmhurmuz). Amidst his men from al-Baṣrah, Sahl went on until they arrived at Sūq al-Ahwāz through which they wanted to get to Rāmhurmuz.

---

470. In a note in the apparatus, it is suggested that it was Ṭabarī himself who identified this Sahl as a brother of Suhayl mentioned above on pp. 80, 87.

471. This is the name of the district between al-Ahwāz and Iṣbahān, see Yāqūt, *Mu'jam*, I, 416–17. See also *EI*[2] s.v. *Īdhadj* (Bosworth).

472. The name of the local Persian chief.

While they were in Sūq al-Ahwāz, the rumor about the battle at Rāmhurmuz reached them. The news came that al-Hurmuzān had withdrawn to Tustar. So Sahl and his men left Sūq al-Ahwāz, taking a direct route from Sūq al-Ahwāz to Tustar. Also al-Nu'mān headed from Rāmhurmuz in the direction of Tustar, and Sulmā, Ḥarmalah, Ḥurqūṣ and Jaz' set out too. All of these descended together on Tustar, with al-Nu'mān commanding the forces from al-Kūfah, directly supported[473] by those from al-Baṣrah.

In Tustar, al-Hurmuzān, together with his forces from Fārs, al-Jibāl and al-Ahwāz, held out in trenches. The Arab commanders wrote about this to 'Umar, and Abū Sabrah asked him for reinforcements. So 'Umar sent them Abū Mūsā, who set out in their direction. Thus we see the people of al-Kūfah commanded by al-Nu'mān, those of al-Baṣrah under Abū Mūsā, while Abū Sabrah was in charge of both contingents together. The Muslims besieged the Persians for months and killed many of them. From the day the siege began until the time God conquered Tustar for the Muslims, al-Barā' b. Mālik[474] killed one hundred adversaries, in
[2554] addition to those he slew on other occasions. Among a number of Baṣrans, Majza'ah b. Thawr, Ka'b b. Sūr and Abū Tamīmah killed similar numbers of enemy soldiers. Among the Kūfans there were also some who killed many enemies, for example, Ḥabīb b. Qurrah, Rib'ī b. 'Āmir and 'Āmir b. 'Abd al-Aswad. Moreover, during that siege there were a number of enemies wounded that have to be added to the numbers killed by them.

During the siege of Tustar, the unbelievers made eighty sorties against the besiegers, beating them off one time, but being driven back another. This continued until, on the day of the last sally, when bitter fighting had broken out, the Muslims said (sc. to al-Barā'), "Barā', beseech your Lord that He rout them for us." So al-Barā' prayed, "Drive them away from us, my God, and let me die a martyr's death."

He said: Then they put the enemy to flight until they drove them into their trenches, whereupon they dived after them. The

473. *Mutasānid* means either "assisting" or "everyone under his own banner," see Lane, 1443 f.

474. He is noted for an allegedly glorious military career, see Ibn Ḥajar, *Iṣābah*, I, 279–82.

enemy fled back to the city. Then the Muslims laid a cordon around it. While they were thus engaged, with the Persian fighters cramming the city, their military efforts wearing them down, a man came to al-Nuʿmān who asked that his life be spared; in exchange he would show the Muslims an entrance into the city via which the Persians could be attacked. (What happened in actual fact was that) an arrow had been shot that landed in the vicinity of Abū Mūsā. (Fastened to it was a message that read,) "I shall put complete trust in you; I ask you to spare my life. In exchange I shall show you a passageway via which you can enter the city. Its conquest may be achieved through this." The Muslims were willing to grant him immunity (which they promised him in a message also shot) with an arrow. Then another arrow was shot in their direction (with a message attached to it that) read, "Attack via the outlet of the water,[475] then you will con- [2555]
quer the city." So he incited and roused (them) in this matter. Then, in answer to his summons, ʿĀmir b. ʿAbd Qays, Kaʿb b. Sūr, Majza'ah b. Thawr, Ḥasakah al-Ḥabaṭī and a large number of other warriors were dispatched to him. They set out for that particular spot in the night. When that man approached him too, al-Nuʿmān charged his companions Suwayd b. al-Mathʿabah, Warqāʿ b. al-Ḥārith, Bishr b. Rabīʿah al-Khathʿamī, Nāfiʿ b. Zayd al-Ḥimyarī and ʿAbdallāh b. Bishr al-Hilālī to go and join him. So they too set out with many warriors and they met with those from al-Baṣrah at that water outlet. Meanwhile, Suwayd and ʿAbdallāh b. Bishr had entered the outlet followed[476] by the men from the one and the other group.

In the end, when they had assembled in it, while the rest of the warriors outside the city walls were ready to pounce, those inside shouted, "God is great." The Muslims outside also shouted, "God is great," whereupon the gates of the city were thrown open and a sword fight broke out in them. They dispatched every enemy fighter and al-Hurmuzān took refuge in the citadel. Those who had entered the city through the water outlet encircled him in the citadel and when they spotted him and advanced upon him,

475. See Appendix II for a description and a plan of the situation as it was at the beginning of this century.

476. I read an eighth form, *fa'ttabaʿahum*.

he said to them, "What do you want? Perhaps you realize that you and I cannot escape one another.[477] But I still have a quiver with one hundred arrows and, by God, you will not lay a hand on me as long as I have still one arrow left. No arrow of mine will fail to find its target. What benefit is there in taking me prisoner, when I kill or wound one hundred of you first?" "What is it you want then?" they asked. He replied,"I would like to place my hand in yours,[478] leaving the decision with 'Umar to do with me as he
[2556] wants." "We agree," they answered, whereupon he threw down his bow and surrendered to them. Next they bound him securely.

The Muslims divided up what God had granted them as *fay*'. Each horseman's share amounted to three thousand (dirhams), while each footsoldier received one thousand.

The man who had shot the arrows drew attention to himself, and he and the man, who had come out of the city in person, came forward, saying, "Who will guarantee us the safety we requested for ourselves and those siding with us?" "Who sided with you then?" the Muslims asked. They said, "Those who bolted their doors against al-Hurmuzān at the time you burst into the city." Then the Muslims granted them immunity.

During that night, many people of the Muslim forces were killed. Among those whom al-Hurmuzān killed personally were Majza'ah b. Thawr and al-Barā' b. Mālik.

They said: Abū Sabrah marched out of Tustar, taking the road to al-Sūs, in pursuit of those who had been defeated and who had fled in that direction. He took al-Nu'mān and Abū Mūsā with him and also al-Hurmuzān was brought along. Finally, they descended upon al-Sūs, the Muslims surrounded the city and wrote to that effect to 'Umar. 'Umar then wrote to 'Umar b. Surāqah that he was to travel to Medina, and he wrote to Abū Mūsā, ordering him to return to al-Baṣrah. In all, he reinstated Abū Mūsā as governor of al-Baṣrah three times in that same year and 'Umar (b. Surāqah) twice. Then 'Umar wrote to Zirr b. 'Abdallāh b. Kulayb al-Fuqaymī to go to Jundaysābūr. Zirr obeyed and arrived there. Abū Mūsā left for al-Baṣrah after he had stayed where he was, waiting for 'Umar's reply. 'Umar put al-Aswad b. Rabī'ah, one of the Banū

477. Literally, the text reads "perhaps you see the straits I and you are in."
478. That is, "I want to surrender."

Rabīʿah b. Mālik, who had the honorific of al-Muqtarib,[479] in charge of the forces in al-Baṣrah. This al-Aswad, as well as Zirr, had been Companions of the Messenger of God. In actual fact, [2557]
they were Muhājirs. In the past this al-Aswad had called upon the Messenger of God saying, "I have come in order to draw nearer to God by associating with you." So the Prophet named him al-Muqtarib.[480] Zirr, too, had once called upon the Messenger of God and said to him, "My clan has died out, but our brothers are numerous; please pray God that He bless us." So the Prophet said, "God, restore Zirr's tribe," whereupon their ranks were indeed filled up again.

Abū Sabrah dispatched a delegation (to Medina) among whom were Anas b. Mālik and al-Aḥnaf b. Qays, and he sent al-Hurmuzān with them. They arrived in al-Baṣrah in the company of Abū Mūsā; then they (alone) set out for Medina. When they were about to enter the city, they arrayed al-Hurmuzān in his own finery, dressing him in his brocaded garment stitched through with gold thread. On his head they placed a crown that was called al-Ādhīn[481] and that was encrusted with rubies. They put on his jewelry so that ʿUmar and the Muslims would see him in his regalia. Then they paraded him in front of the people on their way to ʿUmar's house. But they did not find him there, so they inquired after his whereabouts. They were told, "Just now he was sitting in the mosque to receive a delegation that had come to him from al-Kūfah."

So they left to look for him in the mosque, but they did not find him there either. When leaving, they passed by some local boys who were at play and who asked them, "What are you walking in and out for? If you want to speak to the Commander of the Faithful, he is asleep in the right part of the mosque with his cloak folded under his head for a pillow." ʿUmar had sat there to receive the delegation from the inhabitants of al-Kūfah dressed in a hooded cloak.[482] When he had finished talking to them and they had risen from the audience and left him alone, he took off his

479. See further down.
480. That means "he who draws near."
481. If the reading is correct, this is a Persian word meaning "ornament."
482. In Arabic *burnus*, the English "burnoose" or "burnous."

cloak, folded it to make a pillow and went to sleep. So the people from al-Baṣrah, together with the bystanders, went to look for him. Then, when they spotted ʿUmar, they sat down at a little distance from him. No one else, asleep or awake, was in the
[2558] mosque (at that time). His whip was dangling from his hand. Al-Hurmuzān asked, "Where is ʿUmar?" "There he is," they said, whereupon they gave a sign to the people to keep quiet. Heeding their order, al-Hurmuzān nonetheless asked,[483] "But where are his guards and attendants?" "He has neither," they answered, "nor clerks, nor a chancellery for that matter." "Then he must be a prophet," al-Hurmuzān exclaimed. "No, he is not, but he does the things prophets do," was the reply.

Meanwhile, the number of onlookers had greatly increased and ʿUmar awoke because of the din that they made. He sat upright, spotted al-Hurmuzān and asked, "Is that man al-Hurmuzān?" "Yes," was the answer. ʿUmar looked closely at him and at what he was wearing, and then he said, "I seek my refuge with God from Hellfire and Him I ask for succor. Praise be to God," he went on, "who has humbled this man and his followers through Islam. Hold on to this religion, my fellow Muslims, and be guided by the guidance that your Prophet has given you. Let this material world not make you reckless, for it is a treacherous world." Then the delegation said, "This is the king of al-Ahwāz, speak to him." "No," ʿUmar answered, "not as long as there remains a single item of finery on his body."

So they stripped him of everything he was dressed up in apart from some piece of clothing that covered his nakedness and they made him put on a coarse garment. Then ʿUmar said, "Hey, Hurmuzān, how do you look now upon the evil consequences of your perfidy and the outcome of God's command?" Al-Hurmuzān replied, "In the days before Islam, ʿUmar, God left things between us and you as they were, so we had the upper hand over you, since He was neither with us nor with you. But when He took your side, you gained the upper hand over us." To this ʿUmar replied,

483. Although this is not borne out by the manuscripts, reading *wa-mā aṣghā al-Hurmuzān*, instead of *wa-aṣghā al-Hurmuzān* as Prym has it, would have given a better text: "Not heeding their order, al-Hurmuzān said . . ."

"You only succeeded in defeating us in the days before Islam because you were united, whereas we were divided. But," ʿUmar continued, "what is your excuse or what arguments can you adduce in your defense for going to war against us time after time?"

"I fear that you will kill me before I have told you," al-Hurmuzān answered. "No, do not be afraid," ʿUmar assured him. [2559]
Then, when al-Hurmuzān had asked for something to drink, he was brought water in a primitive cup. "Even if I were to die of thirst, I could not possibly drink from a cup like this," he cried. So he was brought some water in a vessel he approved of. But then his hand began to tremble and he said, "I am afraid that I will be killed while I am drinking." "No harm will come to you," ʿUmar said, "until you have drunk it." Hereupon al-Hurmuzān spilled the water by turning the vessel upside down. "Give him some more," ʿUmar ordered, "so that he will not be bothered by thirst when the time of his execution has come."[484]

Then al-Hurmuzān spoke, "I do not need water; what I want is to ask that you grant me immunity." "I shall certainly kill you," shouted ʿUmar, but al-Hurmuzān cut him short and said, "But you have already granted me immunity." "You lie," roared ʿUmar, but Anas (b. Mālik) intervened and said, "He is right, Commander of the Faithful, you have indeed granted him safety." "Woe unto you, Anas," said ʿUmar to him, "should I grant immunity to the killer of Majza'ah and al-Barā'? By God, think of a subterfuge or I shall surely chastise you!"

But Anas maintained, "You did tell him that no harm would come to him before he had told you what you asked him and you also told him that no harm would come to him until he had drunk the water." Then all those who were standing around ʿUmar joined in, telling him the same thing. ʿUmar approached al-Hurmuzān and said, "You have made a fool of me and, by God, I shall not be hoodwinked by anyone who is not a Muslim."[485] So al-

484. Literally, this sentence reads "Give him some more and do not heap death and thirst upon him together."

485. Contrary to the general rule, we find here a verb VII with the passive meaning "to be cheated," followed by what seems to be the agent introduced by the preposition *li.* This phenomenon is attested also in W. Fischer, *Grammatik des klassischen arabisch,* Wiesbaden, 1972, 98, 138.

Hurmuzān embraced Islam and ʿUmar assigned him a stipend of two thousand (dirhams) and permitted him to settle in Medina.

According to al-Sarī—Shuʿayb—Sayf—Abū Sufyān Ṭalḥah b.
[2560] ʿAbd al-Raḥmān—Ibn ʿĪsā: The day al-Hurmuzān was brought before ʿUmar the translator was al-Mughīrah b. Shuʿbah. (He did all the translating) until the official translator arrived. Al-Mughīrah had been learning some Persian, so ʿUmar ordered him, "Ask him: from what region are you?" whereupon al-Mughīrah said, *"Az kudhām ardīʾī?"*[486] "I am a Mihrijānī," al-Hurmuzān replied. ʿUmar summoned him to adduce arguments in his own defense. "Shall I speak as someone who will live, or as someone who is about to die?" he asked. "No," ʿUmar said, "speak as someone who will live." "You have granted me immunity in that case!" al-Hurmuzān exclaimed.

Then ʿUmar said, "You have played a trick on me and, in wartime, it is for the victim of the trickery used to decide in matters of life and death of the trickster. No, by God, I shall not grant you safety until you have embraced Islam." At that moment, al-Hurmuzān was certain that he had to choose between death and Islam. So he chose the latter and ʿUmar duly assigned two thousand dirhams annually from the treasury to him, allowing him to settle in Medina. Then he addressed al-Mughīrah saying, "I see that you are not at all good at speaking Persian. None of you speaks it well enough without simulating, but he who simulates will betray himself(?). Therefore, be on your guard against this language, for it may devitalize our Arabic language." Then Zayd (b. Thābit)[487] came along and talked to al-Hurmuzān, after which he told ʿUmar what the Persian had said, and he also informed the latter about what ʿUmar had said.

According to al-Sarī—Shuʿayb—Sayf—Muḥammad, Ṭalḥah and ʿAmr—al-Shaʿbī . . . (and Sayf)[488]—Sufyān (b. Ḥusayn b. al-Ḥasan

---

486. This means, "from what region are you?"

487. This Zayd was reputedly famed for his knack for languages. He is reported to have had a working knowledge of Hebrew and Aramaic. He is listed among the Prophet's trusted Companions who allegedly recorded the Qurʾān as it was revealed, and he is also said to have been a legal expert, particularly skilled in the laws of inheritance. See Ibn Ḥajar, *Iṣābah*, II, 592–5.

488. The text reads as if al-Shaʿbī, as well as a certain Sufyān (whom De Goeje identified in the index as al-Thawrī), had both been pupils of al-Ḥasan. But that

al-Wāsiṭī)—al-Ḥasan (al-Baṣrī): ʿUmar said to the delegation (from al-Baṣrah), "Have the Muslims perhaps done harm to the people living under their protection? Or have they perhaps done things to them that caused them to commence hostilities against you?" "No," they answered, "we only know that we acted in good faith and with decency." ʿUmar asked, "Then how did their revolt come about?" But after questioning them, he did not receive any answer from anyone that took away his doubt or through which he gained insight into the situation they described. Only what al-Aḥnaf (told him helped ʿUmar to form a clear picture, for he) said:

"Commander of the Faithful, I shall enlighten you. You forbade [2561]
us to spread out farther into Persian territory, and you ordered us to stay within the borders of the region that we have under our control. However, the king of the Persians is still alive among them, and they will therefore not cease to contend with us for control of the region, as long as their king is among them. Two kings can never govern simultaneously and agree; the one will inevitably oust the other. I have come to realize that we made one conquest after another solely because of their continuous revolts. It is their king who incites them, and this will always be his line of action until you give us permission to venture out into their land so that we separate him from his subjects and expel him from his kingdom by divesting him of his might and authority.[489] Only then will the hope of the Persians be crushed and will they capitulate."

"By God, you have given me a believable picture, and you have explained the situation to me as it is in reality," ʿUmar said. Then he looked into what they were in need of and sent them forth. Next a letter came to ʿUmar informing him of the assembling of the Persians at Nihāwand and of how the people of Mihrijān Qədhaq and those of the districts of al-Ahwāz gravitated toward the point of view and the erstwhile ambitions of al-Hurmuzān. That was what prompted ʿUmar to give the Muslims permission to venture out into Persian territory.

---

solution results in a chronological anomaly. This is clearly a case of an *isnād* ending in two different strains, one with al-Shaʿbī and one with al-Ḥasan al-Baṣrī as oldest authority.

489. For the way in which religious and secular authority were combined in Sasanian kingship, see Morony, *Iraq*, 28–31.

The Conquest of al-Sūs

The historians have different accounts of the conquest of al-Sūs. According to Abū Zayd—al-Madā'inī:[490] When those defeated at Jalūlā' finally reached Yazdajird, who was in Ḥulwān at the time, he summoned his court and the Priest[491] to him and said, "Every time our warriors encounter an enemy force, they suffer defeat at their hands. What do you think we should do?" The Priest answered, "We are of the opinion that you should leave and settle in Iṣṭakhr, for that is the center of the kingdom. Furthermore, keep your treasures with you, and send the soldiers away." Yazdajird
[2562] took his advice and traveled to Iṣbahān. He summoned Siyāh[492] and dispatched him with three hundred men, including seventy Persian aristocrats, with the order to crimp from every village through which they passed as many men as he liked. Siyāh departed, followed by Yazdajird. They finally arrived at Iṣṭakhr, just when Abū Mūsā was laying siege to al-Sūs. So Yazdajird sent Siyāh to al-Sūs and al-Hurmuzān to Tustar. Siyāh then arrived at al-Kalbāniyyah.[493]

Meanwhile, the news of what had happened at Jalūlā' and that Yazdajird had fled to Iṣṭakhr had reached the people of al-Sūs, so they asked Abū Mūsā al-Ash'arī for peace. He complied with their request and then he set out for Rāmhurmuz, while Siyāh was still in al-Kalbāniyyah, the military successes of the Muslims weighing him down.[494] He stayed put until Abū Mūsā set out for Tustar. Only then did Siyāh move to take up a position between Rāmhurmuz and Tustar. He stayed there until 'Ammār b. Yāsir was about to step onto the scene.[495]

At this juncture, Siyāh summoned the chiefs who had left Iṣbahān with him, and said to them, "You remember that we used to

490. He is the famous historian 'Alī b. Muḥammad al-Madā'inī, who died in 235 (850). Precious few of his numerous works have been made available in printed editions, see *GAS*, I, 314–15.

491. In Persian *mōbadh*. For his position at the Sasanian court, see Morony, *Iraq*, 281–2; Christensen, *L'Iran*, 112–13.

492. Siyāh al-Uswārī was the chief of the Asāwirah, Persian nobles first mentioned above on p. 2485 and n. 147; see Morony, *Iraq*, 198.

493. This is the way De Goeje reads this place name and not al-Kaltāniyyah, as Yāqūt, *Mu'jam*, IV, 299, lists it.

494. Or ". . . scaring him."

495. See p. 64 above.

talk about these invaders as people who would bring misery and suffering, who would overpower our kingdom and who would have their animals shit all over the courtyards of Iṣṭakhr and its royal pavilions, even tying up their horses in its orchards. They have subjugated our territory as you have seen, never encountering an armed force without defeating it, never stopping at a stronghold without conquering it. Look for yourselves!" "We concur with what you have said," they answered. Then Siyāh went on, "Let everyone of you protect me with his servants and dependents, for I think we should go over to them and embrace their religion."

They sent Shīrawayh with ten of the Asāwirah to Abū Mūsā to convey the conditions upon which they would embrace Islam. So Shīrawayh approached Abū Mūsā and said to him, "We have [2563]
developed a liking for your religion. We will become Muslims in the understanding that we will fight against Persians on your side, but not against Arab tribes.[496] If any tribesman engages us in a struggle, you will defend us against him; we settle where we want, mingling with those of you whom we want. You will assign us to the ranks of those with maximum stipends,[497] and the Commander (of the Faithful), who is more elevated in rank than you, will personally enter into a pact with us on these conditions."

"No," Abū Mūsā countered, "you will have exactly the same rights and duties as we have," to which they replied, "We do not agree." Then Abū Mūsā wrote to ʿUmar b. al-Khaṭṭāb who, in turn, wrote back to Abū Mūsā, "Give them what they have asked you," whereupon Abū Mūsā told them this by letter. Thus they accepted Islam and participated with Abū Mūsā in the siege of Tustar, but he saw no application or military efforts on their part.[498] Then he turned to Siyāh with the words, "You one-eyed good-for-nothing, you and your comrades do not comport yourselves as we thought you were capable of." "Yes, but we are not as attached to your religion as you are;" Siyāh replied, "we lack

496. The parallel passage in Balādhurī, 372 f., shows many textual similarities to this account of al-Madā'inī. In Balādhurī, this last sentence is worded in clearer language "we will not participate in intertribal warfare."

497. That is how Hinds, "Alignments," 354, interprets *sharaf al-ʿaṭā'*.

498. For this connotation of *nikāyah,* see Lane, 3038.

the enthusiasm you have and, living among you, we have no wives to protect, while you have not assigned the most generous stipends to us (i.e. as we stipulated). And whereas we have weapons and animals, you face the enemy not even wearing helmets!"

Abū Mūsā wrote about this incident to ʿUmar, who duly replied, "Assign to them the highest possible stipends according to their military record, in fact the largest amount any Arab tribesman is paid." So Abū Mūsā decided that one hundred of the Asāwirah were to receive stipends of two thousand (dirhams), while six of them were even given two thousand five hundred: Siyāh, Khusraw—he was the one who had the nickname Miq-
[2564] lāṣ[499]—Shahriyār, Shahrawayh, Shīrawayh and Afrūdhīn. A poet recited the following verse (in *ṭawīl*):[500]

When ʿUmar discovered the extent of their valor
and had been enlightened about their exploits,
He assigned them two thousand, whereas he had given
to ʿAkk and to Ḥimyar[501] no more than three hundred!

Al-Madā'inī said: One day, they laid siege to a fortress in Fārs. At the end of the night Siyāh, dressed in Persian attire, stole away (from the camp of the Muslims) and threw himself on the ground just outside the fortress with his garments streaked with blood. When the people in the fortress awoke in the morning, they saw the prone figure of a man, dressed as they were, so they thought that he was one of them whom they had lost (in a previous battle). They opened the gate of the fortress in order to bring the body inside. Suddenly, he jumped up and began to fight them. In the end they abandoned the gate of the fortress and fled. Thus Siyāh

499. This is the word for a camel that fattens in summer and slims in winter. In his youth the ʿAbbāsid caliph al-Manṣūr was given this nickname too, see Dozy, *Supplément*, II, 395.

500. For an irregularity in the meter, see Appendix I.

501. For more on these South Arabian tribes, see *EI*², s.v. *ʿAkk* (Caskel) and Kaḥḥālah, I, 305–6. Concerning the figures two thousand and three hundred, Puin, 173 ff., has some more information on these. Although the amounts vary in different reports, a stipend of two thousand had been the usual amount assigned to veterans of al-Qādisiyyah. The granting of the same amount to Persians may have caused some bitterness or shock. Three hundred has been mentioned as the amount assigned to the third immigration wave of *rawādif*.

conquered it singlehandedly and the Muslims marched in. Other people say that Siyāh performed this deed at Tustar.

On another occasion, they laid siege to a fortress. Khusraw went forth and moved close to it. A man looking down on him from the parapet spoke to him, whereupon Khusraw shot an arrow at him and killed him.

As for Sayf's account, according to al-Sarī—Shuʿayb—Sayf—Muḥammad, Ṭalḥah, ʿAmr and Dithār Abū ʿUmar—Abū ʿUthmān: When Abū Sabrah, amid his warriors, descended upon al-Sūs and the Muslims had surrounded it under the command of al-Hurmuzān's brother, Shahriyār, they engaged the Persians several times in fights, during which the forces from al-Sūs made casualties among the Muslims. One day, the monks and clerics,[502] looking down upon them from above, said to them, "Hey, you Arabs, among the things our scholars and ancestors have taught us is the story that no one will ever conquer al-Sūs but the Antichrist, or people who have the Antichrist in their midst.[503] If he is [2565]
among you, you will conquer this city, but if he is not, then you might as well save yourselves the trouble of besieging us."

News of the plight of Abū Mūsā reached al-Baṣrah. In lieu of Abū Mūsā, who was laying siege to al-Sūs, al-Muqtarib had been put in charge of the people of al-Baṣrah. Meanwhile, the Persians assembled at Nihāwand. At the head of the people of al-Kūfah, al-Nuʿmān was participating in the siege of al-Sūs with Abū Sabrah, while Zirr, on his part, was closing in on the enemy at Nihāwand. He issued the order to those left behind in al-Kūfah to march under the leadership of Ḥudhayfah and instructed them to join him at Nihāwand. In the meantime, al-Nuʿmān was also preparing himself to march upon Nihāwand, but then he decided to go it alone and, before departing from al-Sūs, he engaged the enemy in combat. Then the monks and the clerics returned (to the battlements) and looked down upon the Muslims, shouting, "Hey, you Arabs, do not bother, for no one will conquer this fortress but the

502. The two Arabic terms used, *ruhbān* and *qissīsūn*, unmistakably point to Christians. See Morony, *Iraq*, ch. 12, for a great deal of material on the Christians under the Sasanids.

503. For more on this enigmatic figure, see *EI²*, s.v. *Dadjdjāl* (Abel).

Antichrist, or forces that have the Antichrist in their midst." Thus they shouted at the Muslims, greatly enraging them. (At the time) Ṣāfī b. Ṣayyād was with al-Nuʿmān among his cavalry. The Muslims attacked the enemy with all their forces, saying, "We will fight them before we withdraw." For Abū Mūsā had not yet pulled out. Then Ṣāfī, furious as he was, strode to the gate of al-Sūs and, kicking it with his foot, shouted. "Open up!" And then it blew open![504] The chains snapped, the locks broke and the other gates were opened too. The Muslims stormed inside and the unbelievers surrendered, stretching out their hands, shouting, "Peace, peace," while trying to grasp the hands of their conquerors. These agreed to peace after[505] they had entered the city by force. They divided everything they found into equal portions before they granted them the peace treaty, and then they dispersed.

Al-Nuʿmān pulled out of al-Ahwāz among his Kūfan troops.
[2566] Finally, he arrived at Māh. Abū Sabrah dispatched al-Muqtarib, who set out until he arrived at Jundaysābūr together with Zirr. After entering Māh, al-Nuʿmān stayed there, until the forces from al-Kūfah joined him there. Then he rode with them to the enemy at Nihāwand. When the conquest of al-Sūs had been completed, Ṣāfī returned to Medina where he stayed until he died.

According to al-Sarī—Shuʿayb—Sayf—ʿAṭiyyah—the one who reported on the conquest of al-Sūs: Someone said to Abū Sabrah, "Here are the remains of Daniel which are buried in this city." "What concern is that of ours?" Abū Sabrah asked and he left the remains there under the supervision of the local people.

ʿAṭiyyah continued with the same *isnād:* Daniel had stayed on in the coastal regions of Fārs after Nebuchadnezzar's death.[506] Without ever having met anyone from those among whom he

504. As two manuscripts have it, I read *fa-ṭāra,* instead of *baẓāri,* which does not seem to convey more than an obscenity (*baẓr* means "clitoris").

505. In the Arabic, *baʿda mā;* since this passage is meant to convey magnanimity on the part of the Muslims, it is perhaps better to translate "*although* they had entered the city by force"; according to the policies of the day, an enemy who had tried to resist being conquered was not entitled to a peace treaty. Translating *baʿda mā* by "although" seems to be attested in Lane, 225, middle column, 9 lines from the bottom.

506. See II Kings, xxiv, and the Book of Daniel.

lived who had voluntarily embraced Islam,[507] he wanted, when the time of his death had come, to preserve the book of God from those who had never wanted to listen to him or accept his teaching and he wanted to entrust it to his Lord. He called his son and said, "Go to the seashore and cast this book into the sea." The lad took it, clasped it to his breast and disappeared for as long as it would have taken him to go (to the shore) and return. He said to his father, "I have done it." The father asked, "And what did the sea do when the book fell into it?" "I did not see it do anything," the son replied. Then the father burst out angrily and said, "By God, you have not done as I ordered." So once more the lad left his father's house, but he did exactly as he had done before, and he went back saying, "I have done it." How did the sea react when it fell into it?" Daniel asked. "It heaved and surged," was the answer. Then the father became even more furious than the first [2567]
time and he said, "By God, you have still not done as I ordered." He adjured his son a third time to go and cast the book into the sea. So the boy left for the seashore and, once there, flung the book into the sea. The sea retreated so that the bottom became exposed. Then the earth split and an abyss of light appeared into which the book vanished. The earth again closed over it and the waters mingled over the bottom. When the son returned for the third time, his father asked him what he had seen. He told him, whereupon the father exclaimed, "Now you have spoken the truth." Daniel died at al-Sūs and there, near his tomb, people used to pray for rain.

When the Muslims conquered the city, Daniel's remains were brought to them, but they left them in the permanent care of the local people. Later, when Abū Sabrah had departed from them and gone to Jundaysābūr, Abū Mūsā came and stayed in al-Sūs. He wrote to ʿUmar about Daniel's grave. ʿUmar wrote back and ordered him to hide it. So Abū Mūsā had the body wrapped in shrouds and the Muslims buried it. Meanwhile, Abū Mūsā wrote to ʿUmar saying that on the body they had found a signet ring that

507. This anachronism of identifying the religion preached by pre-Muḥammadan prophets as Islam is a well-known and frequent feature in stories dealing with those prophets.

they had taken from it. "Return the signet ring to the body," 'Umar wrote back. In the stone of that ring there was the picture of a man between two lions.[508]

In this year, I mean the year 17 (638), the peace treaty of the Muslims with the inhabitants of Jundaysābūr was concluded.

What Happened between the Muslims and the Inhabitants of Jundaysābūr

According to al-Sarī—Shu'ayb—Sayf—Muḥammad, Ṭalḥah, Abū[509] 'Amr, Abū Sufyān and al-Muhallab: When Abū Sabrah had finished what he had to do in al-Sūs, he left with his army and marched until he arrived at Jundaysābūr, where Zirr b. 'Abdallāh b. Kulayb was besieging them. They stayed there, engaging the enemy mornings and evenings in combat and they constantly beset them until someone from the camp of the Muslims shot an arrow in their direction with the message that safety would be granted to them. The conquest of Jundaysābūr and that of Nihāwand took place in a
[2568] timespan of two months. Nothing surprised the Muslims more than the fact that at a certain moment the city's gates were opened. Out came the cattle, the markets emptied themselves and the inhabitants scattered in all directions. The Muslims sent a courier after them who had to ask them, "What has come over you?" They answered, "You have shot us an arrow carrying a message that safety would be granted to us. We have accepted this proposition and we have set aside the *jizā'* payments for you in the understanding that you will grant us protection." "But we did nothing of the sort," the Muslims said. "Nor do we lie," the inhabitants of Jundaysābūr countered. So the Muslims asked around among themselves, and then they came upon a slave, called Muknif, who was in actual fact of Jundaysābūri origin. It was he who had written them the message affixed to the arrow. So the Muslims said, "It was but a slave who sent this message." But they said, "We do not know your slaves from your freeborn; safety has been granted to us, so we have immunity

508. The Muslim version of the story of Daniel differs somewhat from that of the Old Testament. See *EI*[2] s.v. *Dāniyāl* (Vajda), and R. G. Khoury, *Les légendes prophétiques dans l'Islam*, Wiesbaden, 1978, 266–83.

509. This word *Abū* should in all probability be deleted, as Prym suggests.

now since we have accepted your proposition, and we have not changed our minds. But act in perfidy, if you want." Then the Muslims turned away and wrote about these events to ʿUmar, who duly replied, "God holds the keeping of promises in the highest esteem. As long as you hesitate, you will never be true to your word so that you fulfil your pledge. Grant them their immunity and keep your promises to them." So they fulfilled their promise to them and left them.

According to al-Sarī—Shuʿayb—Sayf—Muḥammad, Ṭalḥah, al-Muhallab and ʿAmr: ʿUmar allowed the Muslim forces to spread out into Persian territory in the year 17 (638), having finally adopted this strategy from al-Aḥnaf b. Qays, whom he knew for his virtue and sincerity. He separated commanders and their armed contingents from one another, putting the commanders in charge of the inhabitants of al-Baṣrah as well as others over al-Kūfah, the former as well as the latter implementing what ʿUmar (himself) had ordered. He gave them permission in the year 17 (638) to spread over Persian territory. So they wandered out in 18 (639). He ordered Abū Mūsā to march from al-Baṣrah to the borderland where the protection of al-Baṣrah ceased. Here he stayed until further notice. [2569]
ʿUmar sent the banners for those in command out with Suhayl b. ʿAdī, the confederate of the Banū ʿAbd al-Ashhal. So Suhayl arrived with the banners and he gave the banner of Khurāsān to al-Aḥnaf b. Qays, that of Ardashīr Khurrah[510] and Sābūr[511] to Mujāshiʿ b. Masʿūd al-Sulamī and the one of Iṣṭakhr to ʿUthmān b. Abī al-ʿĀṣ al-Thaqafī, the one of Fasā and Darābajird[512] to Sāriyah b. Zunaym al-Kinānī, and the banner of Kirmān[513] remaining with Suhayl b. ʿAdī himself. The banner of Sijistān Suhayl gave to ʿĀṣim b. ʿAmr, one of the Companions of the Prophet, and the one of Mukrān he handed to al-Ḥakam b. ʿUmayr al-Taghlibī.

They all marched out in the year 17 (638) and set up camp from where they could move out toward their respective districts. Their campaign was not an easy one until the beginning of the year 18 (639). Then ʿUmar reinforced them with fighters from al-

510. This is a district in Fārs of which Shīrāz is the capital, see Yāqūt, *Muʿjam*, I, 199, and Le Strange, *Lands*, 248.

511. Another district of Fārs, see *loc. cit.*

512. See *ibid.*, 290.

513. See *ibid.*, map VII, opposite 323.

Kūfah, sending ʿAbdallāh b. ʿAbdallāh b. ʿItbān to Suhayl b. ʿAdī, while he sent ʿAlqamah b. al-Naḍr, ʿAbdallāh b. Abī ʿUqayl, Ribʿī b. ʿĀmir and Ibn Umm Ghazāl to al-Aḥnaf. He also reinforced ʿĀṣim b. ʿAmr by sending him ʿAbdallāh b. ʿUmayr al-Ashjaʿī, and al-Ḥakam b. ʿUmayr he helped with Shihāb b. al-Mukhāriq al-Māzinī.

Some transmitters say: The conquests of al-Sūs and Rāmhurmuz, as well as the transfer of al-Hurmuzān from Tustar to ʿUmar, all took place in the year 20 (641).

In this year, I mean the year 17 (638), ʿUmar b. al-Khaṭṭāb led
[2570] the people on the pilgrimage. His administrator in Mecca was ʿAttāb b. Asīd; his official in Yemen was Yaʿlā b. Umayyah. He had put ʿUthmān b. Abī al-ʿĀṣ in charge of al-Yamāmah and al-Baḥrayn, in ʿUmān Ḥudhayfah b. Miḥṣan, and in Syria those whose names I have mentioned above. In charge of al-Kūfah and the surrounding territory was Saʿd b. Abī Waqqāṣ; Abū Qurrah was in charge of the judiciary there. In al-Baṣrah and the surrounding territory Abū Mūsā al-Ashʿarī was in command. Above I have mentioned the times when he was relieved from his function and when he was reinstated. Abū Maryam al-Ḥanafī is said to have been in charge of the judiciary of al-Kūfah. I have mentioned above who was in charge of al-Jazīrah and al-Mawṣil.

The Events of the Year 18

(January 12, 639–January 1, 640)

Ṭabarī said: In this year, I mean 18 (639), the people were afflicted by a severe famine and a drought of catastrophic proportions. This is the year that is called the Year of the Drought.[514]

According to Ibn Ḥumayd—Salamah—Muḥammad b. Isḥāq: Then the year 18 (639) began. This was the Year of the Drought in which the epidemic of ʿAmawās occurred, during which the people perished, one after the other.

According to Aḥmad b. Thābit al-Rāzī—Isḥāq b. ʿĪsā—Abū Maʿshar: The Drought was in the year 18 (639).

He continued: In this year the plague of ʿAmawās broke out.
According to al-Sarī—Shuʿayb—Sayf—al-Rabīʿ, Abū al-Mujālid, [2571]
Abū ʿUthmān and Abū Ḥārithah: Abū ʿUbaydah wrote to ʿUmar, "Several Muslims have taken to drinking wine. Among them are Ḍirār (b. al-Azwar al-Asadī) and Abū Jandal (b. Suhayl b. ʿAmr). We asked them about this, but they justified their act with a dictum, saying, "We have been given the choice, and so we have

514. In Arabic *ramādah;* see Lane, 1154, right column, for a catalogue of nuances this name evokes.

chosen."[515] Then someone said[516] to us, "(Do you not remember the verse) 'Will you refrain'?"[517] But that man did not forbid us to drink wine in so many words." Then 'Umar wrote to Abū 'Ubaydah, "This matter is purely between them and me. The Qur'ānic expression 'Will you refrain?' means nothing but 'Stop that practice.' " Then he assembled the people and they all agreed that those who had drunk wine should be given eighty lashes for it, and that they would be held accountable for a 'transgression.'[518] They also agreed that all those who adduced the same dictum to justify their wine drinking should be dealt with in the same manner. If anyone objected, he was to be killed.

'Umar wrote to Abū 'Ubaydah, "Summon all of them. If they claim that wine drinking is permissible, have them killed, and if they claim that it is forbidden, have them flogged with eighty stripes." So Abū 'Ubaydah sent for them and interrogated them in front of all the people. "It is forbidden," they answered. Thereupon he ordered that each one of them be given eighty lashes.[519] So the people who had sinned against this prohibition were to be punished[520] and they repented of their pigheadedness. Then 'Umar said, "People of Syria, may something unexpected occur among you!" whereupon the Drought broke out.

---

515. This dictum bears a close resemblance to an expression ascribed to the Prophet *innī khuyyirtu fa'khtartu*, see *Concordance*, II, 93, left column, when he was asked why he did not refuse to lead the prayer ritual at the grave site of an adversary, the leader of the *munāfiqūn*, 'Abdallāh b. Ubayy. See Wāqidī, III, 1068 ff.

516. The subject of "said" is not expressed. There is perhaps the implication that it was Abū 'Ubaydah, but the syntax of the sentence is too confused to infer this.

517. These are the final words of Q. V, 91; the whole verse reads in translation: "The devil only wants to sow animosity and hatred among you through wine and games of chance, and he wants to turn you away from mentioning God and from the prayer ritual; will you refrain?"

518. The Arabic word *fisq* developed into a technical term for "an act of disobedience against God." For more details, see *EI*[2], s.v. *Fāsiḳ* (Gardet).

519. Strictly speaking, the text says "he flogged them." From what follows, it will become clear that the culprits had the flogging postponed until their return from a campaign against the Byzantines.

520. The Arabic word used is the technical term *ḥadda* "to inflict a punishment detailed in the Qur'ān." For other Qur'ānic punishments, see *EI*[2], s.v. *ḥadd* (Schacht).

Al-Sarī—Shuʿayb—Sayf—ʿAbdallāh b. Shubrumah—al-Shaʿbī gave a similar account.

According to al-Sarī—Shuʿayb—Sayf—ʿUbaydallāh b. ʿUmar—Nāfiʿ: When the letter of Abū ʿUbaydah about Ḍirār and Abū Jandal had reached ʿUmar, he wrote back about the matter to Abū ʿUbaydah and he ordered him to summon them to appear in front [2572]
of the people and to ask them whether wine is forbidden or permissible. "And if they say forbidden, have them be given eighty lashes, and ask them to repent. But if they say permissible, have their heads chopped off!"

Abū ʿUbaydah summoned them to his presence and interrogated them. "No," they said, "wine is forbidden." So he ordered that they be flogged, whereupon they were ashamed and kept to their quarters. But on top of that, Abū Jandal was suffering from a diabolical whispering in his ear.[521] Abū ʿUbaydah wrote to ʿUmar, "Abū Jandal is ridden with fear, which cannot be allayed unless God grants him relief through you. Therefore, write to him and set his mind at rest."[522] So ʿUmar wrote to Abū Jandal and admonished him. This letter read as follows:

"From ʿUmar to Abū Jandal. God will not forgive His being associated with other gods, but He can show forgiveness to whomever He wants for lesser offenses. Repent therefore, raise your head, show yourself again and do not despair, for God says, 'O my servants who have committed an outrage against yourselves, do not despair of God's mercy, for God forgives all sins, He is merciful, compassionate.' "[523]

When Abū ʿUbaydah had read this letter to Abū Jandal, he cheered up again, beaming with happiness. ʿUmar wrote similar letters to the others, so they all showed themselves again. Then he wrote to the people in general, "Take good care of yourselves; he whose behavior is in need of correction, make him change his ways, but do not heap disgrace upon anyone, lest tribulations spread among you."

---

521. See Lane, 2939 f., for this rendition of *waswasa.*

522. The Arabic verb *dhakkara* is given in Lane as "to remind of what might soften the heart by the mention of rewards and punishments."

523. Q. XXXIX, 53.

Al-Sarī—Shuʿayb—Sayf—Muḥammad b. ʿAbdallāh—ʿAṭāʾ gave a similar account, except that there was no mention of ʿUmar writing to the people in general that they should not heap disgrace upon one another.

He[524] said: Those (who were to be punished for drinking wine) said, "The Byzantines are busily regrouping themselves. Let us
[2573] therefore attack them, for if God decrees martyrdom for us, then that will be our destiny, and if not, then you (sc. Abū ʿUbaydah,) will embark upon the line of action that ʿUmar wants." Thus Ḍirār b. al-Azwar died a martyr's death together with a number of men, but the others (found guilty of wine drinking) survived the campaign and were duly flogged. Whereupon Abū al-Zahrāʾ al-Qushayrī composed the following lines (in *ṭawīl*):

Have you never witnessed how fate strikes young men
who lack the ability to turn away death?
E'er patient, unruffled I was, until one day
I yielded, with all my friends dead, to the wine.
Then ʿUmar, our leader, poured all wine away,[525]
while bibbers were weeping around (empty) presses.

According to al-Sarī—Shuʿayb—Sayf—al-Rabīʿ b. al-Nuʿmān, Abū al-Mujālid Jarād b. ʿAmr, Abū ʿUthmān Yazīd b. Asīd al-Ghassānī and Abū Ḥārithah Muḥriz al-ʿAbshamī with their *isnād* and Muḥammad b. ʿAbdallāh—Kurayb: In the reign of ʿUmar the people in Medina and its surrounding territory were afflicted by a drought in which the world was awhirl with dust when the wind blew, as if it rained ashes. That is why this year was called the Year of the Drought.[526] ʿUmar swore an oath that he would not taste butter,[527] milk or meat, until the people found the world once more covered in herbage from the first rains. So he refrained

524. Presumably he is the transmitter Nāfiʿ, introduced on p. 153 above.

525. The text reads *ramāhā bi-ḥatfihā;* literally, this means "he threw the wine away . . . with its death." The word *ḥatf* is a dubious reading and does not seem to admit of a feasible rendering other than "with its deadly effect (on man)."

526. The word used here for "Drought" is *ramādah,* that for "ashes" *ramād(ah),* the former in actual fact being derived from the latter.

527. In Arabic *samn;* strictly speaking we should render this "clarified butter," "ghee," see *EI²*, s.v. *Ghidhāʾ* (Rodinson, II, 1057, right column, of the English edition).

from these until the people did see the world sprouting again from the first rains. Then a skin filled with butter was brought to the market and also a skin filled with milk, whereupon a servant of [2574] ʿUmar bought these skins for forty (dirhams) and brought them to ʿUmar saying, "Commander of the Faithful, God has honored your oath and added to your reward. These two skins, one filled with milk, the other with butter, were brought to the market, so I bought them for forty (dirhams)." But ʿUmar said, "You have spent too much on them; give the contents of both away in alms, for I loathe extravagance in my daily food. How can I show true concern for my subjects," he added, "if I am not smitten by what smites them?"

According to al-Sarī—Shuʿayb—Sayf—Sahl b. Yūsuf al-Salamī[528]—ʿAbd al-Raḥmān b. Kaʿb b. Mālik: This tribulation lasted all during the latter part of the year 17 (638) and the beginning of 18 (638–9). The Drought brought famine, which affected all the people in Medina and the surrounding territory, and spread so much death that the wild animals began to seek food in the settlements of human beings. People even started to slaughter their sheep but then, disgusted with the loathsome appearance of (the meat of) the animals, they would not eat it, although they were starving.

According to al-Sarī—Shuʿayb—Sayf—Sahl b. Yūsuf—ʿAbd al-Raḥmān b. Kaʿb: In this way the population was suffering while ʿUmar was too diffident[529] to approach the people of the garrison cities. One day, Bilāl b. al-Ḥārith al-Muzanī[530] went to ʿUmar, asked permission to enter his house, and said, "I am the emissary of the Messenger of God to you. Thus speaks the Messenger to you, "I have always known you as a resourceful[531] man and as someone who was always ready to act. What is the matter with

528. Not al-Sulamī; see M. Hinds, "Sayf b. ʿUmar's sources on Arabia," 7 and n. 17.

529. For this interpretation of *maḥṣūr*, see Lane, 582, right column, infra.

530. He was a leading spokesman of his tribe and one of its standard bearers. He was present at the battle of al-Qādisiyyah, see Wāqidī, I, 276.

531. For once I must disagree with De Goeje, who suggests in *Glossarium*, p. CDLXII, that the Arabic word used here (*kayyis*) has the meaning of "happy" or possibly "alert." Ullmann (in *WKAS*, I, 492 f.) does not seem to concur either. The same story is related a second time below.

you now?" ʿUmar asked, "When did you dream[532] this?" "Yesterday," was the answer.

Then ʿUmar left his house, had someone call the people to a congregational prayer ritual, and performed two *rakʿa*s with them. After that he stood up and said, "People, I swear to you by God, do you remember that I ever gave you an order that could have been deferred in favor of something better?" "No, by God,"
[2575] they shouted. "Bilāl b. al-Ḥārith," ʿUmar continued, "claims as much." "Bilāl is right," they cried, "ask God and the Muslims (in the garrison cities) for help." ʿUmar then sent a messenger to them after he had been hesitant to approach them. He said, "God is great; our suffering has reached its peak and has manifested itself fully. As a rule, people are not permitted to ask for help unless a catastrophe can be warded off from them by doing so." Then ʿUmar wrote to the commanders in the garrison cities, "Help the people of Medina and the surrounding territory, for their plight has reached its limit."

Next, he ordered the people to leave the prayer meeting for a supplication for rain ritual.[533] He himself left too, on foot, and he brought al-ʿAbbās[534] along with him. (Having arrived at the suitable spot,) ʿUmar delivered a sermon, a short one, then he performed the prayer ritual. After that he fell down upon his knees and prayed, "God, it is You whom we worship, and You we ask for succor.[535] God, forgive us, have mercy upon us, show us Your satisfaction with us." Then he left, and even before the people had reached their homesteads on their way back they had to wade through pools of water!

According to al-Sarī—Shuʿayb—Sayf—Mubashshir b. al-Fuḍayl—Jubayr b. Ṣakhr—ʿĀṣim b. ʿUmar b. al-Khaṭṭāb: For one whole year during ʿUmar's reign, the people suffered from drought and their resources dwindled. The members of a family of the Muzaynah Bedouins said to their chief, "We are near exhaustion. Slaughter a sheep for us." "But they have no meat on them!" the chief protested. However, they persisted until he slaughtered a

532. Messages from the Prophet, it is thought, are transmitted via dreams.

533. In Arabic *istisqā*ʾ, an ancient ritual dating back to the Jāhiliyyah, during which one prayed for rain, see EI^2, s.v. *Istisḳā*ʾ (Fahd).

534. Al-ʿAbbās was an uncle of the Prophet.

535. Q. I, 5.

sheep for them, which was nothing but skin over bleeding bones. "O Muḥammad," he shouted (in despair), whereupon he had a dream in which the Messenger of God came to him and said, "Announce that the rains are coming. Go to ʿUmar, give him my greetings and say to him, "I know you intimately, you are one [2576] who keeps his covenant and you vigorously watch your responsibilities, but, ʿUmar, be resourceful!"

So this chief left and journeyed until he reached the door of ʿUmar's homestead. He said to ʿUmar's servant, "Announce the arrival of the emissary of the Messenger of God." Then the servant went to ʿUmar and transmitted the message to him, whereupon ʿUmar was horror-struck and asked, "Do you think he is insane?" "No," said the servant. "Ask him to come in then," said ʿUmar. The man entered the house and related his story to ʿUmar. ʿUmar left the house, had someone call the people to assemble, climbed the pulpit and said, "I swear to you by him who has guided you to Islam, have you ever witnessed anything from me at which you looked askance?" "No, by God," they shouted, "but why do you ask?" So he told them and they understood the implication. But ʿUmar himself did not. Then they said, "The message implies that it has indeed taken you a long time to enact a supplication for rain ritual. Therefore, hold one with us now."

ʿUmar had someone announce among the people (that a supplication for rain ritual was going to be held). Then he stood up, delivered a sermon, a short one, next he concisely performed two *rakʿa*s and said, "Our allies were unable to help us, by God, our own strength and vigor were lacking, our own souls could not help us, but there is no vigor or strength except in You, O God. So give us rain, and give the people and their lands a new lease on life."

According to al-Sarī—Shuʿayb—Sayf—al-Rabīʿ b. al-Nuʿmān, Jarād Abū al-Mujālid, Abū ʿUthmān and Abū Ḥārithah, all of them—Rajāʾ (b. Ḥaywah); Abū ʿUthmān and Abū Ḥārithah added: According to ʿUbādah (b. Nusayy) and Khālid (b. Maʿdān)—ʿAbd al-Raḥmān b. Ghanm: ʿUmar wrote to the commanders of the garrison cities requesting them to help the people of Medina and the surrounding territory and asking them for supplies. The first to arrive in Medina amid four thousand camels loaded with foodstuffs was Abū ʿUbaydah b. al-Jarrāḥ. ʿUmar charged him with

the distribution thereof among the people who lived around Medina. After he had finished his task and had returned to ʿUmar, the
[2577] latter ordered that four thousand dirhams be given to Abū ʿUbaydah, who said, "Commander of the Faithful, I have no need of this. I only wanted to please God and to help in matters that pertain to Him, and this material world is of no concern to me." But ʿUmar said, "Take it, there is no harm in it since you did not ask for it." Abū ʿUbaydah remained adamant, whereupon ʿUmar repeated, "Take it, for I once took care of certain matters for the Messenger of God under similar circumstances, whereupon he said the same things to me as I said to you, and I answered in the same manner as you did me. But he pressed it upon me." Then Abū ʿUbaydah accepted the money and left for his province, gradually followed by his men. The people of the Ḥijāz were no longer in need of supplies and fully recuperated with the first rains.

They went on with the same *isnād:* Then in answer to ʿUmar's plea for help, there came a letter from ʿAmr b. al-ʿĀṣī which read, "At the time when the Messenger of God first received his mission, a waterway was dug to the Mediterranean that also has an outlet[536] into the Red Sea.[537] But the Byzantines and the Copts have made it unusable.[538] If you want the price of food in Medina to be on the level of that in Egypt, I shall excavate this latter waterway again and build bridges across it."[539] Then ʿUmar wrote to ʿAmr, "Carry out what you suggested and make haste with it." But the people of Miṣr[540] said to him, "Your *kharāj* is now easy to collect and your ruler is satisfied. However, when this work is finished, the paying of the *kharāj* will be discontinued." ʿAmr wrote this to ʿUmar mentioning that the restoring of this canal

536. This is a reference to a canal that the Romans had dug between Babylon (Bāb al-Yūn, near present-day Cairo) and the Mediterranean via the Bitter Lakes north of present-day Suez, see Vasiliev, *History*, I, 203, and also *EI*², s.v. *Baḥr al-Ḳulzum* (Becker); furthermore, Butler, 345–8; idem, *Babylon of Egypt*, 34–6; Jabartī, *Taʾrīkh muddat al-Faransīs bi-Miṣr*, Leiden, 1975, ed. tr. S. Moreh, 60/86.

537. Strictly speaking "the Gulf of Qulzum," an ancient town near present-day Suez.

538. Or ". . . have let it silt up (through long neglect)," as Butler (346) has it.

539. In Ibn ʿAbd al-Ḥakam, 162 ff, the story of ʿAmr reexcavating this canal is related in several versions with many details missing from Ṭabarī's account.

540. Miṣr is the name of Egypt and of a city, see n. 547 below.

might entail the discontinuation of payment of the *kharāj* of Miṣr and its ruination. But ʿUmar wrote back to him, saying, "Work at it and make haste. May God lay waste Miṣr for the sake of the prosperity and salvation of Medina." So ʿAmr applied himself to his task while in al-Qulzum. (Food) prices in Medina reached the level of those in Miṣr, which derived nothing but comfort from it. The inhabitants of Medina never saw anything like the drought again after it was over, until their trading route via the sea was cut off at the time of the murder of ʿUthmān. Then they became weak, poor and downtrodden.

Ṭabarī said: Al-Wāqidī has said that al-Raqqah, al-Ruhā' and [2578]
Ḥarrān were conquered in this year by ʿIyāḍ b. Ghanm and that ʿAyn al-Wardah was taken by ʿUmayr b. Saʿd, but in the foregoing I have already mentioned the accounts of those who disagree with him on this. Al-Wāqidī also says that ʿUmar transferred *al-Maqām*[541] to the spot in which it now lies in the month Dhū al-Ḥijjah of this year, whereas, before that, it used to be propped up[542] against the Kaʿbah itself. Furthermore, he mentioned that during the plague of ʿAmawās twenty-five thousand people died.

Ṭabarī said: Some historians say that in this year ʿUmar asked Shurayḥ b. al-Ḥārith al-Kindī[543] to take charge of the judiciary in al-Kūfah and Kaʿb b. Sūr al-Azdī in al-Baṣrah.

Ṭabarī went on: In this year it was ʿUmar who led the people on the pilgrimage, while his governors in the garrison cities were the same as those in the previous year, that is 17 (638).

---

541. *Al-Maqām* stands here for *Maqām Ibrāhīm*, a stone, allegedly already venerated in the Jāhiliyyah, on which Abraham is believed to have stood when he built the Kaʿbah. See *EI*², s.v. *Kaʿba* (Wensinck-Jomier).

542. The Arabic has *mulṣaq*. Other sources do not throw more light on exactly how the *Maqām* ended up close to, or against, the Kaʿbah, after having been washed away from its old place by a flood (Arabic *sayl*) nicknamed Umm Nahshal. See Azraqī, *Kitāb akhbār Makkah*, ed. Wüstenfeld, Leipzig, 1858, 275.

543. He was allegedly the most famous judge of early Islam, in charge of the judiciary for the incredibly long period of sixty years in al-Kūfah with one or seven years in al-Baṣrah. He is said to have died sometime between 72 (691) and 99 (718) at an equally incredibly advanced age. In Wakīʿ, *Quḍāt*, II, 189–402, there is a large number of judicial decisions ascribed to him. Schacht, *Origins*, 228 f doubts the historicity of Shurayḥ.

The Events of the Year 19

(January 2–December 20, 640)

Ṭabarī said: According to Aḥmad b. Thābit al-Rāzī—his authority—Isḥāq b. ʿĪsā—Abū Maʿshar: The conquest of Jalūlāʾ occurred in the year 19 (640) at the hands of Saʿd (b. Abī Waqqāṣ). Al-Wāqidī agrees. Ibn Isḥāq says that the conquest of al-Jazīrah, al-Ruhāʾ, Ḥarrān, Raʾs al-ʿAyn and Naṣībīn occurred in the year 19 (640).

Ṭabarī went on: In the foregoing we have mentioned the accounts of those who disagreed with them on this issue.

Abū Maʿshar said: In this year, I mean the year 19 (640), Qaysāriyyah was conquered, its governor was Muʿāwiyah b. Abī
[2579] Sufyān, all this according to Aḥmad b. Thābit al-Rāzī—his authority—Isḥāq b. ʿĪsā—Abū Maʿshar, and al-Wāqidī mentions the same details about this as Abū Maʿshar. As for Ibn Isḥāq, he says that the conquest of the Palestinian city Qaysāriyyah, the flight of Heraklius and the conquest of Egypt all took place in the year 20 (641), as related to me by Ibn Ḥumayd—Salamah—himself. But Sayf b. ʿUmar says that Qaysāriyyah and Egypt were conquered in 16 (637). The account of the conquest of Qaysāriyyah was given above[544] and I shall mention the account concerning Egypt and its conquest in the following, together with the ac-

544. Ṭabarī, I, 2397, translated in vol. XII of this series.

count of those who say that it was conquered in the year 20 (641) and the account of those who disagree on this date.

Ṭabarī said: In this year, I mean the year 19 (640), the Ḥarrat Laylā[545] was ablaze with fires, as al-Wāqidī has it. ʿUmar wanted to march out to it with his men,[546] but then he ordered the giving of alms, whereupon the fires went out.

Al-Wāqidī also says that al-Madāʾin and Jalūlāʾ were conquered in this year, but the accounts of those who disagree with him on this have been given above.

ʿUmar led the pilgrimage in this year. His governors and judges in the garrison cities were the same as in the year 18 (639).

---

545. A *ḥarrah* is a stretch of basalt desert that owes its origin to subterranean volcanic action. The Ḥarrat Laylā is such a volcanic field near Medina, but its exact location could not be given in Yāqūt, *Muʿjam*, II, 250 f. See also *EI*[2], s.v. *Ḥarra* (Ed.).

546. Presumably to give help to the local inhabitants.

The Events of the Year 20

(December 21, 640–December 9, 641)

The Campaigns of the Muslims and Other Matters

Ṭabarī said: According to Ibn Ḥumayd—Salamah—Ibn Isḥāq:
[2580] Egypt[547] was conquered in this year. It was conquered in the year 20 (641). Abū Maʿshar has the same (date); according to Aḥmad b. Thābit—his authority—Isḥāq b. ʿĪsā—himself: Egypt was conquered in the year 20 (641), the Muslim commander was ʿAmr b. al-ʿĀṣī.

According to Aḥmad b. Thābit—his authority—Isḥāq b. ʿĪsā—Abū Maʿshar: Alexandria[548] was conquered in the year 25 (646),

---

547. In Arabic, the name of Egypt is Miṣr. This name has given rise to some confusion, since an ancient city, situated south of the fortress of Bāb al-Yūn (in Greek Babylon), but on the opposite bank of the Nile, was also called Miṣr (see Butler, 221 f.). Bāb al-Yūn eventually became the name the whole settlement on the Nile was known by, including the city of Miṣr, which also comprised a part called al-Fusṭāṭ, or Fusṭāṭ Miṣr. It was here that the Arabs allegedly first set up camp, see Butler, *Babylon*, ch. 3. In the following I shall render the name Miṣr by Egypt when I think the country is meant (in which the city of Alexandria does not seem to have been included), and I shall leave it untranslated when I think this ancient city is meant. However, one cannot always be sure which interpretation is correct.

548. In the following I have preferred this name to the Arabic Iskandariyyah.

and al-Wāqidī says, as transmitted from him to me by Ibn Saʿd, that Miṣr and Alexandria were conquered in the year 20 (641). Sayf says, according to al-Sarī—Shuʿayb—himself: Alexandria was conquered in the year 16 (637).

The Conquest of Miṣr and Alexandria[549]

Ṭabarī said: We have mentioned the different opinions of the historians concerning the year in which the conquest of Miṣr and Alexandria took place. Now we will mention the events leading to their conquest and at whose hands this occurred, including the historians' differences concerning this issue too.

As for Ibn Isḥāq, according to Ibn Ḥumayd—Salamah—himself: When ʿUmar had finished taking measures pertaining to all of Syria, he wrote to ʿAmr b. al-ʿĀṣī that he was to march upon Egypt with his army. So ʿAmr departed and finally conquered Bāb al-Yūn[550] in the year 20 (641).

Ṭabarī said: There is a difference of opinion about the date of the conquest of Alexandria. Some say that it was conquered in the year 25 (646), two years after the beginning of the caliphate of [2581] ʿUthmān b. ʿAffān under the supervision of ʿAmr b. al-ʿĀṣī.

According to Ibn Ḥumayd—Salamah—Muḥammad b. Isḥāq[551]— al-Qāsim b. Quzmān, a man of Egyptian origin—Ziyād b. Jazʾ al-Zubaydī, who reported that he was a fighter in the army of ʿAmr b. al-ʿĀṣī when Miṣr and Alexandria were conquered: We conquered Alexandria during the caliphate of ʿUmar b. al-Khaṭṭāb in the year 21 (642) or 22 (643). He went on: When we had conquered Bāb al-Yūn, we advanced on all the villages in the countryside lying between Bāb al-Yūn and Alexandria, one after the other, until we ended up in Balhīb, one of those rural villages,

---

549. The conquest of Egypt has never been analyzed better, it seems to me, than by Alfred J. Butler in his *The Arab conquest of Egypt and the last years of the Roman dominion.* Here the second edition, printed together with two brief treatises that have also been drawn upon, is used. See the Bibliography.

550. Also called Bābilyūn, that is in Greek Babylon; see n. 547 above.

551. The text reads as if the *isnād* ends in Ibn Isḥāq and as if Ṭabarī mentions a new strand, but I think it more feasible to consider this as one *isnād* running from Ṭabarī via Ibn Isḥāq to the eyewitness, Ziyād b. Jazʾ. I therefore propose to delete *wa-* preceding *ḥaddathanī* in l. 2. When verbs like *ḥaddathanī* are preceded by *wa-* in the middle of an *isnād* the compiler of the tradition collection introduces a new *isnād* (strand), which is obviously *not* the case in the present context.

called the Village of Prosperity. In the meantime, the people we had taken prisoner had arrived in Medina, Mecca, and Yemen.

He went on: When we arrived in Balhīb, the ruler of Alexandria[552] sent a message to ʿAmr b. al-ʿĀṣī that ran, "(Listen,) you Arabs, in the past, I used to pay the *jizyah* to people who were more hateful to me than you, Persians and Byzantines.[553] If you want me to pay you the *jizyah,* I am agreeable, on the condition that you will return to me all those people from our region whom you have captured.

The eyewitness went on: Then ʿAmr b. al-ʿĀṣī sent that ruler a message that said, "Above me there is a commander without whose consent I cannot do anything. If you want me to suspend hostilities, while you do the same, so that I can write to him about the proposal you have made to me, (I shall certainly do that). If he accepts that condition from you, I will too, and if he
[2582] orders me to do something else, I will carry out his order." The man agreed. He went on: So ʿAmr b. al-ʿĀsī wrote to ʿUmar b. al-Khaṭṭāb. Our leaders never kept secret for us the letters they wrote. So in this letter he mentioned to him what the ruler of Alexandria had proposed. All the time, the remainder of the Egyptian prisoners had been in our care. Then we stopped at Balhīb and stayed there waiting for ʿUmar's letter, which finally arrived. ʿAmr read it out to us. In it were the words,

"Listen, I have received your letter, in which you mention that the ruler of Alexandria has proposed to give you the *jizyah* on the condition that you return to him all those prisoners of his region who have been captured. Upon my life, a fixed *jizyah* that comes to us, and will be coming to those Muslims who live after us, is in my view preferable to booty, which seems never to have been there once it is divided up. So you must propose to the ruler of Alexandria that he give you the *jizyah* in the understanding that those of their people who were taken prisoner and who are still in your care, be offered the choice between Islam and the religion of their own people. Should anyone of them opt for Islam, then he belongs to the Muslims, with the same privileges and obligations

552. For more on this ruler, see n. 564 below.

553. That is, of course, very unlikely, since the ruler himself was a Byzantine. This is the sort of inconsistency that Butler analyzed so fully, see n. 549 above.

as they. And he who opts for the religion of his own people has to pay the same *jizyah* as will be imposed upon his coreligionists. As for those captives who have been scattered over Arabia and have arrived in Mecca, Medina, or Yemen, those we cannot return and we would not like to enter into a peace treaty with anyone on the condition of a pledge which we cannot fulfill for him."

ʿAmr sent a message to the ruler of Alexandria informing him of what the Commander of the Faithful had written, whereupon this ruler sent a message back that said, "I agree." [2583]

He went on: Then we assembled all those captives who were still in our care, and the Christians among them were grouped together. Then we began to bring forward every single man from among them and we gave him the choice between Islam and Christianity. When he chose Islam, we all shouted, "God is great," even louder than we had done when that village was conquered, and we gathered him within our ranks. When he opted for Christianity, the Christians would snort and pull him back into their midst, while we imposed the *jizyah* on him. All the time we were subject to great uncertainty as if one of us was about to cross over to the other camp. The eyewitness went on: This is how we went about it, until we had dealt with all of them. Among those who were thus brought forward was Abū Maryam ʿAbdallāh b. ʿAbd al-Raḥmān.[554] (The transmitter of this eyewitness), al-Qāsim (b. Quzmān) added at this point: I have set eyes on this Abū Maryam; he was the *ʿarīf*[555] of the Banū Zubayd. The eyewitness went on: We positioned him (i.e., in front of the people) and offered him the choice between Islam and Christianity. Meanwhile, his father, mother and brothers had already opted for Christianity. But Abū Maryam chose Islam, so we made him step into our ranks. However, his father, mother and brothers pounced on him, struggling with us for control of him, until they tore his clothes from his body. Today he is our *ʿarīf*, as you see. Then God conquered Alexandria for us and we could enter the city. This rubbish heap, which you see,[556] Qāsim, is in the vicinity of Alex-

554. For more on him, see further down.
555. For this function, see n. 233 above.
556. It is indeed rare when the words via which an eyewitness directly addresses someone who listens to his story are preserved. We find it here twice. It seems as if Ziyād b. Jazʾ pointed out the rubbish heap to al-Qāsim. It is also conceivable that,

andria. It is meant for garbage.[557] It is enclosed within (a girdle of) stones, (so that) it has not grown or shrunk (in size). He who says something else, for instance that Alexandria and the surrounding villages had no *jizyah* imposed upon them, or that its inhabitants had no pact with us, that man is a liar, by God!"

[2584] Al-Qāsim went on: This account did not fail to give rise to the story that the kings of the Banū Umayyah used to write to their governors of Egypt: "Egypt could only be conquered after we used force.[558] Therefore, the inhabitants are no more than our slaves, whose taxes we can increase if we so desire and with whom we can deal as we want."

Ṭabarī said: As for Sayf, according to al-Sarī—Shuʿayb—himself—al-Rabīʿ Abū Saʿīd, Abū ʿUthmān and Abū Ḥārithah: ʿUmar stayed at Īliyāʾ[559] after its inhabitants had been granted a peace treaty. He entered the city and stayed there a few days. He sent ʿAmr b. al-ʿĀṣī to Egypt and appointed him governor over it, were God to conquer it for him. Then he dispatched al-Zubayr b. al-ʿAwwām after him as reinforcement and he directed Abū ʿUbaydah to al-Ramādah,[560] ordering him, in case God conquered it for him, to return to his province.

According to al-Sarī—Shuʿayb—Sayf—Abū ʿUthmān—Khālid and ʿUbādah: ʿAmr b. al-ʿĀṣī left for Egypt after ʿUmar had returned to Medina. ʿAmr journeyed until he arrived at Bāb al-Yūn. Al-Zubayr followed him in his tracks and joined up with him right at the spot where Abū Maryam,[561] the metropolitan of

---

at this point, Ziyād showed al-Qāsim a sketch he had made of the situation, if he and his audience were not standing in front of it.

557. In Arabic, *li-kunāsatin.* The Cairo edition of Ṭabarī, IV, 106, has *la-kunāsatun* ". . . this rubbish heap is a pile of garbage in the vicinity of Alexandria."

558. This is a reference to the military customs of those days: enemies who surrendered and asked for peace had to pay the *jizyah* and were entitled to Muslim "protection" (*dhimmah*), but those who had been subdued by force had all their belongings confiscated, which were distributed as war booty. For a detailed account of this, see D. R. Hill, *The termination of hostilities in the early Arab conquest*, London-New York, n.d.

559. Another name for Jerusalem.

560. There are various places that bear this name; here the one near al-Ramlah seems to be meant, see Yāqūt, *Muʿjam*, II, 813.

561. Butler (513 f.) thinks this is a distortion of Benjamin. He abandons this surmise in *Treaty*, 60 f.

Miṣr,[562] met them, in the company of the bishop and some people of purpose.[563] The Muqawqis[564] had sent the metropolitan so that they might defend their land. When ʿAmr reached them, they prepared to fight him. Then ʿAmr sent them a message that read, [2585] "Do not prompt us to come down heavily upon you;[565] in a moment you will realize what you can do best." Thereupon they held their fighters back. ʿAmr sent them another message that said, "I shall come forward, let Abū Maryam and Abū Miryām[566] approach me." They consented to this and they granted one another safe-conduct. Then ʿAmr said to the two Christian prelates, "You two are the ecclesiastics[567] of this region. Listen. God sent Muḥammad with the truth and He ordered him to hold to it. Muḥammad transferred to us every command he was given, then he passed away—May God have mercy upon him—having accomplished everything he had been told to do. The instructions that he left us are crystal clear: among the things he enjoined upon us is that we should do our utmost in admonishing the people with whom we come into contact.[568] Therefore, we call upon you to embrace Islam. He who is willing to do so will be like one of us. To him who refuses, we suggest that he pay the *jizyah* and we will give him ample protection. Our Prophet informed us that we would conquer your lands and he has determined that we

---

562. The Arabic term *jāthalīq* is arabicized from the Greek *katholikos*. According to Lane, 369, right column, he is the highest ranking in the Christian hierarchy. However, this title was given to the head of the Christian church under the Sasanids (see Vasiliev, I, 121) and should, strictly speaking, not have been given to an Egyptian Christian. See also Butler, *Treaty*, 58 f.

563. The Arabic reads *ahl al-niyyāt*, literally "the people of the intentions." It is not clear who are meant here, but the "intentions" are probably military rather than religious. At any rate, the reading *niyyāt* is dubious.

564. He is a controversial figure. It seems to me that the most authoritative information on him is given by Butler, 508–26, esp. 521. He identifies him as the viceroy and (Melkite) archbishop of Alexandria, appointed by Heraklius. See also his *Treaty*, 54–83.

565. I base this rendering on Lane's interpretation of *iʿdhār* "taking extraordinary pains in exhortation" (1984, left column, below).

566. Presumably that is the name of the bishop present; this is suggested in note *n* of the previous page, 2584, of the edition. The vocalization is that of Ibn Ḥubaysh.

567. Literally, "the two monks"; perhaps the term is used here to humiliate those addressed.

568. See n. 565 above.

keep you from harm because of our family ties among you. If you accept our proposition, we will give you constant protection. Among the orders we received from our Commander (i.e., in Medina) was the order, "Take the interest of the Copts to heart, for the Messenger of God enjoined their best interests upon us, because they have ties of kinship[569] with us and are therefore entitled to our protection.'"

"It is truly a distant relationship," the prelates answered, "one
[2586] that only prophets can establish. (Hagar[570]) was a well-known and noble woman who was the daughter of our king. She belonged to the people of Manf[571] where the monarchy was established. Then the people of ʿAyn Shams[572] were granted victory over them; they killed them and wrested their kingdom from them, whereupon the people of Manf embarked on a vagrant life. As a result of that she became Abraham's property. He[573] is heartily welcome! Grant us immunity, until we return to you."

ʿAmr answered, "A man like me cannot be deceived, but I will grant you a delay of three days so that you see how things stand with you and can discuss the matter with your people. If you do not promise to return in time, I shall fight you." "Give us more time," they pleaded, so he gave them one day longer. "Give us

---

569. Muslim tradition has it that Hagar, the maidservant of Sarah, by whom Abraham fathered Ishmael (that is, Ismāʿīl, the ancestor of the Arabs), was of Egyptian origin. It is reported that, for this reason, the Prophet had enjoined upon his followers to treat the Egyptians well after they had been subjugated, in particular because of this "kinship." The tradition collector Muslim b. Ḥajjāj (d. 261/875) has preserved a Prophetic *ḥadīth* to this effect in his *Ṣaḥīḥ*, IV, 1970, see also Ibn ʿAbd al-Ḥakam, 2 f. A variant of this report (see the same sources) has *ṣihr* "relationship by marriage" instead of "kinship," taken to be a reference to Māriyah, the Coptic wife of the Prophet and the mother of his son Ibrāhīm; see also Balādhurī, 219, and Maqrīzī, I, 24 f.

570. Although the context refers unmistakably to Hagar, the name itself is lacking in Ṭabarī, and was supplied from parallel versions of this story, for instance Ibn al-Athīr, II, 440.

571. The arabicized name of the ancient city of Memphis, see *EI*², s.v. Manf (U. Haarmann).

572. This is a place at three parasangs (18 kilometers) north of al-Fusṭāṭ, see Yāqūt, *Muʿjam*, III, 762 f; it is probably identical with Heliopolis, which seems to have been bigger than the present-day suburb of Cairo bearing that name (see Butler, 231).

573. It is not clear who is meant. If we read *bi-hi* with the edition, the reference may be taken to point to Abraham, the Prophet or ʿAmr. If we read *bi-kum* with Ibn Ḥubaysh (see apparatus, n. *f*), "welcome to you" gives an understandable text.

more time," they asked again, so ʿAmr gave them one more day. Then they returned to the Muqawqis, who took ʿAmr's proposition into consideration. But Arṭabūn[574] refused to accept it and ordered an attack on the Muslims.

The two prelates addressed the people of Miṣr, "As for us, we shall do our best to defend you and we would not return to the Muslims—after all, four days have passed by now during which you came to no harm—were it not for the fact that we hope that therein might lie immunity for you."

Nothing surprised ʿAmr and al-Zubayr more than the sudden attack of Farqab[575] one night, but ʿAmr was prepared. They confronted the Muqawqis, who was killed with his men. Then the Muslims pursued those who had fled. Thereupon ʿAmr and al-Zubayr headed for ʿAyn Shams, where they had their assembly point, and he sent Abrahah b. al-Ṣabbāḥ to al-Faramā,[576] where he duly arrived, and to Alexandria he sent ʿAwf b. Mālik, who (also) duly arrived there. Each one of them said to the inhabitants of the [2587]
city on which he was ordered to march, "If you surrender, you will be granted immunity." They agreed. Then the Muslims exchanged messages with them and waited there for the Muslim army, (which was at ʿAyn Shams at the time,) to arrive. In the meantime,[577] they took prisoners.

ʿAwf b. Mālik said, "People of Alexandria, how beautiful is your city." They replied, "Alexander the Great once said, 'I shall build a city that is in need of God and can do without people.' Or he said, I shall certainly build a city that is in need of God and can do without people.' That is why its splendor has lasted."

Likewise, Abrahah said to the inhabitants of al-Faramā, "What a ramshackle town this is, people of al-Faramā." "Yes," they answered, "al-Faramā once said, 'I shall build a city that can do

---

574. He is the general of the Byzantines. He is described with a few qualities in vol. XII, 2398, of this series. Butler, 215, maintains that his name should read Aretion.

575. This is the name of the Muqawqis according to Sayf. Butler, 516 f. consistently calls him Cyrus, basing himself on Severus of Ushmūnayn; see also his *Treaty*, 54–83. See also the literature cited in Prym's apparatus.

576. Al-Faramā is ancient Pelusium, a town on the Mediterranean shore near the outlet of the eastern branch of the Nile. Butler, 212, doubts the historicity of this mission.

577. Or possibly, "On their way (from ʿAyn Shams to these coastal cities). ."

without God but not without people.' Thus its splendor has faded." Alexander and al-Faramā were brothers.

Ṭabarī said: Al-Kalbī said: Alexander and al-Faramā were brothers. Then he related a similar story in which both cities were associated with the two brothers. In al-Faramā, something collapsed every day and its outward appearance deteriorated, whereas Alexandria kept its gloss.

According to al-Sarī—Shuʿayb—Sayf—Abū Ḥārithah and Abū ʿUthmān: When ʿAmr descended upon the Egyptians at ʿAyn Shams, a place governed jointly[578] by Copts and Nubians, and al-Zubayr had joined ʿAmr there, the people of Miṣr said to their king, "What do you want to accomplish against warriors who defeated the armies of the Persian king and the Byzantine emperor and overpowered them in their own countries? Conclude a peace treaty with these warriors and enter into a pact with them. Do not resist them and do not order us to resist them." That occurred on the fourth day (since the Muslims' arrival). But (the king) refused.

[2588] So the Muslims attacked them and fought them. Al-Zubayr scaled the wall of the city. When those inside spotted him there, they opened the gate for ʿAmr and rushed out, begging for a peace treaty, to which he agreed. But (inside the wall) al-Zubayr fell upon them with force. In the end he passed through the gate, making his way to ʿAmr together with the Egyptians. After they had taken care[579] of the casualties, they concluded a treaty. The Muslims took the same measures against those who were overpowered by force as they had taken in the case of those who had surrendered on the condition of a treaty. They were all placed under "protection."

The text of their peace treaty reads as follows:

> In the name of God, the merciful, the compassionate.
> This is the text of the covenant that Amr b. al-ʿĀṣī has granted the people of Miṣr concerning immunity for themselves, their religion, their possessions, churches, crucifixes, as well as their land and their waterways. Nothing of these will be interfered with or decreased.

578. Or "alternatively"?
579. Or "taken stock of."

Nubians[580] are not allowed to share their homesteads. It is incumbent upon the people of Miṣr, if they agree on the terms of this covenant and when the rise of the Nile water comes to a halt, to afford the *jizyah*, to wit fifty million (dirhams).[581]

They will have to account for the crimes committed by robbers from among them.

If anyone refuses to comply with the terms of this treaty, *jizā'* obligations will be lifted from them commensurate with their numbers, and we will be exempt from awarding protection to those who do so. If their river fails to reach the highest point when the rise of the water has come to a halt, then, commensurate with the losses suffered, their *jizā'* payments will be reduced.

Those Byzantines and Nubians who are willing to accept the same terms as in the covenant with the people of Miṣr will have the same privileges and duties as the latter.

He who refuses to accept these terms and chooses to depart will enjoy immunity, until he has reached his destination where he can be safe, or has moved out of the territory where our authority prevails.

It is incumbent upon them to comply with the following terms: in three instalments, every third part of the year, they will have to afford one third of what they have to pay.

For the terms of this document the covenant of God and His protection, as well as that of His Messenger, that [2589]
of the Caliph, the Commander of the Faithful, as well as the protection awarded by all the Muslims, are guarantees.

It is incumbent upon the Nubians who have accepted the terms of this treaty that they help (sc. the local government) with so many men[582] and so many horses, in

580. On the Nubians, see Butler, index s.v., especially 432; see also his *Treaty*, 37–46.

581. Butler surmises on reasonable grounds that this amount is a later gloss not to be relied upon, see his *Treaty*, 46–8.

582. Presumably slaves are meant. Butler, *Treaty*, 35, interprets *ra's* as heads (of cattle), but he does mention "contingents of horse and foot" as a possibility

> the understanding that no raids will be mounted against them and that they will not be prevented from trade, export or import.

Al-Zubayr, his sons ʿAbdallāh and Muḥammad, have witnessed the concluding of this covenant, Wardān[583] has put it down in writing and was present.[584]

All the people of Miṣr entered into this covenant and accepted the peace treaty. Then the horses were rounded up.[585]

ʿAmr organized al-Fusṭāṭ as a garrison city, whereupon the Muslims took up residence there. Abū Maryam and Abū Miryām presented themselves and spoke to ʿAmr about the prisoners captured after the battle. ʿAmr said, "Have these prisoners a pact and a covenant with us? Did we not come to an agreement with you two, and were we not attacked the very same day?" Then he kicked them out, whereupon they returned saying, "Everyone you have captured up to the time of our return to you will be placed under your protection!" ʿAmr replied, "Would you launch an attack against us while they are under 'protection'?" "Yes," they answered, "we would." Then ʿAmr divided those prisoners among his men, who distributed them, whereupon they ended up in the lands of the Arabs.

After that, a messenger approached ʿUmar with some fifth parts
[2590] of the war booty.[586] ʿAmr sent emissaries (sc. to Medina). ʿUmar questioned them and they gave him a complete account, until they touched on the story of the metropolitan[587] and his companion. ʿUmar said, "Surely, I think that they showed sense, whereas you acted foolishly, without any sense at all. He who fights you has no immunity, but he who does not fight you, and is subsequently dealt with by you in the same way the villagers[588] were

---

elsewhere. He quotes Caetani, who doubts the authenticity of the inclusion of terms concerning Nubians and labels them as anachronisms, *Treaty*, 51. On the whole, Butler, *Treaty*, 53, thinks that the treaty is possibly authentic in its main outline.

583. He was a client of ʿAmr b. al-ʿĀṣī, see Ibn Saʿd, VII 2, 201.

584. Presumably when it was signed. Butler, *Treaty*, 35, thinks that the subject of *ḥaḍara* was left unmentioned and translates "and there were present. . ."

585. The context does not seem to make clear why.

586. Presumably the fifths of more than one battle or conquest.

587. See n. 562 above.

588. A reference to the prisoners taken in the villages mentioned above on p. 2587.

treated, does have immunity during those five days until they have lapsed." Then he sent messengers in all directions, until all those prisoners who had been captured from among those who had not taken up arms during the five days were returned, except those who had engaged in fighting afterwards. Thus the Muslims sent those captives back to Egypt, one after the other, except those who belonged to that last category.[589]

Meanwhile, some Copts had come to ʿAmr's living quarters. He was informed that they had been saying, "How worn out these Arabs look, how little care they take of themselves; we are of the opinion that people like us should not be obedient to people like them." So ʿAmr feared that this appearance of the Arab warriors would prompt the Copts to rebellion. Therefore, he ordered that several camels be slaughtered and cooked in water and salt. Then he ordered the army commanders to assemble, after they had notified their troops to do likewise. ʿAmr sat down and beckoned to the people of Miṣr to join him. Then the meat and the broth were served. (Servants[590]) handed it out to the Muslims, who began to eat in typically Arab fashion, tearing at the meat with their teeth and slurping the broth, dressed in their woolen cloaks and unarmed. After a while, the people of Miṣr dispersed with [2591]
their ambitions and courage boosted.

The next day, ʿAmr sent word to the army commanders to come (i.e. to his tent again) with their troops. He ordered them to come dressed in Egyptian clothes and footwear, bidding them that they order their troops to do likewise. They complied. Then ʿAmr invited the people of Miṣr again who saw something completely different from what they had seen the previous day: erect figures[591] dressed in Egyptian colors standing by, the Arabs eating Egyptian food, behaving in an Egyptian manner. The Copts dispersed, perturbed this time, muttering, "We have been made fools of!"

ʿAmr sent word to his army that they had to arm themselves for the roll call to be held the next day. Then he went to the parade

589. Sc. those who had joined in the battle after the five days of truce.

590. The subject is not expressed. Grammatically, the Copts could be the subject, but I do not think that that is meant.

591. Presumably of servants. The dictionaries do not seem to list a connotation for *quwwām* that fits the present context. Conceivably, it could also be "banners" or "standards."

and permitted the Copts to be present. He showed his troops to them and said, "I am aware that you considered yourselves to have panache when you saw the frugality of the Arabs and their simple life style. But I fear lest you perish. Therefore, I wanted to show you what sort of people they really are, under what circumstances they lived in their own country, then what they have come to in yours, and how ready they are for war. They have defeated you, warfare is their life. They were anxious to take
[2592] possession of your country even before they appropriated its customs as you saw on the second day. And I also wanted you to realize that those you saw on the third day will not abandon the life you saw depicted on the second day, nor will they resume the lifestyle you saw depicted on the first day." Thereupon the people of Miṣr dispersed saying to one another,[592] "The Arabs have smitten you with this one hero of theirs."

News of these events reached ʿUmar, who said to his companions, "By God, ʿAmr's military campaign has become truly easy, no more attacks or assaults like the ones in battles against others. ʿAmr is indeed a crafty fellow!" Then he installed ʿAmr as governor of Miṣr, where he stayed.

According to al-Sarī—Shuʿayb—Sayf—Abū Saʿīd al-Rabīʿ b. al-Nuʿmān—ʿAmr b. Shuʿayb: When ʿAmr and the Muqawqis came face to face at ʿAyn Shams and their respective cavalries began to do battle with one another, the Muslims started to swerve some way toward the far end (i.e. of the battlefield), but ʿAmr urged them to attack. Then a certain man from Yemen said, "We are not made of stone or iron!" "Shut up, you dog!" ʿAmr shouted, but the man retorted, "In that case you are the upper dog."[593]

The transmitter went on: When that contingent began to draw more closely together, ʿAmr shouted, "Where are the Companions of the Messenger of God?" Then those Companions who had participated in the evasive action[594] came along and ʿAmr roared, "Advance, through you God will grant victory to the Muslims." So they went forward. Among them that day were Abū Burdah and Abū Barzah.[595] The other warriors attacked the enemy, close-

---

592. Or, conceivably, "to their countrymen upon their return."

593. Literally, "the commander of the dogs."

594. Admittedly, a wordy rendering of *man shahidahā*.

595. They could not be identified with certainty.

ly following the Companions. Then God granted victory to the Muslims who vanquished the enemy in a glorious manner. Miṣr was conquered in the month Rabīʿ I of the year 16 (April 637); there the authority of Islam stood firm. [2593]

On the whole, Islam began to spread over peoples and kings. Thus the people of Egypt started to engulf (Ifrīqiyah[596] and its ruler) al-Ajall,[597] likewise the people in Mukrān overran Rāsil and Dāhir,[598] the people in Sijistān overpowered the Shāh and his nobles, and the people in Khurāsān and Bāb (al-Abwāb)[599] their respective Khāqāns,[600] as well as less powerful nations. ʿUmar held the conquering armies back out of concern for the lives of the Muslims. Had he allowed them to go where they liked, they would have gone anywhere where water was available.[601]

According to ʿAlī b. Sahl—al-Walīd b. Muslim—(ʿAbdallāh) b. Lahīʿah—Yazīd b. Ḥabīb:[602] When they had conquered Miṣr, the Muslims launched an attack on (northern)[603] Nubia. But they returned having sustained injuries and with many people having been blinded because of the Nubians' superior bowmanship. That is why the Nubians were nicknamed "the eye shooters." When ʿAbdallāh b. Saʿd b. Abī Sarḥ governed Egypt, over which ʿUthmān b. ʿAffān had appointed him, he concluded a peace treaty with the Nubians on the condition that they offer a gift, namely a number of people from among them (i.e., to be used as a labor force), whom they were to deliver into the hands of the Muslims. In exchange, every year the Muslims would present them with certain specific foodstuffs and equally well-specified garments.

According to ʿAlī—al-Walīd—Ibn Lahīʿah: ʿUthmān and those governors and commanders who lived after him stuck to this

596. In this particular context, it is the name of the North African coastal regions west of Egypt; but see *EI*², s.v. *Ifrīḳiya* (Talbi), for the many different definitions of this name.

597. According to a gloss in Ibn Ḥubaysh (Berlin), this is the title of the ruler of Ifrīqiyah; it means something like "the most noble." He is mentioned once more in a subsequent volume of this series.

598. These are the names of local rulers.

599. This is a city on the western shore of the Caspian Sea, north of Baku. Nowadays it is called Derbent. See Yāqūt, *Muʿjam*, I, 437–42.

600. This is the (Persian) title of local rulers.

601. Literally, "they would have reached every watering place."

602. On this important Egyptian historian, see *GAS*, I, 341 f.

603. In Arabic, Nūbat Miṣr, probably that part of Nubia bordering on Egypt.

peace treaty and ʿUmar b. ʿAbd al-ʿAzīz confirmed it out of consideration and concern for the well-being of the Muslims.

[2594] Sayf said: When the month Dhū al-Qaʿdah of the year 16 (November–December 637) had begun, ʿUmar stationed the armed forces of Egypt along all the coastal regions, the reason for this being that Heraklius was launching attacks on Egypt and Syria from the sea while he assaulted the people of Ḥimṣ in person. That occurred after three and a half years of ʿUmar's reign had elapsed.

Ṭabarī said: In this year, I mean 20 (641), Abū Baḥriyyah al-Kindī ʿAbdallāh b. Qays made a raid into Byzantine territory. It is alleged that he was the first to invade it, but another opinion has it that Maysarah b. Masrūq al-ʿAbsī was the first to do so and to return safely, laden with booty.

(Ṭabarī) said: Al-Wāqidī said: In this year, ʿUmar dismissed Qudāmah b. Maẓʿūn as governor from al-Baḥrayn and had him flogged for wine drinking. In the same year, ʿUmar installed Abū Hurayrah[604] as governor of al-Baḥrayn and al-Yamāmah.

Ṭabarī said: In the same year, ʿUmar married Fāṭimah bt. al-Walīd, the mother of ʿAbd al-Raḥmān b. al-Ḥārith b. Hishām.

He continued: Also in the same year Bilāl b. Rabāh[605] passed away. He was buried in the cemetery of Damascus.

In the same year, ʿUmar relieved Saʿd from the governorship of al-Kūfah on the strength of complaints filed against him. People said that he could not perform the *ṣalāt* properly.

In the same year, ʿUmar divided Khaybar[606] among the Mus-

---

604. He was reputedly a major Companion of the Prophet, whose role in the dissemination of prophetic *ḥadīth* has occupied scholars in East and West until the present day. For his biography, see the somewhat uncritical study of him by Helga Hemgesberg, *Abū Huraira, der Gefährte des Propheten*, Frankfurt/Main, 1965, and for his alleged role in *ḥadīth* transmission, see Juynboll, *Authenticity*, ch. VII, idem, *Muslim tradition*, 190–206.

605. He is described as a black Ethiopian slave who had embraced Islam very early. After Abū Bakr had bought him from his cruel Meccan master, he manumitted him. Bilāl later became Muḥammad's official *muʾadhdhin*, the man who called the faithful to prayer. See Ibn Ḥajar, *Iṣābah*, I, 326 f.

606. Khaybar is an oasis comprising settlements, cultivated soil and palm-groves, ninety-six miles/154 kilometers north of Medina, captured by Muḥammad in 7 (628); it used to be occupied by Jews. See *EI*², s.v. *Khaybar* (Veccia Vaglieri).

lims and expelled the Jews from it. He sent Abū Ḥabībah[607] to Fadak;[608] he granted them half[609] the fruit produce and the value of the land in gold and silver and let them keep that. (The other half he confiscated), then he went to the Jews of Wadī al-Qurā[610] and (confiscated their property) to divide it. Also in this year, ʿUmar drove the Jews out of Najrān to al-Kūfah, as al-Wāqidī has it. [2595]

Al-Wāqidī said: In this year, I mean the year 20 (641), ʿUmar organized the *dīwāns*.[611] Ṭabarī said: We have already mentioned the accounts of those who disagree on this chronology.[612]

In the same year, ʿUmar sent ʿAlqamah b. Mujazziz al-Mudlijī overseas to Ethiopia, and this because it was rumored that Ethiopia had made a sudden attack on some border regions of the Islamic domain, but the Muslim forces were annihilated. Then ʿUmar imposed upon himself that he would never send anyone again on a mission overseas. As for Abū Maʿshar, according to Aḥmad b. Thābit—his authority—Isḥāq b. ʿĪsā—himself: The campaign against the land of the blacks was one overseas, in the year 31 (651–2).[613]

Al-Wāqidī said: In the same year, Usayd b. al-Ḥuḍayr[614] passed away in the month Shaʿbān (July–August).

Also in this year, Zaynab bt. al-Jaḥsh[615] died.

---

607. Who this man was could not be established with certainty.

608. A village not far from Khaybar, see *op. cit.*, which surrendered to Muḥammad when he marched on Khaybar, as it says in the sources.

609. Ṭabarī's text appears to have a lacuna; my translation is based upon Prym's emendation, which is derived from Balādhurī, 29, 32. See also Yāqūt, *Muʿjam*, III, 855, and Wāqidī, II, 721, which has *nakhl* "palms."

610. Wādī al-Qurā is a *wādī* running from Medina to Syria in which there were several villages. The Jews who lived there were said not to have been expelled, since Wādī al-Qurā is not part of the Ḥijāz but of Syria.

611. The registers in which stipends, etc. were entered; see the monograph of G. R. Puin.

612. In vol. XII of this series.

613. That is, during ʿUthmān's reign.

614. Usayd was a nobleman from the Jāhiliyyah, who could write Arabic and was an excellent swimmer and archer. He who possessed these qualities was called *al-Kāmil* "the perfect one." He embraced Islam early, see Ibn Saʿd, III/2, 135–7.

615. This Zaynab was the wife of the Prophet's adopted son Zayd b. Ḥārithah. When the Prophet married her, after Zayd had repudiated her, it is reported that

In this year, ʿUmar led the pilgrimage. His governors in the garrison cities were the same in this year as in the previous year with the exception of those whom I have mentioned as dismissed or replaced by others. The same applies to his judges, who were the same persons as in the previous year.

---

the Qur'ān abolished adoption. Thus Muḥammad could not be accused of incest by marrying his "son's" wife. This episode has been analyzed by western as well as oriental scholars, but with quite different results. For an interesting account of both treatments, see Muḥammad Ḥusayn Haykal, *Ḥayāt Muḥammad* (first published Cairo 1935, now also in English translation) ch. XVII, latter half.

The Events of the Year [2596]

21

(December 10, 641–November 29, 642)

Ṭabarī said: In this year the battle of Nihāwand occurred as related in the account of Ibn Isḥāq according to Ibn Ḥumayd—Salamah—himself. Abū Maʿshar has the same according to Aḥmad b. Thābit—his authority—Isḥāq b. ʿĪsā—Abū Maʿshar. Al-Wāqidī says likewise. As for Sayf b. ʿUmar, he has it that the battle of Nihāwand took place in the year 18 (639), in the sixth year of ʿUmar's reign, according to al-Sarī—Shuʿayb—Sayf.

The Battle of the Muslims and the Persians at Nihāwand[616]

The beginning of this episode was as follows according to Ibn Ḥumayd—Salamah—Ibn Isḥāq: (A basic element) of the story of Nihāwand was that al-Nuʿmān b. Muqarrin was governor of Kas-

---

616. For a detailed source analysis of this battle and a comparison with the accounts concerning the conquest of Iṣfahān, see the fundamental study of Noth, "Iṣfahān-Nihāwand," in *ZDMG*, CXVIII (1968):274–96.

kar.[617] He wrote to 'Umar to inform him that Sa'd b. Abī Waqqāṣ had employed him to levy the *kharāj*. He wrote, "I would have loved to wage Holy War, indeed I am craving it."

Then 'Umar wrote to Sa'd, "Al-Nu'mān has written to me mentioning that you have employed him to gather the *kharāj*. However, he loathes this function and would much rather go and fight in the Holy War. Send him, therefore, to your most important objective, to wit Nihāwand."

He said: In the meantime, the Persians had assembled in Nihāwand under the command of (Bahman Jādhawayh) Dhū al-Ḥājib,[618] a certain Persian. Then 'Umar wrote to al-Nu'mān b. Muqarrin, "In the name of God, the merciful, the compassionate. From the servant of God, 'Umar, the Commander of the Faithful, to al-Nu'mān b. Muqarrin. Peace be upon you, I praise God to you, beside Him there is no other god. Listen. It has reached me that
[2597] numerous bands of Persians have assembled against you at the city of Nihāwand. When this letter has reached you, I want you to march out against them, by order of God, with His help and His support, together with those Muslims who are with you at present. Do not let your fighters tread on rugged ground lest you bring harm to them, do not deny them their rights lest you have to make up for that to them, and do not make them enter swampy areas. For one Muslim man is dearer to me than one thousand dīnārs. Fare you well."

So al-Nu'mān marched out toward his goal with the most important Companions of the Prophet accompanying him, such as Ḥudhayfah b. al-Yamān, 'Abdallāh b. 'Umar b. al-Khaṭṭāb, Jarīr b. 'Abdallāh al-Bajalī, al-Mughīrah b. Shu'bah, 'Amr b. Ma'dī Karib al-Zubaydī, Ṭulayḥah b. Khuwaylid al-Asadī and Qays b. Makshūḥ al-Murādī.[619] When al-Nu'mān b. Muqarrin finally arrived with his army at Nihāwand, the enemy spread iron spikes over

---

617. This is the name of the district that lies between al-Kūfah and al-Baṣrah. The main town in it in later times is Wāsiṭ, founded half-a-century later, see Le Strange, *Lands*, 39.

618. That may mean "he in charge of the screen." Was he a chamberlain? See n. 17 above. In other sources, such as Balādhurī, 303, he is called Dhū al-Ḥājibayn "he in charge of the two screens." Elsewhere (below, and Balādhurī, 302) he is Mardānshāh Dhū al-Ḥājib. It should be borne in mind, though, that Dhū al-Ḥājibayn can also mean "he with the (big) eyebrows."

619. For the three last-mentioned, see n. 93 above.

the ground against him. Al-Nuʿmān sent out spies who approached unaware of the caltrops. One of them urged his horse which had just stepped with its leg into a spike forward, but it would not budge. The man dismounted and inspected his horse's foot and then he found the caltrop lodged in its hoof. He brought it to al-Nuʿmān and told him what had happened. Then al-Nuʿmān asked his men what they thought should be done. They answered, "Move away from the position that you have taken here, so that they think that you are fleeing away from them. Then they might come out of their stronghold to pursue you."

Thus al-Nuʿmān moved away from that position. The Persians swept the caltrops out of their path and left their stronghold in pursuit of the Muslims. Then al-Nuʿmān turned around to face them once more. He set up camp, drew up his platoons in battle array and addressed them as follows, "If I am killed, Ḥudhayfah b. al-Yamān will be your new commander; if he is slain, obey Jarīr b. ʿAbdallāh, and if he gets killed too, then Qays b. Makshūḥ will command you."

Al-Mughīrah b. Shuʿbah was resentful that al-Nuʿmān had not asked him to succeed him. So he went up to al-Nuʿmān and asked
him, "What is your plan of action?" Al-Nuʿmān replied, "After I [2598]
have performed the noon *ṣalāt,* I shall fight them, because I have seen that the Messenger of God preferred it that way."[620] "If I had been in your place," al-Mughīrah remarked, "I would have engaged them very early in the morning." Then al-Nuʿmān said, "(On several occasions in the past) you may perhaps have engaged the enemy in fighting early in the morning, which did not result in your face being blackened by God,[621] but today happens to be Friday."

So al-Nuʿmān said to his army, "With God's permission, we will first perform the *ṣalāt,* and then we will confront our enemy after the *ṣalāt.*" When they had arranged themselves in rows for

620. This is a reference to a *ḥadīth* (Bukhārī, II, 293; Abū Dāwūd, III, 49; Tirmidhī, IV, 160; Ibn Ḥanbal, V, 444 f.). Although ascribed to the Prophet, its originator was most probably Ḥammād b. Salamah (d. 167/784), a fact highlighted by Noth *op. cit.*, 274. A reason why Ḥammād might have brought this *ḥadīth* into circulation is hard to give. For an account of a later time in the day when the struggle is reported to have started, see below, on pp. 187–88.

621. This is an expression conveying that God renders someone's face expressive of sorrow or displeasure, or "to disgrace" (Lane, 1461, left column).

the prayer ritual, al-Nuʿmān spoke to his fighters, "I shall shout 'God is great': after the first time everybody should fasten his sandal straps and adjust his gear. After I have shouted it a second time, everybody should fasten his belt and prepare himself to attack straightaway. After the third time, you must launch an all-out assault against them. I shall attack too."[622]

The Persians went forth, having fastened themselves to one another with chains so that they could not flee.[623] The Muslims attacked them and fought them. Al-Nuʿmān was hit by an arrow, as a result of which he died. His brother Suwayd b. Muqarrin wrapped him in his garment and concealed the fact that his brother had been slain, until God granted victory to the Muslims. Then Suwayd gave the standard to Ḥudhayfaḫ b. al-Yamān. God killed Dhū al-Ḥājib and Nihāwand was conquered. After this, the Persians never amassed an army of that size again.

Ṭabarī said: According to what I was told, ʿUmar had sent al-Sā'ib b. al-Aqraʿ, a client of Thaqīf[624] (i.e., to Nihāwand). Al-Sā'ib could write and was good at arithmetic. ʿUmar told him, "Join the army there and stay with them. If God grants the Muslims victory, you must divide the booty among them. And set aside the fifth that belongs to God and the fifth of His Messenger. This army has suffered losses. Go into the countryside, for low land is better than elevated land."[625]

Al-Sā'ib said:[626] When God had conquered Nihāwand for the Muslims, they acquired enormous masses of booty. So, by God, I took pains to divide it justly among the fighters, when someone

622. Or, conceivably, "I shall carry (our standard)." The carrying of flags and standards as a prominent feature in early Muslim war tactics is studied in Juynboll, "The Qur'ān reciter on the battlefield and concomitant issues," in *ZDMG*, CXXV (1975): 11–27.

623. Enemy troops tying themselves up in chains out of cowardice is a *topos* observed in various sources, see Noth, 122, and idem, "Isfahān-Nihāwand," 280.

624. This man was highly praised for his intellectual powers. For more stories about him, see Ibn Ḥajar, *Iṣābah*, III, 16 f.

625. This seems to suggest that ʿUmar advised the Muslim warriors to recuperate from their war effort in the countryside, where they could hide themselves and where they were less conspicuous. The opposition *bāṭin/ẓāhir* is very much in evidence in the opposition *baṭn/ẓahr*. However, this expression as used here could not be traced to other sources.

626. This whole story is interrupted so often by the word *qāla* "he said" that for once I deemed it proper to leave it out altogether in what follows.

from the local people came to me and said, "Will you grant me, my wife and my family immunity? For my part I will show you the treasures of al-Nakhīrajān. These are the treasures of the royal family, which will be for you and your commander without anyone else sharing with you in them." "All right," I said, whereupon that man said, "Send someone with me whom I can show where they are." I dispatched someone with him. That man returned to me with two huge baskets filled with nothing but pearls, chrysolites and rubies. When I had finished dividing the booty among the men, I took these two baskets with me and traveled to ʿUmar b. al-Khaṭṭāb, who said, "What happened, Sā'ib?" "Good news, Commander of the Faithful," I answered, "God has granted you the most glorious victory and al-Nuʿmān b. Muqarrin died a martyr's death." Then ʿUmar exclaimed, "Verily, we belong to God and to Him we will return,"[627] and burst into tears, weeping like a child, (bending his head forward so) that I saw the uppermost part of his shoulders above his neck. When I saw how he grieved, I said to him, "By God, Commander of the Faithful, apart from al-Nuʿmān nobody who could be considered important died." "The weak are also Muslims," ʿUmar retorted, "but He who has honored them with martyrdom knows their prominence and lineage, and of what they achieve. ʿUmar, his mother's son, is aware (too)."[628] Then he stood up to enter his house. So I said, "I have enormous riches that I have brought along with me," whereupon I told ʿUmar the story of the two baskets. "Bring them to the treasury," ʿUmar ordered, "we will see later what we will do with them. And you should once more join your army unit." [2599]

So I brought the baskets to the treasury and soon afterwards left for al-Kūfah. [2600]

The same night that I departed for al-Kūfah, ʿUmar rested, but when he awoke the next morning, he dispatched a messenger after me. By God, he only caught up with me the moment I was about to enter al-Kūfah. When I made my camel kneel, he made his camel kneel right beside mine. "Go back immediately to the Commander of the Faithful," he shouted. "He sent me to fetch

627. Q. II, 156.
628. Rendition tentative.

you but I only caught up with you this very moment." "Damn you," I said, "what is all this about and why should I?" "I (honestly) do not know," he answered.

So I rode back with the messenger. Finally, I approached ʿUmar, who the moment he spotted me said, "What shall I tell the son of al-Sāʾib's mother, or rather what can he tell me?" "Commander of the Faithful," I asked him, "what is all this about?" "Damn you, by God," ʿUmar replied, "hardly had I gone to sleep that night in which you left Medina, when the angels of my Lord came to me to escort me to those two baskets that shone like flames, while the angels said, "We are going to brand you with them." Then I said, "I shall divide their contents into equal shares among the Muslims." Therefore, Sāʾib, go and take them away from me, you bastard, do not let them out of your sight. Sell them so that with the proceeds the stipends and annuities of the Muslims can be paid." Thus I left with the baskets. (Having arrived in al-Kūfah,) I deposited them in the mosque, whereupon the tradesmen descended upon me. It was ʿAmr b. Ḥurayth al-Makhzūmi who bought them from me for two million dirhams. He left with them for the land still under control of the Persians and sold them there for four million. Consequently, he remained ever after the wealthiest man in al-Kūfah.

According to al-Rabīʿ b. Sulaymān—Asad b. Mūsā—al-Mubārak b. Fuḍālah—Ziyād b. Jubayr—his father (sc. Jubayr b. Ḥayyah): ʿUmar b. al-Khaṭṭāb said to al-Hurmuzān when he granted him immunity, "Do not fear, will you give me advice?" "I will,"
[2601] al-Hurmuzān replied. Thereupon ʿUmar said, "Suppose Persia is today like a head and two wings." "Then where is that head?" al-Hurmuzān asked. "In Nihāwand," was the answer, "under the command of Bundār,[629] for he has the royal brigade of the Asāwirah[630] and troops from Iṣbahān with him." "And where are the wings?" al-Hurmuzān asked. ʿUmar mentioned a region that I have forgotten. "Cut off the wings," the Persian suggested, "then the head will weaken." "You speak lies, enemy of God," ʿUmar

629. This is thought by De Goeje to be a corruption of Mardānshāh (Dhū al-Ḥājibayn), see *Glossarium*, p. DCXXII.

630. See n. 147 above.

retorted, "no, I shall go for the head first, which I shall cut off; when God has struck off the head, the wings will no longer resist Him."

He went on: Then ʿUmar intended to march on Nihāwand himself, but his associates said, "For God's sake, may we remind you, Commander of the Faithful, that you intend to march on the élite cavalry of the Persians? If you are slain, the Muslims will no longer have a binding force. But by all means, send military forces." So ʿUmar sent men from Medina. One of them was his son ʿAbdallāh, but Muhājirs and Anṣār were also among them. Then he wrote to Abū Mūsā al-Ashʿarī, "March out with the people of al-Baṣrah," and to Ḥudhayfah b. al-Yamān, "March out with the people of al-Kūfah," and to both ". . . until you all come together near Nihāwand. When you are assembled," the letter went on, "then your commander will be al-Nuʿmān b. Muqarrin al-Muzanī." When the Muslims gathered at Nihāwand, Bundār, nicknamed the Sturdy One, sent them a message that said, "Detail someone to us so that we may speak to him." So al-Mughīrah b. Shuʿbah was commissioned.

He went on: It is as if I still see him: a man with long hair and only one eye. They sent him to the Persian commander. When he came back, we questioned him. Al-Mughīrah said," (When I came into their presence,) I learned that a short while ago the Persian commander had sought the advice of his associates by asking them, "For what good reason shall we allow this bedouin to behold our stateliness, grandeur and regality? Or should we present ourselves to him in an unkempt state, hiding from him what we are really like, so that he turns away in disgust?" "No," they shouted, "let us adorn ourselves in the most splendid possible way, in full armor. Let us array ourselves in our gear, and when [2602]
we ride against them, our spears and lances will glitter so brilliantly that it will almost affect their eyesight."

(Al-Mughīrah entered and) lo, there was Bundār, with a crown on his head, (stretched out) on a golden throne, with (the nobles) standing around its head end, looking (vainglorious) as devils.[631]

631. In Lane, 1552, middle column, a devil is described in terms of insolence, audacity and pride, among other characteristics. Hence my use of "vainglorious."

Al-Mughīrah continued: I walked a few steps, (shabbily dressed) as I was, and bowed. But I was pushed and held back.[632] "This is not the way emissaries are treated," I protested. But they said, "You are nothing but a dog." "God forbid," I retorted, "among my own people I hold a higher rank than he among his." But they jeered at me, hollering, "Sit down!" pushing me to a place to sit.

He went on: Someone translated for me[633] the words Bundār spoke. "You bedouins, of all people you are the farthest removed from anything that is beneficial; you have been hungry longer than anyone else, you are the most wretched, live in the greatest squalor and in the most remote homesteads. Nothing prevents me from ordering these knights around me to shoot the lot of you with a barrage of arrows[634] except the fear of all your corpses polluting the air, for you are filth. If you go away, we will let you do so, but if you persist, we will show you the spot where you will be slaughtered."

Al-Mughīrah went on: I praised God and extolled Him and then I spoke, "By God, everything you said to describe and characterize us is absolutely correct. It is true, of all people we have the most remote homesteads, our hunger has been most severe, we were the most wretched and we were farther removed from anything beneficial than anyone, until God sent us His Messenger and promised us victory in this world as well as Paradise in the Hereafter. And by God, since His Messenger came to us, we have never experienced anything from our Lord but conquest and victory. Finally, we have come to you, and I swear by God, we will never
[2603] return to that misery until we have vanquished you, acquiring everything you own, or otherwise get killed in your land." Hereupon Bundār said (i.e. to his entourage), "Forsooth, this one-eyed scoundrel has given you a truthful rendering of what he thinks deep down."

632. In parallel reports (for instance, Balādhurī, 303) the reason why al-Mughīrah was jostled was that he had torn the carpet with his spear and had seated himself next to the Persian general on the latter's throne, apparently just to provoke them.

633. The text has "for him," but I have opted for a suggestion made in the apparatus.

634. This is the translation suggested in *Glossarium* for form VIII of *naẓama*.

Al-Mughīrah continued: Then I stood up and I swear that I had rattled the lout[635] with my determination.

Thereupon the Sturdy One[636] sent us a message that said, "Either you cross over to us in Nihāwand, or we will cross over to you." Al-Nuʿmān ordered, "Let us cross over to them."[637]

He[638] went on: I swear by God, I have never seen a spectacle as on that day, the Persians advancing like mountains of steel, having tied themselves[639] to one another lest they flee from the Arabs. In units of seven they had bound themselves to their peers with ropes,[640] and they threw iron spikes behind their backs, thinking that, if someone fled, he would wound himself on the spikes. When al-Mughīrah saw how numerous they were, he said, "I have never seen such vacillation.[641] Our enemies are left free to prepare themselves without any pressure being exerted on them. But I swear, had I been in command, I would not have hesitated a moment to attack them." Al-Nuʿmān b. Muqarrin, however, was a mild-mannered man, who said to him, "God will see to it that you witness similar battles (sc. in future, in which your preferred tactics are followed). Let your point of view not sadden you or reproach you, for I swear, nothing prevents me from attacking them except something I witnessed from the Messenger of God: When he went on a campaign, he never fought at the beginning of the day, not seeking a speedy outcome, but he waited until the time for the sunset[642] *ṣalāt* had come and the wind had freshened. As a consequence, fighting could be expected

---

635. The Arabic has *ʿilj* "strong," "sturdy," "coarse," a term especially used to indicate unbelievers. It is unclear whether *ʿilj* is here an honorific of Bundār or a term of abuse. I have translated it as a double entendre.

636. See previous note.

637. For this *topos*, see n. 425 above.

638. He is Jubayr b. Ḥayyah again, the transmitter of this report introduced above on p. 184.

639. This verb *tawāthaqa* also permits of the translation "they had made promises to one another."

640. For the words *qarana* and *qirān*, see Lane, 2987 f. For the *topos* of enemy troops binding themselves to one another out of cowardice, see n. 623 above.

641. He probably means "in our strategy."

642. Although the text in Ṭabarī does not specify this *ṣalāt* as the one performed at sunset, parallel texts in the *ḥadīth* (referred to above in n. 620) have it coincide with sunset (. . . *ḥattā tazūla al-shams*).

to be more vigorous. That is really the only reason that holds me back. Almighty God, I beg You to gladden my eyes today with a victory in which there is prestige for Islam and an ignominy in which the unbelievers are humiliated. Then gather me unto You as a martyr after (victory has been won). And now, all of you, say 'Amen' to that. May God have mercy upon you." So we all said, "Amen," and wept.

Then al-Nuʿmān b. Muqarrin went on, saying, "When I wave my banner, you must hold your weapons ready. When I wave it a second time, you must prepare yourselves for fighting your en-
[2604] emies and when I wave it a third time, let every man attack the enemy nearest to him, secure in the blessing of God."

Meanwhile, the enemy had scattered the iron stakes. Al-Nuʿmān, however, waited until the time of the sunset *ṣalāt* had come and the winds had freshened. Then he shouted, "God is great," whereupon we answered with, "God is great." After that al-Nuʿmān said, "May God answer my prayer and grant me victory." Al-Nuʿmān waved the banner, so we prepared to fight. Then he waved it a second time, whereupon we positioned ourselves facing the enemy. After that he waved it a third time. Al-Nuʿmān shouted, "God is great," and the Muslims did likewise saying, "Victory will be ours with which God will honor Islam and its adherents." Then al-Nuʿmān ordained, "If I am slain, then Ḥudhayfah b. al-Yamān will lead the troops, and if Ḥudhayfah is slain, then so-and-so, and if he is also killed, then such-and-such." (He went on mentioning names) until he had enumerated seven leaders, the last of whom was al-Mughīrah. Then he waved the banner a third time, whereupon every fighter attacked the enemy nearest to him. By God, on that day I do not know of a single Muslim who wanted to get back to his family; (everybody kept fighting) until he either got killed or defeated his adversary. We attacked as one man, but the enemies stood their ground against us. The only sound we heard was iron clashing on iron, until the Muslims had sustained serious losses. However, when the Persians saw our endurance and our reluctance to leave the battlefield, they lost their confidence. As soon as one man fell down, seven others fell down too, one on top of the other, still being chained together. So all of them were slain, while others sustained injuries from the caltrops that they had spread about behind them. Al-Nuʿmān shouted, "Bring the banner forward." So we began to move the banner forward. We killed the enemy and routed them. When al-Nuʿmān realized that God had answered his prayer, and when he saw that victory was ours, an arrow was shot at him that struck him in his flank and killed him.

Then Maʿqil, his brother, went to him and covered him with a cloak. He took the banner and joined the fight again. Next he [2605]
shouted, "Forward. Let us kill and rout them." When the warriors had assembled, they asked, "Where is our commander?" Then (pointing to the body) Maʿqil said, "Here is your commander. God has gladdened his eye with victory and has sealed this with his martyrdom." After that the warriors gave the oath of allegiance to Ḥudhayfah and also to ʿUmar in Medina, asking (God) to grant him victory and invoking God's blessing upon him, as is done for pregnant women.

News of the victory was recorded in a letter for ʿUmar that was delivered by one of the Muslims. When he had arrived at ʿUmar's abode, he said to him, "Rejoice, Commander of the Faithful, in a victory with which God has honored Islam and His subjects and with which He has disgraced unbelief and its advocates." ʿUmar said, "Praise be to God. Has al-Nuʿmān sent you?" "Prepare yourself (for bad news and God's blessing), al-Nuʿmān (was slain),[643] Commander of the Faithful." ʿUmar burst into tears and cried, "Verily, we belong to God, and to Him we will return,[644] who else was killed, you bearer of bad news?" The man mentioned such-and-such and so-and-so, until he had enumerated many people for him, concluding with the words, "And the others, Commander of the Faithful, you would not know." "It will not hurt them that ʿUmar does not know them. In any case God certainly knows them," ʿUmar said tearfully.

As for Sayf, according to al-Sarī—Shuʿayb—himself—Muḥammad, al-Muhallab, Ṭalḥah, ʿAmr and Saʿīd: What precipitated the fighting at Nihāwand was that, after the fighters from al-Baṣrah had overpowered al-Hurmuzān and had forestalled the people of

643. The Arabic expression *iḥtasaba fulānan* conveys that someone may reap a reward from God for his composure upon hearing about the death of someone dear, see Lane, 565, right column, below.

644. Q. II, 156.

Fārs by preventing them from annihilating the army force of al-ʿAlāʾ[645] and had trampled them underfoot, the people of Fārs wrote to their king, who was at the time in Marw, to prompt him to take action. The king wrote to the inhabitants of al-Jibāl, namely those of al-Bāb, al-Sind, Khurāsān and Ḥulwān, who were duly roused. They exchanged letters and some even rode to others. They agreed that they would show up at Nihāwand and sort out their matters there.

One after the other, the first contingents of Persians began to arrive at Nihāwand. Qubādh (b. ʿAbdallāh al-Khurāsānī), the commander at Ḥulwān, sent news of this to Saʿd, who in turn wrote to ʿUmar. Meanwhile, Saʿd was being beleaguered by certain[646] people,
[2606] who incited against his authority in the time that elapsed between the exchange of letters among the Persians and their assembling at Nihāwand. But the latter were not concerned with the commotion that their maneuvers caused the Muslims. Among those people who recalcitrated was al-Jarrāḥ b. Sinān al-Asadī amidst a group of followers.

ʿUmar wrote back, "Proof that not everything is in order among you lies in your[647] rising up just at the moment when those who are preparing to fight you are getting ready. But I swear by God, this crisis will not prevent me from looking into your situation first, even if the Persians attack you." Then ʿUmar sent Muḥammad b. Maslamah.[648] In the meantime, the Muslim forces were getting ready to fight the Persians, while the Persians were concentrating their forces. Muḥammad b. Maslamah was the overseer of the governors, whose task it was at the time of ʿUmar's reign to investigate the administrative measures taken by those against whom complaints had been filed.

So Muḥammad went up to Saʿd to be escorted amongst the inhabitants of al-Kūfah, while deputations meant for the people of the garrison cities were sent in the direction of Nihāwand. Saʿd escorted Muḥammad along the mosques of the people of al-Kūfah.[649] Muḥammad did not address himself in secret to any

---

645. See above, pp. 129–31.

646. Who these people were will become clear further down.

647. Presumably, ʿUmar refers only to those malcontents siding with al-Jarrāḥ.

648. In the past he had also acted as ʿUmar's trouble-shooter, see pp. 73–74 above.

649. Various clans and tribal groupings had their own prayer sites, also used for local public meetings.

question raised about Sa'd, since in those days problems related to people's circumstances were never dealt with behind closed doors. Muḥammad did not stop at a prayer site in order to interrogate the people about Sa'd without receiving the answer, "We know nothing but good (about him), we do not wish him to be replaced, we will not say anything that discredits him and we will help no one against him." (All expressed these and similar ideas) except those who supported al-Jarrāḥ b. Sinān and his associates. The last-mentioned had kept silent, not saying anything detrimental, nor had Muḥammad given them permission (to speak for that matter). They had also deliberately abstained from uttering salutations. Finally, the investigation committee reached the abode of the 'Abs. Muḥammad addressed them, "I swear by God, let anyone who knows the truth speak up."

Then Usāmah b. Qatādah said, "If you adjure us, by God, (to be frank with you), Sa'd does not divide the booty equally among us, he does not act justly among his subjects and he does not mount campaigns (sc. that might bring in spoils)." Hereupon Sa'd exclaimed, "By the almighty God, if he has told a deliberate lie for everybody to see and hear, then, God, blind him, give him numerous children,[650] and expose him to tribulations that will make him take leave of his senses!" And indeed, (in the time that followed), Usāmah did become blind. Moreover, in the end he had [2607]
ten daughters, having heard about a woman whom he went to seek out, until he felt his way toward her. Later, when people bumped into him, he would say, "(The state in which I am is the result of) an imprecation of Sa'd, that blessed man."

Then, in conformity with his imprecation, Sa'd addressed (al-Jarrāḥ's) hangers-on and said, "O God, if they have stepped out of line in brazen impertinence with false pretenses, mete out a severe punishment to them." And indeed, the afflictions that befell them were great: al-Jarrāḥ was cut down by sword blows on the day he pounced on al-Ḥasan b. 'Alī to kill him at Sābāṭ;[651] Qa-

650. A reference to one of man's most serious misfortunes, to have many children and little means, expressed in a saying later ascribed to the Prophet: *jahd al-balā' kathrat al-'iyāl ma'a qillat al-shay'*. See Juynboll, "The ḥadīṯ in the discussion on birth-control," in *Actas IV Congresso de estudos árabes e islâmicos*, Leiden, 1971, 373–9.

651. This event is described in more detail in Abū al-Faraj al-Iṣfahānī, *Maqātil al-Ṭālibiyyīn*, ed. Aḥmad Ṣaqr, Cairo, 1949, 64.

bīṣah (b. Ḍubayʿah al-ʿAbsī) was stoned to death;[652] Arbad was killed as a result of emasculation and blows with sword scabbards. In addition, Saʿd said, "Remember that I was the first man to shed the blood of unbelievers.[653] The Messenger of God asked that both his parents be held ransom for me[654] and that was something he had never done for anyone before. At one time I saw that I comprised one-fifth of the adherents of Islam.[655] And now these yokels from Asad claim that I cannot perform the *ṣalāt* correctly and that I am solely concerned with hunting." Muḥammad (b. Maslamah) took Saʿd and those men from Asad with him back to ʿUmar. When they had arrived at ʿUmar's abode, Muḥammad reported to him, whereupon ʿUmar said, "Woe unto you, Saʿd, how *do* you perform the *ṣalāt*?" "I take my time in performing the first two (*rakʿa*s)," Saʿd replied, "and I shorten the last
[2608] two." "But that is merely your own private interpretation,"[656] ʿUmar said and he went on, "Had it not been for their (lack of) circumspection (in their accusations), their line of action would have been clearly (justified)." Then he asked, "Saʿd, who is your deputy in al-Kūfah?" "ʿAbdallāh b. ʿAbdallāb b. ʿItbān," Saʿd answered. ʿUmar confirmed this appointment and nominated him as governor. The prelude to the battle of Nihāwand and the beginning of deliberations and missions concerned with it occurred during the time of Saʿd's governorship, as for the actual battle, that took place in the time of ʿAbdallāh.

They said: What happened among other things was that the Persians responded to the letter of king Yazdajird and set out for

652. He was an associate of the Shīʿite agitator Ḥujr b. ʿAdī (on him, see *EI*[2] s.v. *Ḥudjr* (Lammens)). For more on Qabīṣah, see Ṭabarī, II, 128–43.

653. This is a reference to an incident during which Saʿd is reported to have dealt someone from the (still unbelieving) Quraysh a blow when he and a group of early converts to Islam were harassed during their prayer ritual. See Abū Hilāl al-ʿAskarī, *al-Awāʾil*, ed. M. al-Miṣrī and Walīd Qassāb, Damascus, 1975, I, 308.

654. This is a reference to an ancient custom. If someone is about to embark on a dangerous mission, well-wishers pray that a parent be held ransom in order to secure his safety. The Prophet is reported to have said when Saʿd was about to mix in the fray at Uḥud, *fidāka abī wa-ummī* "may my father and mother be held ransom for your (safe return)," see Bukhārī, III, 81. Compare also l. 1 of the poem on p. 25 above.

655. He is even recorded as having considered himself one-third of the adherents to Islam, see Bukhārī, II, 439.

656. In other words: This is not the established norm according to which four *rakʿa*s should be performed.

Nihāwand. Thus, one after the other, there arrived those living in the territory between Khurāsān and Ḥulwān, those living in the territory between al-Bāb and Ḥulwān and those living in the territory between Sijistān and Ḥulwān. The cavalry of Fārs and of the Fahlūj, the inhabitants of al-Jibāl,[657] joined forces. Those hailing from the territory between Bāb (al-Abwāb) and Ḥulwān numbered thirty thousand troops, those hailing from the territory between Khurāsān and Ḥulwān numbered sixty thousand and those hailing from between Sijistān and Fārs and Ḥulwān numbered sixty thousand. They all assembled under the command of al-Fayruzān and they all set out to him, one after the other.

Mūsā—Ḥamzah b. al-Mughīrah b. Shu'bah—Abū Ṭu'mah al-Thaqafī, who was a witness to these events, concurred with the last-mentioned transmitters: The Persians said to one another, "This man, Muḥammad, who has brought this religion to the Arabs, never wanted to undertake anything against us. Then, after his death, they were ruled by Abū Bakr, who did not undertake anything against the Persians either, except on one campaign during which he attacked them.[658] For the rest he concentrated on military maneuvers in that part of the Sawād bordering on Arab territory. Then, after Abū Bakr, the Arabs were ruled by 'Umar. His rule has lasted for some time and he has become so powerful that he could grapple with you and conquer the Sawād and al-Ahwāz little by little.[659] Now he has trampled these territories underfoot, but he will not be satisfied until he has attacked the people of Fārs and the monarchy in the very heart of their country. If you do not rush upon him now, he will certainly launch an offensive against you, after he has destroyed the seat of your monarchy and invaded the heartland of your royal family.
The crisis will not be over until you have expelled the last of [2609]
'Umar's warriors from your country and razed their two gar-

657. I have not found another reference to them. But see Paul Schwarz, *Iran im Mittelalter nach den arabischen Geographen*, VII, Stuttgart-Berlin 1936, 829.

658. Probably a reference to the campaign led by Khālid b. al-Walīd, which resulted in the conquest of al-Ḥīrah, a city that had been under a Persian governor for some time. See *EI*², s.v. *al-Ḥīra* (Shahid). For the controversy about Khālid's mission to Iraq, see *EI*², s.v. *Khālid b. al-Walīd* (Crone).

659. This connotation for *intaqaṣa* is suggested in Lane, 2841, middle column, below.

risons.[660] After that you will have to keep ʿUmar occupied with (defending) his own country and security."

Thereupon, the Persians concluded pacts and covenants among one another. They exchanged letters about this matter among themselves, pledging to help each other in this. News of this reached Saʿd who had just appointed ʿAbdallāh b. ʿAbdallāh b. ʿItbān as his deputy. Having left (al-Kūfah, he went to) meet ʿUmar to tell him the news in person. Before that he had notified ʿUmar by letter, in which he had said, "The people of al-Kūfah request your permission to spread out into enemy-held territory in order to attack the Persians first." In the past, ʿUmar had forbidden the Muslims to invade al-Jabal. But also ʿAbdallāh (b. ʿAbdallāh b. ʿItbān) as well as other Muslim commanders had written to ʿUmar to tell him that a Persian army force of fifty thousand fighters was being concentrated, arguing, "If they march on us before we have mounted an offensive against them first, they will increase in courage and strength. But if we forestall them, that will be to our advantage and to their disadvantage."

The messenger who carried this letter to ʿUmar was named Qarīb b. Ẓafar al-ʿAbdī. After this messenger, Saʿd left al-Kūfah and set out for consultations with ʿUmar. When the messenger had presented himself to ʿUmar with the letter containing the news, and ʿUmar had read it, he asked, "What is your name?" "Qarīb." "And who is your father?" "I am the son of Ẓafar," the messenger replied. ʿUmar regarded this as a good omen, saying, "Victory is nigh,[661] if God wills it, for there is no power except in Him."

Then a congregational prayer meeting was announced among the people, who flocked together. Right at this moment, Saʿd presented himself to ʿUmar, who saw a favorable omen in the fortuitous presence of Saʿd b. Mālik.[662] ʿUmar climbed the pulpit to deliver a speech. He informed the congregation of the news and

---

660. A reference to al-Baṣrah and al-Kūfah.

661. A play on the messenger's name, *ẓafar* "victory" and *qarīb* "close at hand."

662. Unlike in the case of Qarīb b. Ẓafar, the supposedly good omen in Saʿd b. Mālik's name seems less obvious, but a *yawm saʿd* is a "lucky day" and *mālik* means "master," "possessor" as in Q. I, 4, where God is called *mālik yawm al-dīn* "the master of the Day of Reckoning."

asked the people's advice, saying, "Today is a day that will be decisive for the future,[663] but one thing is constantly on my mind. I will disclose this to you; therefore, listen to it, inform me of your views and be concise, '. . . and do not quarrel so that you lose heart and your vigor disappears.'[664] Do not use too many arguments and avoid longwindedness, lest you lose sight of your goal[665] and your suggestions turn out to work against you. Is there anyone who proposes that I should march out amidst my men and whomever else I succeed in persuading to follow me, until I have reached a position between our two garrison cities? Shall I call upon them to launch an offensive, while I am there to support them, until God grants them victory and carries out what He desires? If He grants them victory, I suggest that I order the Muslims to pursue the enemy far into his lands and to wrest their monarchy from him." Then ʿUthmān b. ʿAffān, Ṭalḥah b. ʿUbaydallāh, al-Zubayr b. al-ʿAwwām and ʿAbd al-Raḥmān b. ʿAwf stood up among other Companions of the Messenger of God considered to be people of sound judgment, and they deliberated for a while. They said, "We do not think that (you yourself should set out on this campaign), but your authoritative opinion should not be withheld from the Muslim forces (sc. in Iraq)." [2610]

Several Arab chieftains, horse-owning knights and eminent leaders held the opposite view, as well as those whose associates had scattered, whose leaders had been killed and who had engaged in military activities even more extensive than the one (that lay ahead). They said, "They[666] have asked you leave to invade enemy territory without asking for your support. Give them your permission, send them your orders and pray for their well-being." The one who was critical of ʿUmar's opinion, when he was asked to give his views, was al-ʿAbbās.

According to al-Sarī—Shuʿayb—Sayf—Ḥamzah (b. al-Mughīrah)—Abū Ṭuʿmah: ʿAlī b. Abī Ṭālib stood up and said, "The people have arrived at the right decision, Commander of the [2611]

663. See n. 122 above.

664. Q. XLVIII, 46.

665. This rendering is suggested in *Glossarium*, p. CDIV, but is not recorded in the available dictionaries. Going by what is given there, one may translate "lest you are swamped by circumstances."

666. Presumably the Muslim fighters in al-Baṣrah and al-Kūfah.

Faithful, for they have insight into the circumstances you were informed about by letter. The outcome of this perilous situation will not be determined by victory because of superior numbers in one army or by defeat because of inferior numbers in the other army. No, the determining factors will be His religion, with which He prevails, and His army, which He has made powerful and which He has strengthened with His angels,[667] so that it may achieve its goal. For we can count on a promise from God. God will fulfill His promise and He will grant victory to His army. For them you are the string on which the beads of a necklace are threaded and held together. When the string is broken, all the beads on it will scatter and be lost, and they will never be gathered together again. Although few in number, today the Arabs are numerous and powerful through Islam. So stay (in Medina) and write to the people of al-Kūfah, for they comprise the most eminent leaders of the Arabs as well as those people who do not even pay attention to others who might have a more numerous following, better weapons[668] and greater application than they themselves. Let two-thirds of the people of al-Kūfah march on the Persians, with one-third staying behind. And write to the inhabitants of al-Baṣrah to reinforce those of al-Kūfah with some of their men."

ʿUmar was delighted with their sound advice and he expressed his admiration for them. Then Saʿd stood up and said, "There is no need to strike such a belligerent note, Commander of the Faithful, the people will march out because they want revenge."

According to al-Sarī—Shuʿayb—Sayf—Abū Bakr al-Hudhalī: When ʿUmar had told the people the news (sc. about the Persians concentrating their troops at Nihāwand), and had asked their advice, adding that they should avoid prolixity and not be longwinded lest they lose track of their objectives, he said, "Know that this is a day that will be decisive for the future.[669] Speak up."

667. This is probably a reference to the celestial hosts that descended from heaven to help the early Muslims in their struggle against the Meccans. See Juynboll, "Fighting angels," in *Ohio Journal of Religious Studies*, II/1 (1974):85–7.

668. This rendering is based on Lane's connotation (525, middle column, 6 lines from the bottom) *dhawū ḥaddin* "possessors of arms." In *Glossarium*, p. CLXXXIII, the connotation "élite troops" is suggested.

669. See n. 122 above.

Then Ṭalḥah b. ʿUbaydallāh stood up. He was one of the major [2612]
public speakers from among the Companions of the Messenger of God. After he had uttered the formula of the unity of God he said, "Listen. You, Commander of the Faithful, have been fortified by circumstances and tested by tribulations. Your experience has rendered you sound in judgment. Do as you deem fit and proper. We will not withdraw from our obligations to you and we will never tire from serving you. With you rests the decision to be taken in this matter. So, if you give us your orders, we will obey them. If you call upon us, we will oblige. If you give us mounts,[670] we will ride them. Detail us and we will go, lead us and we will be led. For you are in charge of this matter, having been tested, tried and examined.[671] No outcome of God's decree has been revealed to you that was not favorable."

Ṭalḥah sat down. Then ʿUmar returned to the pulpit and said, "Today is a day that will be decisive for the future. Speak your minds." After that, ʿUthmān b. ʿAffān stood up and, having uttered the formula of God's unity, he said, "Commander of the Faithful, I propose that you write to the people in Syria. Let them march out from their territory. I also propose that you write to the people of Yemen to march out from theirs. Furthermore, I suggest that you, together with the people of these two holy cities,[672] march out in the direction of the two garrison cities, al-Kūfah and al-Baṣrah, in order to confront the assembled unbelievers with all the Muslim forces. For if you march out with your allies as well as your (Ḥijāzi) followers, then the enemy's forces, although increasingly mobilized, will no longer pose so much of a problem to you. You will be more powerful and numerous, Commander of the Faithful. After the tribal warriors have given their utmost, you will not leave the least bit of your energy unused. You are not the man to carry the goods of this world away for yourself, nor the man to seek refuge from it in a shelter. Today is a day that will be
decisive for the future. Be present at this crucial day with your [2613]
good counsel and your allies, and do not absent yourself from it."

670. Literally, the text reads "if you carry us, we will ride." My rendering is suggested by Lane, 647, left column, lines 4 ff.

671. Instead of the active verbs of the text, I opt for the passives suggested in the apparatus.

672. That is, Medina and Mecca.

At this ʿUthmān sat down. ʿUmar returned to the pulpit and said, "Today is a day that will be decisive for the future. Speak your minds." Then ʿAlī b. Abī Ṭālib stood up and said,

"Listen. If you order the people of Syria to leave their country, Commander of the Faithful, then the Byzantines will pounce on their offspring, and if you order the people of Yemen to leave theirs, the Ethiopians will pounce on their offspring. And if you depart from this land, rebellions may break out against your authority from all sides and regions to the point that what you left behind, namely your wives and children, may become more important to you than what lies ahead of you. Let those tribesmen stay in their garrison cities, and write to the people of al-Baṣrah ordering them to divide themselves into three groups—one to remain behind to protect the women and children, another to remain behind to keep an eye on the conquered people who have treaties with the Muslims, lest they rebel against them, and the third to march out to their brethren in al-Kūfah as reinforcements for the latter. If the Persians lay eyes on you some day in the near future, they will say, 'This is the Commander of the Arabs on whom the whole nation of the Arabs depends,' and that will only increase their desire to defeat you. Thus you will have incited them against you. You also mentioned that the enemy has mobilized; God abhors that even more than you do, and He is more powerful to alter a situation He abhors. And as for the consideration you mentioned—that the enemy is (so) numerous—in the past we never had superior forces, but we fought assured of divine support."

"Yes, indeed," ʿUmar exclaimed, "by God, if I leave this land, the whole area may start a rebellion against me from all quarters
[2614] and regions. If the Persians see me in person, they will certainly not leave the battleground (of Nihāwand) and they will surely be reinforced by those who have never given them help (in the past). They will say to their forces, 'This is the man on whom the Arabs depend; if you cut him down, you will have severed the spine of the Arab nation.' Advise me, what man shall I entrust with handling the situation in that border region in the days to come?"

The people answered, "You yourself have better ideas and are more competent to decide." But ʿUmar went on, "Give me some name and let it be someone presently in Iraq." They answered "Commander of the Faithful, you know the people in Iraq and the warriors in your army better than we. They have sent you a delegation; you have seen them and spoken with them." "By God," ʿUmar said, "I shall certainly place the command over them in the hands of a man who will surely face the first of their spears when he confronts the enemy in a few days' time." "Whom do you have in mind, Commander of the Faithful?" he was asked. "Al-Nuʿmān b. Muqarrin al-Muzanī," he answered, whereupon they said, "He will be the man to face them."

At that time al-Nuʿmān was in al-Baṣrah, surrounded by several army commanders from the people of al-Kūfah, with whom ʿUmar had reinforced the people of al-Baṣrah at the time of the insurrection of al-Hurmuzān. They conquered Rāmhurmuz and Īdhaj and helped them against Tustar, Jundaysābūr and al-Sūs. Through Zirr (b. ʿAbdallāh) b. Kulayb and al-Muqtarib al-Aswad b. Rabīʿah, ʿUmar sent a letter to al-Nuʿmān with the news of his appointment: "I have given you the command to fight the enemy. So march out immediately and go on as far as Māh.[673] In the meantime, I have written to the people of al-Kūfah to join you there. When all your troops have assembled under your command, advance on al-Fayruzān and all those people from Fārs and the others who joined him. Pray God to grant you victory, and frequently repeat the words[674] 'There is no power or strength except in God.'"

As to ʿUmar's motive for sending al-Nuʿmān b. Muqarrin to [2615]
Nihāwand, according to Muḥammad b. ʿUbaydallāh b. Ṣafwān al-Thaqafī—Umayyah b. Khālid—Abū ʿAwānah—Ḥuṣayn b. ʿAbd al-Raḥmān—Abū Wā'il: While al-Nuʿmān was governor over Kaskar,[675] he wrote to ʿUmar, "The way I feel here in Kaskar is like a young, vigorous man who is beside a prostitute who has put on make-up for him and has perfumed herself. I swear to you by God

673. That is Nihāwand. Māh is the Persian word for chief city, Arabic *qaṣbah.* Because it paid its tribute after the conquest in particular to al-Baṣrah, Nihāwand was called Māh al-Baṣrah. In the same manner Dīnawar was called Māh al-Kūfah. See n. 15 above, and Le Strange, *Lands,* 196 f.

674. A common expression, probably based on Q. 18, 39.

675. See n. 617 above.

that when you have relieved me of my function in Kaskar and have sent me to one of the armies of the Muslims (I shall perform great feats!)"

He said: Then ʿUmar wrote to him (saying), "Join the troops at Nihāwand, for you will be their commander."

He said: The armies came face-to-face, and al-Nuʿmān was the first to be killed. His brother, Suwayd b. Muqarrin, took the flag (that al-Nuʿmān had dropped). Then God granted the Muslims victory, and they, that is the Persians, never assembled a host like that again. Henceforth, the inhabitants of every garrison city launched campaigns against their enemies in the countryside near their cities.

The Account Is Resumed Once More by Sayf

Through Ribʿī b. ʿĀmir, ʿUmar wrote to ʿAbdallāh b. ʿAbdallāh (b. ʿItbān), "Call up so-and-so many men from al-Kūfah to accompany al-Nuʿmān. I have written to him ordering him to go from al-Ahwāz to Māh, and these troops are to join him there. He is to march with them to Nihāwand. I have appointed Ḥudhayfah b. al-Yamān as their commander until he meets up with al-Nuʿmān b. Muqarrin. In the meantime, I have written to al-Nuʿmān, 'If something happens to you, Ḥudhayfah b. al-Yamān is to take charge of the troops, and if something happens to Ḥudhayfah, then Nuʿaym b. Muqarrin is to be the new commander.'"

[2616] ʿUmar sent Qarīb b. Ẓafar back (to Iraq), accompanied by al-Sā'ib b. al-Aqraʿ as ʿUmar's confidential agent. To the latter he said, "If God grants you victory, you must divide the booty that God has made available to them in equal shares among the troops, and do not swindle me out of what is due to me[676] by setting aside worthless goods for me. And if our warriors suffer a disastrous defeat, you and I will never see each other again."

The two emissaries arrived in al-Kūfah carrying ʿUmar's letter with his marching orders. Among the people of al-Kūfah, the quickest to respond were the 'newcomers',[677] who were eager to have their faith tested and to be given a share in the booty.

---

676. That is, the fifth part.

677. See n. 253 above for an explanation of the term *rawādif*.

Ḥudhayfah b. al-Yamān left with the troops accompanied by Nuʿaym. After a while they joined al-Nuʿmān at al-Ṭazar, and they concentrated the cavalry at Marj al-Qalʿah[678] under the command of al-Nusayr (b. Thawr al-ʿIjlī).[679] To Sulmā b. al-Qayn, Ḥarmalah b. Murayṭah, Zirr (b. ʿAbdallāh) b. Kulayb, al-Muqtarib al-Aswad b. Rabīʿah and the Persian commanders, who had settled in the region between Fārs and al-Ahwāz,[680] ʿUmar had written a letter saying, "Prevent the Persians from bothering your brethren and, for that purpose, protect your manpower and your land from all sides. Furthermore, stay at the borders of the area between Fārs and al-Ahwāz, until new orders from me reach you."

Then ʿUmar sent Mujāshiʿ b. Masʿūd al-Sulamī[681] to al-Ahwāz and said to him, "Withdraw from there in the direction of Māh." So off he went. Some time later, when he was near Ghuḍā Shajar,[682] al-Nuʿmān ordered him to stay where he was. Thus Mujāshiʿ made camp between Ghuḍā Shajar and Marj al-Qalʿah. Sul- [2617]
mā, Ḥarmalah, Zirr and al-Muqtarib went forth, ending up at the district borders of Iṣbahān and Fārs, thereby blocking the access routes to be taken by reinforcements from Fārs intended for the enemy at Nihāwand. When the Kūfan troops joined al-Nuʿmān at al-Ṭazar, a letter from ʿUmar, delivered by Qarīb, reached him, that read, "In your army you have the best fighters from the tribes as well as their heroes of long standing.[683] Let them see action rather than those whose experience of warfare is less extensive. Ask for their support and follow their good counsel. Ask advice also from Ṭulayḥah, ʿAmr and ʿAmr,[684] but do not give them any

678. Al-Ṭazar and Marj al-Qalʿah were two localities in al-Jibāl, see Le Strange, *Lands*, 191 f., Yāqūt, *Muʿjam*, III, 537, IV, 488.

679. According to De Goeje's index, he may be identified with the man mentioned in n. 214 above.

680. Presumably they are the leaders of Persian deserters, such as the Ḥamrā' and the Asāwirah.

681. A colorful figure whose military career is described in Ibn Ḥajar, *Iṣābah*, V, 767 f.

682. A locality between al-Ahwāz and Marj al-Qalʿah, see Yāqūt, *Muʿjam* III, 804.

683. Literally "in the Jāhiliyyah."

684. For their full names, see a little further down. Two of these were mentioned above in n. 93 as erstwhile leaders in the *riddah* wars; one ʿAmr, the son of Abū Sulmā, seems a less well-known person.

commanding function." Thereupon al-Nuʿmān sent Ṭulayḥah and the two ʿAmrs ahead on patrol so that they might furnish him with military intelligence, and he ordered[685] them not to penetrate too deeply into enemy territory. So Ṭulayḥah b. Khuwaylid, ʿAmr b. Abī Sulmā al-ʿAnazī and ʿAmr b. Maʿdi Karib al-Zubaydī left. When they had been gone for a day and the evening was nigh, ʿAmr b. Abī Sulmā returned. "What caused you to turn back so soon?" he was asked. "I was in the land of the enemy," he replied. "A country can kill someone who does not know it, whereas someone who does know a certain country will not die crossing it."[686]

Meanwhile, Ṭulayḥah and (the other) ʿAmr pressed on until, by the end of the night, the latter came back too. "What made you return so soon?" people asked him, whereupon ʿAmr replied, "We had been gone for a day and a night without spotting anything suspicious, and I began to have fears that the route we had taken would be seized by the enemy."

Ṭulayḥah pressed forward, not paying attention to the other two (and stayed away so long that) the people said to one another, "Maybe he has turned his back on Islam again."[687] So Ṭulayḥah forged ahead, until he finally reached Nihāwand. From al-Ṭazar to Nihāwand is a distancc of more than twenty parasangs.[688] He learned the whereabouts of the enemy and gathered intelligence;
[2618] then he himself returned. When he finally came in sight, approaching the Muslim army, the people shouted, "God is great." When he asked them what the commotion was about, they told him about their anxiety for him, but he said, "By God, were religion nothing more than being Arab, I would not be inclined to let these barbarous Persians be slaughtered by us noble Arabs."[689]

Then al-Nuʿmān came and sat down with Ṭulayḥah, who told

685. For this connotation of *taqaddama*, see Lane, 2985, right column.

686. Literally, "whereas someone who does know a certain country can kill it." ʿAmr's explanation is couched in two short proverbs. My rendition is based upon an analysis of both proverbs in G. W. Freytag (ed.), *Arabum proverbia*, Bonn 1838–43, II, 271; the reference is Prym's.

687. Literally, "he has apostatized a second time," a reference to his alleged role in the *riddah* wars.

688. Twenty parasangs equal sixty miles; see Lane, 2369, left column, where other numbers are also given.

689. Rendition tentative. Is Ṭulayḥah here at his most cynical?

him everything that had happened and informed him that, between the spot in which they were and Nihāwand, there was nothing that might cause him alarm, in fact there was not a soul. Thereupon al-Nuʿmān issued the order to saddle the animals, and he told the men to line up. To Mujāshiʿ b. Masʿūd he sent word that he was to take charge of the rearguard.[690] Al-Nuʿmān marched at the head of his formations, his brother Nuʿaym leading the vanguard, his brother Suwayd and Ḥudhayfah b. al-Yamān leading the wings, with al-Qaʿqāʿ b. ʿAmr in command of the cavalry[691] and Mujāshiʿ commanding the rear. In the meantime, reinforcements from al-Madīnah had joined al-Nuʿmān. Among these were al-Mughīrah (b. Shuʿbah) and ʿAbdallāh (b. ʿUmar b. al-Khaṭṭāb). They ended up at al-Isbīdhahān.[692]

The enemy was stationed in their formations on this side of Wāya Khurd[693] under the command of al-Fayruzān, with al-Zarduq and Bahman Jādhawayh, who had been appointed in the place of Dhū al-Ḥājib, commanding the wings. They had been joined at Nihāwand by everyone from the border regions, including princes and several nobles, who had not participated in the battle of al-Qādisiyyah or in those battles immediately preceding it. In all, they were no less in number[694] than those who had been present at the battles preceding al-Qādisiyyah, that of al-Qādisiyyah and [2619]
its aftermath.[695] In command of the Persian cavalry was Anūshaq.

When al-Nuʿmān spotted the enemy, he shouted, "God is great." This was repeated by the men who were with him, something that greatly upset the Persians. Halting his mount, al-Nuʿmān ordered that the luggage be unloaded and that the tent[696]

690. Or, conceivably, "to urge the men on from the rear."

691. This word is problematic. De Goeje suggests (*Glossarium*, p. CLXII) "contingent of cavalry." In his partial translation of Ṭabarī, Kosegarten, 257, seems to have opted for "lightly armed footsoldiers" (Latin *velites*). See Lane, s.v. *jarīdah*, but also s.v. *mujarrad*. Below, on pp. 205–6, the context seems to suggest that horses are involved.

692. A locality near Nihāwand; see Yāqūt, *Muʿjam*, I, 239.

693. According to Yāqūt, *Muʿjam*, IV, 896, a riverbed near Nihāwand. On p. 209 below it is described as a ravine.

694. Or, conceivably, "more numerous," the preposition *dūna* used here being a *ḍidd*, admitting of two opposite connotations "more than" and "less than."

695. See n. 114 above.

696. Presumably the one from which the battle is directed.

be pitched. So while al-Nuʿmān waited there, his tent was set up. The nobles from al-Kūfah hurried to him to pitch a tent for him, racing each other to get there first. Arriving ahead of their peers were the following fourteen persons: Ḥudhayfah b. al-Yamān, ʿUqbah b. ʿAmr, al-Mughīrah b. Shuʿbah, Bashīr b. al-Khaṣṣāṣiyyah, Ḥanẓalah b. al-Rabīʿ the secretary, Ibn al-Hawbar, Ribʿī b. ʿĀmir, ʿĀmir b. Maṭar, Jarīr b. ʿAbdallāh al-Ḥimyarī, al-Aqraʿ b. ʿAbdallāh al-Ḥimyarī, Jarīr b. ʿAbdallāh al-Bajalī, al-Ashʿath b. Qays al-Kindī, Saʿīd b. Qays al-Hamdānī and Wāʾil b. Ḥujr. Never before had Iraq witnessed such illustrious people setting up a tent (together).

After the luggage had been unloaded, al-Nuʿmān announced that fighting was to begin. They fought for two days, the Wednesday and the Thursday, both armies scoring alternate successes. This took place when seven years of ʿUmar's reign had elapsed, in the year 19 (640). On Friday, the Persians took refuge in their
[2620] trenches with the Muslims encircling them. They launched a fair number of attacks against them, but the Persians fared well, only leaving their trenches when they wanted. This exasperated the Muslims, who feared that the struggle might turn into a lengthy one. Finally, one Friday,[697] the wise men among the Muslims assembled and talked things over, saying, "We see that the enemy is faring well against us." So they raised the matter with al-Nuʿmān and told him their views; then they confronted him (with their point of view,[698]) while he pondered over the very same matter. Finally, he said, "Take it easy; do not leave your position." Then al-Nuʿmān sent for the remaining people of steadfastness[699] and strategic acumen, whereupon they made their way to him. He addressed them as follows,

697. Literally, it says "one day on a Friday of Fridays." This seems to suggest that, after the skirmishes of Wednesday and Thursday mentioned above, the two armies spent one week or more facing each other. Assuming that *jumʿah* is here used in the sense of "congregation," usually *jamāʿah* in Arabic, we may translate "one day at one of the prayer meetings." This solution seems to make more sense, while *jumʿah* in the sense of *jamāʿah* is listed in Lane, 457, middle column, supra.

698. The reading is dubious. The Arabic verb used here is *wāfaqa*, which usually means "to agree with." This does not seem to suit the present context at all, however, and that is why I have opted for a connotation suggested in Lane, 3057, middle column, line 5 (*ṣādafa* "to encounter someone").

699. See n. 47 above.

"You probably witnessed how the unbelievers sought refuge in their fortified trenches and settlements.[700] They do not make sorties unless they feel like it, while the Muslims are unable to stir or incite them to battle unless the Persians let them (do so). You may have also seen how exasperated[701] the Muslims are as a result of the situation in which they find themselves, and how successful the enemy is in that same situation when they make sallies. What is the proper strategy for us to stir them up and lure them into an open confrontation and make them abandon their shilly-shallying?"

The first to speak was ʿAmr b. Thubayy.[702] He was at that time the oldest warrior among them, since they only rose to speak in order of seniority. He said, "Their being entrenched is harder for them to bear than the delay of getting to grips with them is for you. Let them be. Do not exert pressure on them to come forth and vie with them in pertinacity. Fight only with those enemies [2621]
who attack you."

But all of those assembled rejected this proposal, saying, "We are certain that our Lord will keep His promise to us." Then ʿAmr b. Maʿdī Karib rose to speak and said, "Attack them, try to defeat them and do not fear them." But again, all the others rejected this suggestion, saying, "All you want us to do is to run with our heads against their walls, but these walls are their friends in need against us."

Then Ṭulayḥah began to speak and said, "Those two have said what they think, but what they suggest is not appropriate. As for me, I think that you should send forth armed horsemen to surround the enemy and shoot at them, feigning to open hostilities and thus inciting them to battle. When the enemy is provoked in this way and they are about to leave their trenches in order to engage our horsemen, these must retreat in simulated flight[703] back to our position. All the time that we have been doing battle

700. The Arabic has *madāʾin* "cities," but that seems too grand a rendering in the present context.

701. Or "how constrained they are in their movements."

702. This man is identified by De Goeje with ʿAmr b. Abī Sulmā mentioned above on p. 2617.

703. In Arabic, *istiṭrād;* see Lane, 1839, left column, below, for a detailed description of this ancient Arab stratagem.

with them, we have never made use of this stratagem against them. Therefore, if we resort to it now and they see us behaving like this, they may develop the ambition to inflict a crushing defeat upon us and they will not have second thoughts. They will leave their trenches and fight with us, whereupon we will (turn around and) fight them, until God decides between them and us as He likes."

Then al-Nuʿmān ordered al-Qaʿqāʿ b. ʿAmr, the commander of the cavalry,[704] (to do as Ṭulayḥah suggested). Al-Qaʿqāʿ obeyed. At first the Arab cavalry kept themselves at a distance from the Persians, but then they suddenly rushed upon them as if to open hostilities, while gibing[705] at them. When the enemy was about to leave the trenches, al-Qaʿqāʿ withdrew little by little, whereupon, expecting to acquire booty, the Persians did exactly as
[2622] Ṭulayḥah had thought they would. Shouting, "Hurry up, get a move on!" they rushed forth from their trenches. No one stayed behind except those who stood guard for them at the gates. They followed the Arabs closely, until al-Qaʿqāʿ had retreated to the Muslim army, in doing so, partly cutting off the Persians from their prepared positions.

Meanwhile, al-Nuʿmān b. Muqarrin and the Muslim warriors were drawn up in battle array on that particular Friday.[706] It was still morning. Al-Nuʿmān had issued orders to his men to the effect that they were to remain where they were and not to fight the enemy until he gave permission to do so. Accordingly, they stayed put, hiding behind their shields against the enemy's arrows. The unbelievers advanced upon them, shooting at them and causing many Arabs to sustain injuries. The Arabs complained to one another about this and said to al-Nuʿmān, "Do you not see that we are in a spot? Do you not see what they have to endure from the enemy? What are you waiting for? Give our warriors permission to engage the enemy in combat."

"Take it easy, take it easy," al-Nuʿmān replied, thus soliciting the same complaint from his men several times and each time calming them down with the same words. Then al-Mughīrah

704. See n. 690 above.
705. By making a clicking noise with their tongues.
706. I prefer the reading *al-jumʿah* in Co.

said, "Had I been in command here, I know exactly what I would have done." But again al-Nuʿmān answered, "Easy does it—mind your own business! In the past, when you were in command, you did a good job. But God will not forsake us, nor you for that matter. We expect the same result from staying put as you do from rushing forth." So al-Nuʿmān started to postpone doing battle, until that particular hour of the day had arrived in which the Messenger of God preferred facing the enemy in battle, to wit when the sun has begun its decline, shadows lengthen, and [2623] breezes start to blow.[707]

When this hour had almost come, al-Nuʿmān stood up and rode through the army, seated on a dark brown, short-legged hack. He stopped at every banner and, after praising and extolling God, he said:

"You know how far God has honored you with this religion and what victory He has promised you. So far He has realized the neck and the chest of His promise; only the rump and the hind legs remain to be fulfilled.[708] But God will realize His promise and He will make sure that the final stage thereof will follow its initial stage. Remember what has happened, how weak you were, and how much you have achieved in this situation now that you are powerful. At present you are the veritable servants and protégés of God. You know that you are cut off from your brethren in al-Kūfah; you know well how they will benefit if you are granted a glorious victory and what a difficult task awaits them if you are defeated and disgraced. You may have seen what enemies you are facing. You may be aware of your exertions against them and theirs against you. As for what they stake, that is these paltry chattels and the land you see around you, but what is at stake for you is your religion and your nobility.[709] There is no comparison between what you and they put at stake. Surely there is no one who protects his worldly goods as zealously as you protect your religion. The most God-fearing person is he who believes in God, [2624] puts himself to the test and does so wholeheartedly. You have two excellent choices, anticipating either one of two beneficial

707. All these seem to point to approximately 5 p.m.
708. The imagery is derived from the horse.
709. The word *bayḍah* also admits of the interpretation "territory."

courses: everlasting martyrdom in which you will be well provided, or a quick conquest and easy victory.

Every man is to look to the adversary in front of him," he went on, "nobody may leave the grappling with his opponent to his brother, so that the latter is suddenly faced by his brother's adversary as well as his own, for that is ignominious. Even a dog sometimes fights in defense of its mate. Therefore, every one of you is held responsible for the adversary facing him. When I have finished issuing my marching orders, get ready. I shall shout three times 'God is great!' When I shout it the first time, let anyone who is not yet ready get ready. After I have shouted it a second time, everybody is to gird himself with his sword and get himself prepared to rush forward, and after the third time, I shall attack,[710] if God wills it. Then you must attack with me. O God, honor Your religion and grant Your servants victory! Make al-Nuʿmān the first martyr today, so that You may strengthen Your religion and ensure victory for Your servants!"

When al-Nuʿmān had finished doing his rounds among the fighters in their respective positions, and had issued his marching orders to them, he returned to his former position and shouted "God is great!" three successive times, whereupon the troops listened, obeyed and got ready to rush forward, some of them (in their haste) brushing aside others from their path. Al-Nuʿmān charged and so did the troops. The flag that al-Nuʿmān was hold-
[2625] ing swooped down upon the enemy like an eagle.[711] al-Nuʿmān himself was recognizable by his white cloak and bonnet.[712]

The armies fought a tremendous battle with their swords, causing such a clamor that those who heard it had never heard in any battle a din louder than this. In the period between late afternoon and early darkness, they killed so many Persians in this battle that the battlefield was inundated in blood and warriors and animals lost their footing in it. Several Muslim horsemen lost their lives in this way, having slipped in the blood. So too the horse of

710. Or, conceivably, "I shall carry (the banner) forward." Compare n. 622 above.

711. Compare the report in which the Prophet is said to have had a flag called *al-ʿuqāb* "the eagle"; see Juynboll, "The Qur'ān reciter on the battlefield and concomitant issues," in *ZDMG*, CXXV (1975):26.

712. For the *topos* of distinctive clothing worn during battle, see also the paper mentioned in n. 667 above.

al-Nuʿmān stumbled and threw off his rider. Thus al-Nuʿmān was killed when his horse lost its footing and he was flung down. Nuʿaym b. Muqarrin took hold of the flag before it fell down, and he covered al-Nuʿmān in a garment. Then he brought the flag to Ḥudhayfah and gave it to him. The banner was already with Ḥudhayfah. He made Nuʿaym b. Muqarrin take his place and he himself took up the position previously occupied by al-Nuʿmān. Then he stuck the banner in the ground. Al-Mughīrah suggested to him, "You must hide the fact that your commander has fallen so that we will see what decision God will take between us and the enemy, lest our forces lose heart."

They fought until the night cast its shadow over the warriors, and the infidels took to their heels. They ran away, with the Muslims constantly harassing them and pursuing them. In the end the enemy forces lost their sense of direction in the dark, so they abandoned that course and directed their steps toward the ravine in which they had made their camp at Isbīdhahān. They fell into this ravine, and nobody tumbled down into it without shouting "*wāyah khurd.*" That is why to this day this ravine is called Wāyah Khurd.[713]

In that place, one hundred thousand enemy warriors, or even [2626]
more, lost their lives, in addition to those who were killed on the battlefield, who were also very numerous. Nobody escaped except a few stragglers. Amidst the slain on the battlefield, al-Fayruzān found a way to safety. Amidst those stragglers he fled in the direction of Hamadhān. Nuʿaym b. Muqarrin pursued him and sent al-Qaʿqāʿ to head him off. Finally, just as al-Fayruzān arrived at the mountain road to Hamadhān, al-Qaʿqāʿ overtook him. This road was chock-full of mules and donkeys loaded with honey, so the animals prevented him from escaping his death. In that mountain pass Al-Qaʿqāʿ killed al-Fayruzān after he had duly defended himself.[714] Hence the Muslims have a saying, "God recruits soldiers even from honey."[715] The Muslims led away the

713. None of the experts I consulted is sure what the name might mean; Prym pointed out that *wāyah* may mean "woe"; this is supported by D. N. MacKenzie (Göttingen). "Woe has consumed (us)" may then be a tentative interpretation.

714. For this interpretation of *imtanaʿa*, see Lane, 3024, right column, in form V.

715. Prym gives a reference to the proverb listed in Freytag (ed.), *Arabum proverbia*, I, 10: *inna li 'llāhi junūdan minhā 'l-ʿasalu* "God has soldiers, honey is one of them."

animals laden with the honey and all the other goods they carried besides, and marched on. That is why that mountain road is called the Honey Pass. When al-Qaʿqāʿ closed in on al-Fayruzān, the latter dismounted and clambered away in the mountains, since he could not find a passage to ride through them. Al-Qaʿqāʿ clambered after him, pursuing him until he caught him.

With the Muslim cavalry hot on their heels, the vanquished Persian warriors ran on until they arrived at the city of Hamadhān.[716] They entered the city. The Muslims descended upon them and laid a cordon around the city and its immediate vicinity. When Khusrawshunūm[717] saw this, he sought to obtain immunity from the Muslims and he accepted their preconditions, namely that he would surrender to them Hamadhān and Dastabā,[718] and that the Muslims would not be attacked by Persians living in that area. The Muslims accepted the Persians' guarantees and granted them immunity. So the Persians were safe and everyone who had run away returned.

After the defeat of the unbelievers at the battle of Nihāwand, the Muslims entered the city itself and laid a cordon around it and
[2627] its immediate vicinity. They collected the enemy's armor and chattels, and handed them to the overseer of the spoils, al-Sā'ib b. al-Aqraʿ. While the Muslims were thus engaged, operating from their camp and waiting for those of their brethren who were at Hamadhān to make their way to them, the Hirbadh, that is the overseer of the fire temple,[719] came forward seeking immunity. Ḥudhayfah was notified of his arrival (and received him). The hirbadh said, "Will you grant me immunity provided that I tell you what I know?" "All right," Ḥudhayfah replied. Then the hirbadh said, "Al-Nakhīrajān has deposited in my care a treasure of the king. I will produce it on the condition that I, as well as those people I shall name, will be granted immunity." When Ḥudhayfah had given him this guarantee, the hirbadh brought

716. One of the main cities of al-Jibāl lying about forty miles (sixty-four kilometers) north of Nihāwand; see Le Strange, *Lands*, 194 ff.

717. He was a Persian general whom we encountered as the one left in charge of Ḥulwān after the king had vacated that city.

718. A city northeast of Hamadhān, see Le Strange, *Lands*, the map opposite 185.

719. For more details on this functionary, see Morony, *Iraq*, 284 f.

him the royal treasure consisting of gems that the king held in readiness for the deputies of his reign.[720] The Muslims looked into this matter and agreed with one another that they should submit this treasure to ʿUmar, so they kept it apart and delayed sending it off, until they had finished amassing all the booty. Then, finally, they sent it away together with the fifths[721] that were due.

Ḥudhayfah b. al-Yamān distributed shares in the booty equally among his men, the share of a mounted warrior at Nihāwand being six thousand dirhams and that of a footsoldier two thousand. Before that, Ḥudhayfah had handed out free shares[722] from the fifths among those fighters "of tested strength,"[723] who had participated in the battle of Nihāwand and whom he had selected himself. All that remained from the fifths he handed over to al-Sā'ib b. al-Aqraʿ. Al-Sā'ib took possession of it and departed with it, as well as with the royal treasure, to ʿUmar.

After he had written about the victory at Nihāwand to ʿUmar, Ḥudhayfah stayed there and waited for ʿUmar's reply and orders. His messenger carrying the news of the victory was Ṭarīf b. Sahm, the brother of the Banū Rabīʿah b. Mālik.

When the news had reached the people in charge of Māh (al-Baṣrah) and Māh (al-Kūfah)[724] that Hamadhān had been taken and that Nuʿaym b. Muqarrin and al-Qaʿqāʿ b. ʿAmr had made camp there, they followed Khusrawshunūm's example and corre- [2628]
sponded with Ḥudhayfah, who reacted positively to what they were asking. They agreed on accepting Ḥudhayfah's invitation and set out to meet him. But they were deceived by one of them, a man called Dīnār. He was a king[725] (in his own right) but of lesser nobility than the others, all of them being more exalted in status than he, with Qārin[726] the noblest of them all. Dīnār had said to them, "Do not present yourselves to these Arabs in full regalia,

720. In Arabic, *nawā'ib al-zamān.* I base my rendering on Lane, 1254, middle column, lines 1–3, and Steingass, *A comprehensive Persian-English dictionary* (London 1957), 621, left column, above.

721. See nn. 88, 117 above.

722. See nn. 88, 94 above.

723. In Arabic *ahl al-balā'*; see n. 94 above.

724. Two regional centers; see Le Strange, *Lands*, 189, 197, and n. 15 above.

725. See Morony, *Iraq*, 186, for this use of the title "king."

726. See *loc. cit.*, where the noble Persian family of Qārēn is mentioned.

but assume a shabby appearance when you confront them." So they did, but Dīnār acted otherwise; he approached the Arabs dressed up in brocaded garments and jewelry. He paid the Muslims the necessary respect,[727] bringing them presents that they appreciated. So the Muslims concluded a treaty with him while disregarding his (fellow aristocrats, the outcome of this being that) the latter saw no other way than to yield to Dīnār and to accept his authority. That is why Nihāwand came to be called Māh Dīnār.[728]

Ḥudhayfah went by Māh Dīnār. Some time earlier, al-Nuʿmān had concluded a pact with Bahrādhān based on the same conditions as mentioned above. Hence this pact was associated with Bahrādhān. Ḥudhayfah charged al-Nusayr b. Thawr with the taking of a citadel to which a number of people had sought refuge. Al-Nusayr engaged these people in battle and conquered the citadel, which was henceforth associated with him.

In his distribution of the booty of Nihāwand Ḥudhayfah included those left behind in Marj al-Qalʿah and those who were still in Ghuḍā Shajar, as well as the forces occupying the strong points, in the same manner as he had distributed it among those who had participated in the actual battle. This was because the aforementioned three categories of warriors could have been called upon as reinforcements for the Muslims fighting in the battle, so that they would not be attacked from one (unforeseen) direction or another.

In that same night, which was destined for the encounter of the Muslims (and their adversaries at Nihāwand), ʿUmar was restless,
[2629] so he left his house to seek further news. In the meantime, a certain Muslim, who had gone out to attend to some business of his and had returned to the city in the dark, was overtaken by a rider, who himself was on his way to Medina. (This was) in the course of the third night after the battle of Nihāwand. The man asked him, "Hey, ʿAbdallāh, where have you come from?" "From Nihāwand," the other answered. "What is the latest news?" the first man asked. "The news is good," the other replied, "God has

727. The text seems corrupt and my rendition is tentative.

728. Literally, "the district of Dīnār." For the exact meaning of the Middle Persian word *māh*, see also Le Strange, *Lands*, 190 n.

granted al-Nuʿmān victory and a martyr's death. The Muslims have divided the booty of Nihāwand among themselves, each mounted warrior receiving six thousand dirhams." The rider accompanied the man until he was swallowed up in the dark in Medina. The first man entered his house and slept. The following morning he started telling this story. The news spread around until it reached ʿUmar, who was as restless as ever. He sent for the man and questioned him, whereupon the other gave him the news. ʿUmar said, "That traveler spoke the truth, and so have you. This was ʿUthaym, the messenger of the jinn; he must have seen the messenger sent by the people at Nihāwand."

Then, somewhat later, Ṭarīf (b. Sahm) came to ʿUmar with the news of the victory. ʿUmar said, "Give me all the news." The man replied, "I have no more information than just the news of the victory. When I left, the Muslims were busily pursuing the enemy and still on full alert." But from ʿUmar he hid everything except that which might please him. After that, ʿUmar went out accompanied by his companions. ʿUmar insisted on receiving more news. Then a rider was pointed out to him. He said to his companions, "Tell me who he is." Then ʿUthmān b. ʿAffān said, "He is al-Sā'ib (b. al-Aqraʿ)," so ʿUmar exclaimed, "Al-Sā'ib?" When al-Sā'ib had come closer, ʿUmar asked him, "What happened to you?" "I have glad tidings for you and news of victory," al-Sā'ib replied. "How did al-Nuʿmān fare?" ʿUmar wanted to know. "His horse stumbled in the blood of the enemies," al-Sā'ib replied, "so he was thrown down and died a martyr's death." ʿUmar went home accompanied by al-Sā'ib. He asked him about the number of Muslims who got killed, so al-Sā'ib told him their number—which was small—and also that al-Nuʿmān was the first to die a martyr's death on the "day of the victory of victories." That is how the men of al-Kūfah and the Muslims referred to that day.[729]

As ʿUmar was entering the mosque, the loads were being taken off (the camels of al-Sā'ib) and deposited in the mosque. ʿUmar [2630]
ordered some of his companions, among whom were ʿAbd al-

729. In Ibn al-Athīr, III, 12, we read that the battle of Nihāwand was so called because, after that, the Persians never succeeded in mobilizing such an army again and the Muslims remained in control of their land. Noth, 118, identifies the expression as a *topos*.

Raḥmān b. ʿAwf and ʿAbdallāh b. Arqam, to spend the night in the mosque guarding these loads. He himself entered his house followed by al-Sā'ib b. al-Aqraʿ with these two baskets.[730] The latter gave him the news concerning the two baskets and information about the Muslim warriors. "Son of Mulaykah," ʿUmar said, "by God, the warriors did not know about these baskets and you are no longer there with them to tell them about them. Quickly, go back where you came from. Go to Ḥudhayfah and let him dole out the contents of these baskets in equal shares among those to whom God has granted them as booty." So al-Sā'ib went back again and journeyed until he came to Ḥudhayfah at Māh, where he offered the baskets for sale. In due course he sold them and received four million dirhams for them.

According to al-Sarī—Shuʿayb—Sayf—Muḥammad b. Qays al-Asadī: While they were encamped at Nihāwand, a man called Jaʿfar b. Rāshid said to Ṭulayḥah, "We suffer from lack of supplies. Do you know one more of those wonderful jingles, which might be of use to us?" "Stay where you are," Tulayḥah answered, "I will see what I can do." He took a garment, wrapped himself loosely in it[731] and declaimed,

By far the best news
    Is the dihqān's ewes
(They roam) in a meadow
    Dispelling our sorrow.

[2631] When they entered the enclosure, they found the sheep to be well fed.

According to al-Sarī—Shuʿayb—Sayf—Abū Maʿbad al-ʿAbsī and ʿUrwah b. al-Walīd—someone from their tribe: On a certain day, while we were laying siege to the enemy in Nihāwand, they made a sortie against us. They engaged us in close combat and we did not have to wait long before God put them to flight. Simāk b. ʿUbayd al-ʿAbsī pursued one of the enemies who was escorted by

---

730. See p. 183 above.

731. A reference to Ṭulayḥah's former status as a *kāhin* ("soothsayer") turned false prophet at the time of the *riddah*. For the custom of wrapping oneself in a cloak before uttering the soothsayer's "jingle," which was often, as is the case here, in rhyming prose (*sajʿ*), see Toufic Fahd, *La divination arabe*, Strasbourg, 1966, 65, esp. n. 2.

eight horsemen. Simāk challenged them to fight him and whoever accepted the challenge was killed. Then Simāk advanced on them, he attacked the man whom the others were escorting and took him prisoner. He divested him of his weapons and called for someone called ʿAbd to guard him. When Simāk had entrusted him to ʿAbd, the prisoner spoke, "Bring me to your commander to conclude a peace treaty with him in respect of this region and to pay him the *jizyah.* And you yourself may ask your prisoner[732] for whatever you want, for you have been merciful toward me by not killing me. From now on I shall be your servant. If you present me to your king and bring us together, you will find me grateful and you will be like a brother to me."

Then Simāk let him go and granted him immunity. He asked him, "Who are you?" "I am Dīnār," was the answer. The ruling family in those days was that of Qārin.[733]

When he was brought before Ḥudhayfah, Dīnār told him about the valor of Simāk and how many enemies he had killed. He also gave evidence of his own respect for the Muslims. Ḥudhayfah granted him a peace agreement in exchange for payment of the *kharāj*. Thus Māh was called after Dīnār, who entered into a close relationship with Simāk and gave him presents. He used to come to al-Kūfah whenever the collected taxes of his area had to be submitted to the Kūfan governor.

One day during the caliphate of Muʿāwiyah, Dīnār came to al-Kūfah, addressed the people there and said,

"Inhabitants of al-Kūfah, from the moment you first came into contact with us, you have behaved irreproachably and you have stayed the same throughout the reigns of ʿUmar and ʿUthmān. But thereafter you changed and four qualities have gained the upper [2632]
hand among you: niggardliness, deceit, perfidy and narrow-mindedness, although not one of these marked you in the past. I have been watching you and I have found these characteristics in your new generation.[734] I also know where you got them. Deceit you derived from the Nabateans, niggardliness from the Persians, per-

732. I have opted for *min* from Ibn Ḥubaysh, rather than *ʿan* in Prym's edition.

733. See n. 726 above.

734. In Arabic: *fī muwalladīkum.* Strictly speaking, a *muwallad* is a person of non-Arab origin who has grown up among Arabs having embraced Islam.

fidy you copied from the Khurāsānians, and narrow-mindedness from al-Ahwāz."

According to al-Sarī—Shu'ayb—Sayf—'Amr b. Muḥammad—al-Sha'bī: When the prisoners taken at Nihāwand were brought to Medina, a servant of al-Mughīrah b. Shu'bah, Abū Lu'lu'ah Fayrūz, could not meet any young captive without caressing his head and bursting into tears, wailing, "'Umar has consumed my liver!"[735] Fayrūz was a Nihāwandī whom the Byzantines had taken prisoner in the days of the Byzantine-Persian war and who, after that, had been captured by the Muslims. That is why he was supposed to hail from Nihāwand.

According to al-Sarī—Shu'ayb—Sayf—'Amr b. Muḥammad—al-Sha'bī: Of those who tumbled into the ravine, eighty thousand lost their lives, while on the battlefield thirty thousand got killed, being chained together,[736] apart from those who were slain when they were pursued (while running for safety). The Muslims numbered thirty thousand (on that day). The city of Nihāwand was conquered in the beginning of the year 19 (640), just after the year 18 (639) had come to a close, after seven years (had elapsed) of 'Umar's caliphate.

According to al-Sarī—Shu'ayb—Sayf—Muḥammad, al-Muhallab and Ṭalḥah: The texts of the two documents that al-Nu'mān and Ḥudhayfah presented to the inhabitants of the two regions called Māh read, "In the name of God, the merciful, the
[2633] compassionate. This is the covenant that al-Nu'mān b. Muqarrin has granted to the inhabitants of Māh Bahrādhān.[737] He has guaranteed them immunity for their person, their property and their lands; they need not give up any religious custom and they will not be prevented from implementing any of their own laws. They will enjoy protection as long as every year they pay the *jizyah* to the governor in charge. This is incumbent upon every adult in respect of himself and his possessions, each according to his ability. They will also enjoy protection as long as they show the way to travelers, keep the roads in good repair and extend hospitality

735. This expression is supposed to mean (*Glossarium*, p. CDLXIV) "he has caused me great pain."

736. See n. 623 above.

737. See p. 212 above.

for a day and a night to Muslim warriors who pass by and seek refuge with them, and as long as they fulfill their promises and give sound advice. But if they act dishonestly and change their conduct, our obligation to protect them will lapse." Witnesses to this document were ʿAbdallāh b. Dhī al-Sahmayn, al-Qaʿqāʿ b. ʿAmr and Jarīr b. ʿAbdallāh (al-Bajalī), and it was written in the month Muḥarram of the year 19 (January 640). (The second document read), "In the name of God, the merciful, the compassionate. This is the covenant that Ḥudhayfah b. al-Yamān has granted the inhabitants of Māh Dīnār. He has guaranteed them immunity for their person, their property and their lands; they need not give up any religious custom and they will not be prevented from implementing any of their own laws. They will enjoy protection as long as every year they pay the *jizyah* to the Muslim governor in charge. This is incumbent upon every adult in respect of himself and his possessions, each according to his ability. They will also enjoy protection as long as they show the way to travelers, keep the roads in good repair and extend hospitality for a day and a night to Muslim warriors who pass by and seek refuge with them, and as long as they give sound advice. But if they act dishonestly and change their conduct, our obligation to protect them will lapse." Witnesses (to this second document) were al-Qaʿqāʿ b. ʿAmr, Nuʿaym b. Muqarrin and Suwayd b. Muqarrin, and it was written in the month Muḥarram.

They said: ʿUmar assigned to each of those who had been present at the battle of Nihāwand, and those newcomers[738] who had fought valiantly, two thousand dirhams, putting them in the same category as the veterans of the battle of al-Qādisiyyah.

738. For this term, see n. 253 above.

Appendix I

*The Poetry and Saj*ʿ *in This Volume*

Throughout this translation I have tried to render the poetry, as well as a few fragments of rhymed prose (*saj*ʿ), into rhythmic English.

The majority of translations of Arabic occasional poetry hitherto published in western languages occurring in works such as this are anything but poetic, and are distinguishable from the surrounding prose only by the way these translations are printed. In the present volume an attempt is made to set off the scattered verses against their backdrop more distinctly than is usually the case in translated histories of this sort.

The poems and one-liners found in this text are on the whole of little artistic merit and constitute no more than the endeavors of alleged eyewitnesses at *Gelegenheitsdichtung,* commemorating mostly military events. But as with all classical Arabic poetry, this poetry has a strict meter and rhyme, and in my translation I have tried to substitute the various meters with something similar that, it is hoped, might be felt to fall easily on anglophone ears. Where possible, I have included rhyme in the one-liners.

In the following pages, I have collected some comments on the poetic fragments in the order in which they appear in this volume. These comments are of a slightly more technical nature and sometimes contain a host of details; that is why I have chosen not to include them in the footnotes.

Pp. 2419f.: The final syllable *-bu* of the first word of line 1 has to be read as long so as to make it fit the *rajaz* meter.

P. 2434: Occasionally I have shortened certain Arabic words or names so as to make them fit the English rhythm, for example, Madā'in for al-Madā'in; I also had to resort to this device in some of the poetic fragments that follow.

Pp. 2445f.: These six lines in my view present by far the most intriguing problem of all the poetry found in this volume.

Before I dwell for some time on a metrical anomaly in ll. 1 and 2, let me make some remarks about ll. 3 to 6.

The word *khiṣām* in l. 3 may be taken as a double entendre, conveying on the one hand "fray" and on the other "squabble (over the distribution of the booty)."

The verb *falaja* in l. 3 also seems to permit two interpretations; constructed with *shu'ūna* as direct object, it means "cleaving" (as in my rendition); on the other hand, constructed with *bi-* it means "acquiring," namely, the mule. Translated thus, ll. 3 and 4 should then be rendered:

They acquired the mule in the struggle
by means of every sharp-cutting blow to the sutures of skulls.

In l. 6, the apparatus gives a variant *ba'run* "dung" for *na'mun* "cattle," which makes equally good sense; I have preferred to read *na'mun,* though, because of the following qualification *mina 'l-an'āmi,* which constitutes a well known stylistic device as described in Wright, II, 136. It is true that the voweling *na'mun* is far less common than *na'amun,* but the former is duly listed in *Lisān al-'arab,* XVI, 64, l. 12.

Finally, ll. 1 and 2 deserve a short digression.

Although I have rendered the first two lines in an equal number of syllables as are found in the rest of the lines, the Arabic originals contain three long syllables more than ll. 3 to 6. Literally translated, ll. 1 and 2 read:

May my maternal and paternal uncles be held ransom for my men;
they recoiled at the river from deserting and surrendering me.

However, since *akhwāl* (maternal uncles) and *aʿmām* (paternal uncles) in l. 1, and *khidhlān* (deserting) and *islām* (here: surrendering) in l. 2, are near-synonyms, I chose to ignore them in my translation for the following reasons:

Although I have no evidence for this other than the otherwise unattested peculiarity of three long syllables too many in the first two lines, I contend that these lines may have been "doctored." Who may have been responsible for this "doctoring" is anybody's guess; everyone in the *isnād* qualifies, from the eyewitness(es) to Ṭabarī himself or, conceivably, even a later copyist of a manuscript, from which the presently available manuscripts are (in)directly derived.

In any case, we have here two lines with three long syllables too many to make them fit in with the following four, totally regular, *rajaz* lines. Furthermore, in each of these lines we find two seemingly superfluous near-synonyms of the crucial rhyme bearers *aʿmāmī* and *islāmī*. Both words happen to comprise three long syllables. Is this just a coincidence, or may we dig into this a little bit more deeply?

Now, it is good practice not to interfere with the original text, any original text, and even if we have to bend over backwards in an attempt to account for seemingly insoluble "peculiarities," that is what we mostly do because that is what we have been taught. In this case, however, we may find some justification for doing our best to restore the regular *rajaz* meter also in the first two lines, because the "peculiarity" of three long syllables extra is recorded nowhere else, as far as I have been able to ascertain. Should this anomaly—as I now term it—turn out to be attested elsewhere, or even to be unexpectedly common, then the following suggested emendation loses its *raison d'être*. But for the time being I feel free to go ahead.

A feasible way to create an orthodox *rajaz* meter in ll. 1 and 2, it seems to me, is to take away the penultimate words, near-synonyms as we saw of the rhyme bearers, as well as the two immediately following particles *wa-* that, without the synonyms, no longer make sense. We then have:

Fidan li-qawmī 'l-yawma — aʿmāmi
    Hum karihū bi 'l-nahri — islāmi

All that remains to be done is to look for a suitable word or particle of one long syllable to insert in the place of —, which stands for the invariably long fourth syllable of the second foot in both lines. But that is a lot easier said than done, as the following may show. The syntax seems to require a preposition.

In l. 1 *min* appears to fit nicely; see Wolfdietrich Fischer, *Grammatik des klassischen Arabisch,* Harrassowitz, Wiesbaden, 1972, 141, l. 18, 163, l. 19, 164, l. 15.

However, in l. 2 the choice is not so easy. *Kariha,* at least in old Arabic, always takes its direct object in the accusative, and the line therefore seems to exclude the insertion of a preposition. We do find in *WKAS,* I, 157, l. 17–18, the object of *kārihun* mentioned as sometimes introduced by *fī,* which would suit admirably, but this is a later usage that is not yet attested in early Arabic.

On the other hand, we might conjecture that we are confronted with a case of contamination. Suppose that *before* it was "doctored" the line read:

hum raghibū *bi 'l-nahri* ʿan *islāmi*

and we have exactly the same meaning as

hum karihū bi 'l-nahri . . . islāmi

Whatever the right solution may be, this brings me to the important question: If we assume that the lines were indeed interfered with, what induced the "culprit" to tamper with them at all? Translated literally, the reconstructed l. 2 reads in translation

They hated to desert me at the river

but it could just as well be interpreted as

They were disgusted with my (having embraced) Islam

and that interpretation may, in actual fact, have caused our tamperer to resort to some padding; he selected an equivalent of *islāmī* in the sense of "surrendering," coming up with *khidhlānī,* and inserted it in order to make absolutely sure that the word *islāmī* could not be taken as "my (having embraced) Islam" but only in the sense indicated, in fact prompted, by the insert *khidhlānī.*

Let us suppose that what happened may be reconstructed as

follows: Someone in the *isnād* of the report containing the four *rajaz* lines under scrutiny found two lines that permitted of the interpretation:

> Although these brave warriors of mine were disgusted with the fact that I had embraced Islam, let my uncles be ransom for them today.

Let us furthermore assume that the eyewitness/transmitter felt that he could not let that pass without doing something to the lines in an attempt to do away with this odious ambiguity. Before the advent of Islam, the verb *aslama/yuslimu* usually meant "to surrender" or "to desert," more often than not in a wartime situation, as the majority of occurrences in Ibn Isḥāq's *Sīrah,* for instance, seem to indicate. But in later times the verb was almost exclusively used in the connotation "to surrender to the new religion." The obviously ancient usage of *islāmī* in the poem had to be made unequivocally clear to readers no longer familiar with this usage, hence the insert of *khidhlānī wa-*, which in turn resulted in the insertion of *akhwālī wa-*.

Now, it could be argued that the word *islāmī* in the poem could have been substituted by another verbal noun of form IV ending in *-mī,* allowing of the same, or a cognate, interpretation as *khidhlānī.* Did our tamperer think of that solution? A study of the standard dictionaries yields only a limited number of eligible roots and none seem to fit effortlessly. *Idhāmī* and *ighmāmī* both mean "to grieve me," *is'āmī* means "to disgust me" and *iʿdāmī* "to put me to death." Any of these four might just have suited the context, but it is my contention, expressed with due caution of course, that it is precisely the occurrence of the slightly ambiguous term *islāmī* that induced our tamperer to try his hand at some, in his eyes probably indispensable, "doctoring," *without* having to rewrite l. 2.

P. 2484: Like the preceding verses, this short piece of rhyming prose (*sajʿ*) solicits a few comments.

At first glance, it sounds like a pastiche of Qur'ān verses or, to be more precise, verses commonly ascribed to the first Meccan period. This fragment of *sajʿ*, preserved for us by Ṭabarī, but as far as I was able to ascertain never commented upon, bears all the hallmarks of those early Qur'ān verses that still bespeak the pre-

Islamic setting of *kāhins*, the soothsayers: oaths taken on heaven, earth, wind and stars, with a loose cadence and a consistent rhyme. For more on early *saj*ʿ, see Wellhausen, *Reste*, 135 f., and Fahd, 159–70.

A few more points deserve our attention, I think.

All but the first and the last line are purely pre-Islamic; the new religion is not yet discernible. The first line may have been purely pre-Islamic as well, but is now provided with an introductory vocative *Allāhumma*[*yā*] *rabba*. . . The second line may also have been "islamicized" by the insertion of *rabba* before *al-arḍi*. In fact, all the following lines may be interpreted as equally well "islamicized" by reading *rabba* between *wa-* and, respectively, *al-rīḥi, al-nujūmi, al-biḥāri, al-shayāṭīni* and *al-khiṣṣāni* (which I read for the nonsensical *khiṣṣāṣi*). Then the lines translate:

> Lord of the earth . . .
> Lord of the wind . . .
> Lord of the stars . . .
> Lord of the seas . . . etc.

It looks like a *kāhin*'s formulaic oath partly padded by "islamifying" elements. The final line "Bless us . . ." then seems to round off the oaths with a prayerlike request, no longer built of soothsayers' material but of Islamic ingredients, and it concludes seven short, consistently rhyming lines in *-at* with the cripple *thabāt*. (My stressmark on "firmnèss" is an equally awkward attempt at having it rhyme with "possess").

Who composed this piece of *saj*ʿ? Possible solutions are many but, as yet, incapable of substantiation. Two points should be made:

The piece could be an original part of the Qur'ān that failed to become part of the first tentative redaction then allegedly in the process of being compiled; if the historical accounts about Abū Bakr and ʿUmar toying with the idea of compiling the scattered fragments of revelation into one generally recognized corpus have never been satisfactorily authenticated in the eyes of western historians, the *likelihood* that they may have done so is only scorned by those whose skepticism effectively precludes them from arriving at any acceptable *Geschichtsbild* at all.

The piece could be a pastiche of the usual opening lines of an early Qur'ān chapter dating to what we now call the first Meccan period. Muslims may be prevented from comparing anything with the Qur'ān on an equal basis due to the doctrine of the "inimitableness" of the Holy Book, but western readers may be struck by certain unmistakable similarities:

For l. 1, see Q. XCI, 5: By Heaven and what it has built; see further LXXXV, 1, and LXXXVI, 1.

For l. 2, see XCI, 6: By the Earth and what it has spread.

For l. 3, see LXXVII, 1–2: By the Winds like horses' manes and the mighty hurricanes.

For l. 4, see LIII, 1: By the Star when it sets, see further LXXVII, 8, and LXXXI, 2.

For l. 5, see LXXXI, 6, and LXXXII, 3.

However, the final two oaths have no obvious Qur'ānic equivalents. If such oaths were ever part of it, they were removed by those responsible for our *textus receptus.* The word *shayṭān* in the connotation "inspiring demon" is fairly common in the Qur'ān; compare also the occurrences of the word *qarīn,* which has the same meaning.

In any case, whatever we assume the breeding ground of this piece of *saj*ʿ to be, speculations as to who composed it increase with the whole, or even partial, acceptance of the analytical description given of it in the foregoing.

P. 2528: The two hemistichs contain six derivatives of one root *ṣanaʿa* "to make."

P. 2536: The first two lines of the first poem contain the stylistic device *paranomasia,* two words from different but similarly sounding roots, juxtaposed because of the homophonous effect. This did not find expression in my translation.

P. 2536: The second poem does not translate easily. In the first place, it contains several rare words whose meanings can only be guessed.

Jumāhir seems to mean "bulky," "thick"; I rendered it here "big" (l. 4).

ʿAdīd (l. 4), usually meaning "numerous," here seems to be a noun for "large tribe." My rendering (l. 6) ". . . not even a pin" is, to say the least, tentative; *iḥdā 'l-hanāti 'l-bahātiri* means literally "one of the short (insignificant?) problems," and even that is not entirely certain. May we rephrase this line as ". . . so there remained (hardly) one insignificant problem for us (to solve) among them"? Recapitulating, ll. 5–6 seem to convey: "We drove the Nabateans away from the Persians and so the only thing that we had to solve among them was (hardly more than) an insignificant little problem."

In line 7 we encounter the words *al-ʿArab al-ʿalyāʾ*, which is an expression for "Arabs living in high places"; here Tamīm are probably meant. See Lane's introduction, XI, n., and 2147, right column. The word *ʿulyā* from line 1 can also be understood in this way.

The word *buḥūr* in ll. 7–8, literally "seas," is here used in the connotation "land with green plants and plenty of water," see Lane, 156, right column, *ad finem.*

P. 2564: This *ṭawīl* meter contains an irregularity: the first syllable of the first hemistich is missing. This phenomenon is alluded to in Stanislas Guyard, "Théorie nouvelle de la métrique arabe . . ." in *Journal Asiatique,* VII série, VIII (1876):120, and is called *kharm;* see also G. W. Freytag, *Darstellung der arabischen Verskunst,* 88. In the Leiden manuscript of Ibn Ḥubaysh, this "irregularity" is "rectified" by an added *wa-* preceding *lammā.*

Appendix II

A Modern Description of Tustar

"Attack via the outlet of the water, then you will conquer the city." This hint at a secret entrance into the city of Tustar, nowadays Shushtar, intrigued me enough to look for a modern description and see what truth there was in it. In the following I shall briefly quote my findings:

The "outlet" is probably a tunnel dug in the bank of the river through which water was led into the city at the foot of the rock on which the citadel was built. This outlet, or passageway as it is called in the text, seems still to have been in place when a Dutch scientist, D. L. Graadt van Roggen, gave a detailed description of it in *Mémoires publiés sous la direction de M. J. de Morgan. Tome VII. Recherches archéologiques*, deuxième série, Paris 1905, 177 f [see map provided there].

Under the heading "*Tunnels sous la citadelle*" we read the following remarkable description:

"A environ 300 mètres en amont du pont, on trouve deux tunnels perçant la roche sur laquelle est bâtie la citadelle de Chouster (=Shushtar/Tustar -J.). Ce châteaufort existait certainement avant l'époque sassanide. Nous en voyons, dans Yakout, le récit de la prise par les troupes arabes sur la garnison persane de Yezdegerd III. [This is erroneous; at the time Yazdajird was presumably in Marw, see p. 2551 above, and al-Hurmuzān was the commander of the city -J.] Ces canaux se réunissent à une centaine de mètres au delà du mur d'enceinte de cette forteresse (fig. 471) pour former un seul canal. . . . Ces tunnels ont de 3 à 4 m.50 de largeur sur environs 100 mètres de longueur; ils étaient munis, d'un coté, d'*une voie de passage qui est en partie éboulée*" [italics mine -J].

Furthermore, we read in *Early adventures in Persia, Susiana, and Babylonia including a residence among the Bakhtiyari and other wild tribes before the discovery of Nineveh* by A. Henry Layard, London 1894, 234:

"The houses [sc. of Shushtar/Tustar -J] are mostly built of stone, and . . . are provided with extensive 'serd-âbs,' or underground apartments, known in Khuzistan as 'shâdrewan,' which are excavated to a considerable depth in the rock, and are ventilated and kept cool by lofty air chimneys."

The word *shâdrewan* used here is the same as *shādhurwān*, a word mentioned in Yāqūt, *Muʿjam*, I, 848, by which the same water conduit is meant. This connotation is not listed in the major Persian dictionaries.

Figure 1. General plan and detail (above) of Tustar after D. L. Graadt van Roggen, "Notice sur les anciens travaux hydrauliques en Susiane," Délégation en Perse, *Mémoires,* VII, 2e sér., Paris, 1905, 178.

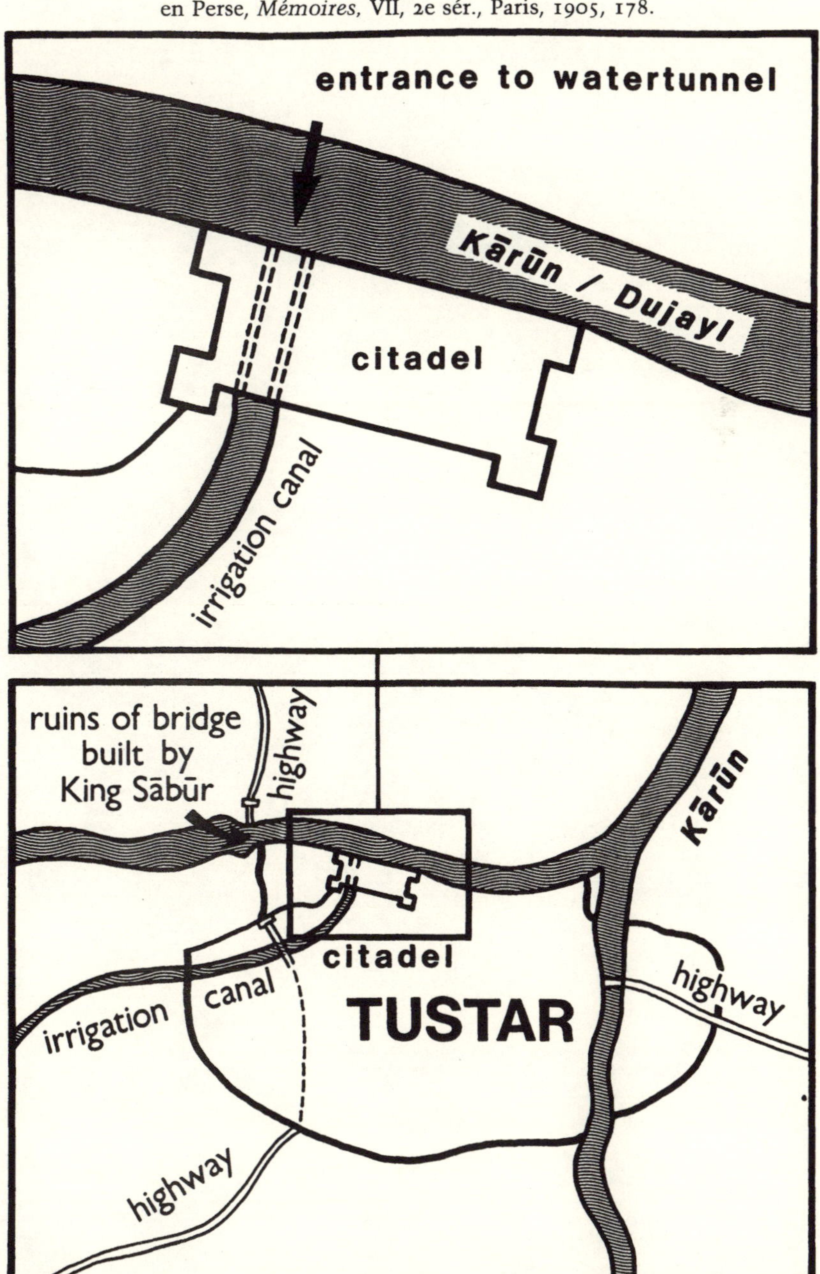

Bibliography of Cited Works

Abū Dāwūd. *Sunan*. 4 vols. Ed. M. M. ʿAbd al-Ḥamīd. Cairo, 1935.

Abū ʿUbayd. *Kitāb al-amwāl*. Ed. Muḥammad Khalīl Harrās. Cairo, 1968.

Balādhurī. *Futūḥ al-buldān*. 3 vols. Ed. M. J. de Goeje. Leiden, 1866.

Bravmann, M. M. *The Spiritual Background of Early Islam. Studies in Ancient Arab Concepts*. Leiden, 1972.

Bukhārī. *Ṣaḥīḥ* 4 vols. Ed. L. Krehl and Th. W. Juynboll. Leiden, 1862–1908.

Butler, A. J. *The Treaty of Miṣr in Ṭabarī. An Essay in Historical Criticism*. Oxford, 1913. Repr. in Butler, *The Arab Conquest of Egypt*.

———. *Babylon of Egypt. A Study in the History of Old Cairo*. Oxford, 1914. Repr. in Butler, *The Arab Conquest of Egypt*. . . .

———. *The Arab Conquest of Egypt and the Last Years of Roman Dominion*. 2nd ed. Oxford, 1978.

Caskel, W. See al-Kalbī.

Christensen, A. *L'Iran sous les Sassanides*. Copenhagen, 1936.

Concordance et indices de la tradition musulmane. 7 vols. Ed. A. J. Wensinck *et al*. Leiden, 1936–69.

Dennet, D. C. *Conversion and the Poll Tax in Early Islam*. Cambridge, Mass., 1950.

Donner, F. M. *The Early Islamic Conquests*. Princeton, 1981.

Dozy, R. P. A. *Supplément aux dictionnaires arabes*. 2 vols. Leiden, 1881.

Fahd, T. *La divination arabe*. Strassburg, 1966.

Fīrūzābādī. *al-Qāmūs al-muḥīṭ*. 3rd impr. 4 vols. Cairo, 1935.

Fischer, W. *Grammatik des klassischen arabisch*. Wiesbaden 1972.

Glossarium. See Ṭabarī, *Annales . . . at-Tabari*.

Hinds, M. "Kûfan Political Alignments and Their Background in the

Mid-Seventh Century A.D." *International Journal of Middle East Studies*, 2, 1971, 346–67.
Hinz, W. *Islamische Masse und Gewichte.* Leiden, 1955.
Ibn ʿAbd al-Ḥakam. *Futūḥ Miṣr.* Ed. Ch. C. Torrey. New Haven, 1922.
Ibn al-Athīr. *al-Kāmil fī al-taʾrīkh.* 14 vols. Ed. C. J. Tornberg. Leiden, 1867–76.
Ibn Ḥajar. *Fatḥ al-bārī.* 20 vols. Cairo, 1959.
———. *al-Iṣābah fī al-tamyīz al-ṣaḥābah.* 8 vols. Ed. ʿA. M. al-Bajāwī. Cairo, 1383–92 [1963–72].
Ibn Ḥanbal, Aḥmad b. Muḥammad. *Musnad.* 6 vols. Cairo, 1313 [1895–96]. 15 vols. Ed. A. M. Shākir. Cairo, 1949–56.
Ibn Hishām. *al-Sīrah al-nabawiyyah.* 4 vols. Ed. M. al-Saqā, I. al-Ibyārī, and ʿA. Shalabī. Cairo, 1936.
Ibn Isḥāq. See Ibn Hishām.
Ibn Kathīr. *al-Bidāyah wa al-nihāyah.* 14 vols. Cairo, 1351–58 [1932–39].
Ibn Manẓūr. *Lisān al-ʿArab.* 20 vols. Būlāq, 1883–91.
Ibn Saʿd. *Kitāb al-ṭabaqāt al-kabīr.* 9 vols. Ed. E. Sachau *et al.* Leiden, 1905–17.
Juda, J. *Die sozialen und wirtschaftlichen Aspekte der Mawālī in frühislamischer Zeit.* Tübingen, 1983.
Juynboll, G. H. A. *The Authenticity of the Tradition Literature. Discussions in Modern Egypt.* Leiden, 1969.
———. *Muslim Tradition. Studies in Chronology, Provenance and Authorship of Early* Ḥadīth. Cambridge, Eng., 1983.
Kaḥḥālah, ʿU. R. *Muʿjam al-qabāʾil al-ʿarab al-qadīmah wa al-ḥadīthah.* 3 vols. Damascus, 1949.
al-Kalbi, Hishām b. Muḥammad. *Ǧamharat an-Nasab. Das Genealogische Werk des Hišām b. Muḥammad al-Kalbī.* 2 vols. Ed. W. Caskel. Leiden, 1966.
Lane, E. W. *Arabic-English Lexicon.* 8 vols. London and Edinburgh, 1863–93.
Le Strange, G. *The Lands of the Eastern Caliphate.* 2nd ed. Cambridge, Eng., 1930.
Lisān. See Ibn Manẓūr.
Løkkegard, F. *Islamic Taxation in the Classic Period.* Copenhagen, 1950.
Mālik b. Anas. *al-Muwaṭṭaʾ.* 2 vols. Ed. M. F. ʿAbd al-Bāqī. Cairo, 1951.
Maqrīzī. *Kitāb al-mawāʿiẓ wa al-iʿtibār bi dhikri khiṭaṭ wa al-āthār.* 2 vols. Būlāq, 1853.
Morony, M. G. *Iraq after the Muslim Conquest.* Princeton, 1984.
Muslim b. al-Ḥajjāj. *Ṣaḥīḥ.* 5 vols. Ed. M. F. ʿAbd al-Bāqī. Cairo, 1955–56.
Noth, A. *Quellenkritische Studien zu Themen, Formen und Tendenzen frühislamischer Geschichtsüberlieferung.* Bonn, 1973.

Pellat, Ch. *Le milieu baṣrien et la formation de Ǧāḥiẓ*. Paris, 1953.
Puin, G. R. *Der Dīwān von ʿUmar Ibn al-Ḫaṭṭāb. Ein Beitrag zur frühislamischen Verwaltungsgeschichte*. Bonn, 1969.
Qāmūs. See Fīrūzābādī.
Schacht, J. *the Origins of Muhammadan Jurisprudence*. Oxford, 1950.
———. *An Introduction to Islamic Law*. Oxford, 1964.
Ṭabarī. *Annales Regum atque Legatorum Dei*. 3 vols. Ed. and tr. J. G. L. Kosegarten. Greifswald, 1831–53.
———. *Annales . . . at-Tabari. Introductio, Glossarium, Addenda et Emendanda*. Ed. M. J. de Goeje. Leiden, 1901.
———. *Taʾrīkh al-mulūk wa al-rusul*. 10 vols. Ed. M. A. Ibrāhīm. Cairo, 1960–69.
Tabātabāʾī, H. M. *Kharāj in Islamic Law*. London, 1983.
Tāj. See al-Zabīdī.
Thesiger, W. *The Marsh Arabs*. Penguin ed. Harmondsworth, Eng., 1967.
Tirmidhī. *al-Jāmiʿ al-ṣaḥīḥ*. 5 vols. Ed. A. M. Shākir *et al.* Cairo, 1937–65.
Vasiliev, A. A. *History of the Byzantine Empire*. Vol. 1. Madison, Wisc., 1928.
Wakīʿ. *Akhbār al-quḍāt*. 3 vols. Ed. ʿA. M. al-Marāghī. Cairo, 1947–50.
Wāqidī. *Kitāb al-maghāzī*. 3 vols. Ed. J. M. B. Jones. London, 1966.
Wellhausen, J. *Reste arabischen Heidentums*. Berlin, 1897.
———. *Skizzen und Vorarbeiten*. Vol. VI. Berlin, 1899.
Wright, W. *A Grammar of the Arabic Language*. 3rd ed. 2 vols. Cambridge, Eng., 1955.
Yaʿqūbī. *Taʾrīkh*. 2 vols. Ed. M. Th. Houtsma. Leiden, 1883.
Yāqūt. *Muʿjam al-buldān*. 6 vols. Ed. F. Wüstenfeld. Leipzig, 1866–73.
al-Zabīdī, M. M. *Tāj al-ʿarūs*. 10 vols. Cairo, 1306–07 [1888–90].

Index

This index, comprising names as well as concepts, serves at the same time as a glossary of some technical terms. In the alphabetization *b.* (*ibn* "son"), *bt.* (*bint* "daughter"), and the Arabic article *al-* have been disregarded.

A

B

C

D

E

I

L

M

N

T

U